the great vegetable plot

'A vegetable garden is a beautiful thing to make, with the extra bonus of producing the best possible things to eat. If you get it right, the whole place can become your market, your haven and your playground.'

sarah raven

the great vegetable plot

delicious varieties to grow and eat

photographs by jonathan buckley

Left **A broad bean tip.**
Opposite **Nasturtiums look
wonderful in a salad and
have a strong peppery taste.**

Contents

Introduction

I love growing my own vegetables because I love the harvest, walking through the garden picking delicious meals. I enjoy the propagation, the sowing of the seed, but most of all I love the baskets of tomatoes and aubergines, the wads of herbs, the colanderfuls of salad, the barrow-loads of pumpkins that you can so easily produce. That's the garden I want to create – a rich and fruitful place, generous with all the things I want to eat.

This is not about growing for self-sufficiency's sake, or growing as a chore – it's about growing for pleasure. I can't stand a glut of one thing in a great mountain, so I successionally sow small quantities of things many times in the year. I don't bother to plant many maincrop potatoes, parsnips and cabbages, which are easy to buy and whose flavour doesn't suffer when they are stored. And I avoid things that are tricky to grow, such as celery. My life's too busy for that. I concentrate on the real life-enhancers – vegetables that are easy to grow and that make every meal more fun to cook.

The vegetables I love fall into three distinct groups. For my first batch of choices I simply let taste decide. I want to grow what I call the 'fresh-as-a-daisy veg' – tomatoes, asparagus, sweetcorn, small tasty carrots, newly picked peas, and waxy new potatoes just out of the ground, all things that taste completely different when picked and eaten straight away. With these, in a blindfold flavour test, you'd know which were bought and which home-grown from every single mouthful.

I also want to produce more unusual veg – varieties that in this country you'll find difficult to buy. How many greengrocers sell onion squash, viola or nasturtium flowers, borlotti beans and pea tips? And what about some of the unusual herbs? Where can one buy lovage, sorrel, lemon verbena and chervil, each one invaluable in the kitchen, a cinch to grow, and yet rarely to be seen? They are what I call the 'unbuyables', and these form my second batch of choices.

My third group may not seem to be the most glamorous of vegetables, but they are more than just a third team. To me, these are the real stars – life-savers in more ways than one. I can't let producing lots of delicious food take up all my time. I have a full-on working life and a family, a husband, two daughters and three stepsons. I've found that there are certain vegetables that produce lots of food over a long period with very little input from me, *and* they're versatile enough in terms of flavour so you can eat them in many different ways. These are what I call the 'desert island plants', the things that I would grow if I genuinely had to produce my own food efficiently. They are the plants that should form the backbone of any vegetable garden, the varieties with which everyone should start.

If time and garden space are limited, don't aim to grow every vegetable, salad and herb that you eat, but be selective. Concentrate your time and energy on varieties that are really worth growing, as opposed to buying.

I aim for minimum input for maximum reward from my vegetable garden, and so I concentrate on the three categories mentioned above. Their guaranteed tasty productivity enables me to eat delicious home-grown food as a meal, or part of a meal, every day of the year, without the kitchen garden taking over my life.

I have a garden and cookery school at home, and we grow lots of the food for the demonstrations and the students' lunches. I have two areas for vegetables, which together come to about 1000 sq m (10,765 sq ft), a bigger space than I would need if I were growing food only for my family and friends. We also spend more time on it. For most households of four or five, think of having a patch similar in size to a traditional allotment – about 250 sq m (2700 sq ft) – which should be do-able on a couple of hours' gardening a week.

The nicest possible place to be

My garden is there to produce lots of fantastic things to eat, but I also want it to be beautiful. I have a tunnel of sweet peas, which is fragrant from 10m (30ft) away. I can't eat them, but the garden wouldn't be as lovely if they weren't there. There's an avenue of borlotti beans scrambling up over frames of silver birch sticks. There are woven willow teepees hung with lantern-like squashes, and a bank of silver, jagged-leaved globe artichokes. There are carpets of closely planted salad leaves, herbs and lettuce, with different colours and shapes in stripes across the bed. There are avenues of crimson-black and blood-red dahlias, sprinklings of gladioli and mounds of chunky, stately kales. There's an aspagarus bed, and the plumped-up cushions of the courgette plants. There's plenty of chaos mixed in here too – areas that need weeding and replanting – but overall it feels marvellous, with good, frivolous, inedible splashes of colour and scent to make my patch the nicest possible place to be.

A vegetable garden is a beautiful thing to make, with the extra bonus of producing the best possible things to eat. If you get it right, the whole place can become your market, your haven and your playground. For me, life would not be complete without one!

1

What to grow

My first category of must-have vegetables contains the things that are immeasurably different in flavour if you grow your own. I call these 'fresh-as-a-daisy veg'. To be at their best, they have to be recently picked. If you asked a whole table of people to taste and then tell you which plate had been grown in the garden and picked only hours before, and which had been bought from the farm shop down the road, you'd get an almost 100 per cent correct result every time. These are the things whose sugars turn to starch very quickly on storing, or that lose their all-important water-filled texture. If you want to eat these vegetables at their best, you've got to grow them yourself.

Page 10 **Chips made from red and blue potatoes, 'Highland Burgundy Red' and 'Salad Blue'.**
Page 11 top **Just-picked peas and broad beans.**
Page 11 centre '**Red Kuri' pumpkin.**
Page 11 bottom **A bowl of summer salad.**
Opposite **The beautiful sweetcorn 'Inca Rainbow'.**

Tomatoes are the obvious example, and certain tomato varieties are my number one choice of must-haves. If you grow the right cordon types in a greenhouse – 'Sungold' being the prime example – you'll be picking tasty sugar bombs from July until November. From ten plants, you can pick enough tomatoes for frying or grilling and eating on toast for breakfast, to make a salad with basil and mozzarella for lunch, and to make soup or pasta sauce in the evening two or three times a week.

Peas also have to be included. To get them sweet, with a good crunch eaten raw, and that crucial bounciness as you bite, they must be only hours old. Most taste good if quickly frozen, but then you don't have the luxury of eating them raw mouthful by mouthful stripped straight from the pod. Fresh peas are one of my favourite additions to a summer salad – small, raw peas, mixed with young spinach leaves and feta cheese – and to get this, you've got to grow your own.

Sweetcorn is another vegetable that passes the blindfold taste test almost every time. This is in spite of breeding programmes that have been run for many years to produce the sweetest taste possible. It's true that the new F1 hybrids have some sweetness left when cooked a few days later, but nothing in comparison to the delicious sugariness and crunchiness of cobs just picked.

You may be surprised to find new potatoes included here, but their flavour and texture is one hundred times better when they are dug up and plunged straight into the pot of salty, minty water. If you're adding anything to them in mash, or even baking them and dousing them in butter, it doesn't matter quite as much, but if you're eating them just as they come, as boiled new potatoes, that's when you can really tell which is which.

The same is true of carrots, lettuce and asparagus, where it's as much the texture as the taste that makes the difference. These three do go downhill, with their sugars converting to starch, but less rapidly than the other 'fresh-as-a-daisy veg'. In fact they may not lose their perfection for a day or two, but there aren't many vegetable supply chains that can guarantee to get them from the ground to your plate in such a short time. If you've got room, try to grow these three as well.

Left **Our pizza oven is in constant use when the new crop of tomatoes is harvested.**

Tomatoes

Home-grown tomatoes taste far better than bought ones – there's no argument about that. You'd have a hard task putting the same case for onions, leeks and cabbage, but tomatoes pass the blindfold taste test every time. Picked from your garden, they are tasty and sweet, and if you eat them straight away, they have that characteristic smell too – a cross between parsley and tobacco.

These are the ultimate 'fresh-as-a daisy veg' – best eaten warm from the plant – but they're very much 'desert island veg' too. If you grow cordon types, the ones that need tying up and training, they will crop over three or four months at a stretch, producing an amazing amount of tomatoes from one single plant. I grow six or seven pots of the sweet, thin-skinned, golden-coloured 'Sungold', and we pick these almost every day for eating raw or cooked right the way through the summer and into the autumn. My daughter Rosie's favourite breakfast involves going down to the polytunnel before school and picking a good handful for eating as we drive in.

I think most of us want a few ripe tomatoes a day, a drip-drip production, rather than a short, overwhelming gush. Cordons give you the drip-drip, bush types the gush – large quantities of fruit all reaching perfection at much the same time, for a limited four- or five-week season. That's how commercial growers prefer it, with one area cropping hugely, but briefly. They can harvest one lot, clear it and then move on to the next, leaving the first area to be replanted, but that doesn't suit the way most households eat. You can't consume the mountain of tomatoes that you'll get from lots of plants of a bush type. You can freeze them as sauce, which is a bonus in the winter if you've got plenty of room in your freezer, but that's not as good as several months' supply of the real thing, fresh and raw in a salad. Cordons are the ones to choose – marvellous varieties like 'Sungold', 'Costoluto Fiorentino' and 'Brandywine' (see pages 231–2).

If you can't spare the soil or greenhouse space to grow them, use a pot or a growing-bag on a patio or windowledge. Even if your garden's jam-packed with other things, or if you don't have much of a garden, go on – make room for a few tomatoes.

Sowing and growing tomatoes

I used to think that there were too many things to remember for me to be any good at growing tomatoes – all that tying in, pinching out, watering and feeding (see below), but once you've done it for one year, you realize it's just a therapeutic ten-minute walk through your plants about once a week. You'll need to water them more often than this, but we produce fantastic tomatoes with minimal preening and feeding.

Sowing

Tomatoes are half-hardy annuals – they can't withstand the frost. If you're going to grow them in an unheated greenhouse or outside, sow them under cover in early March. On a cold night you may need to protect them with fleece, which protects to -5°C (22°F), but sown at this time, they'll be at the right stage for planting when the frosts finish in May. If you have a frost-free greenhouse, you can get going a bit earlier. I do, luckily, and so I aim to sow my tomatoes on Valentine's Day.

Germination

As with most other half-hardy annuals, after sowing, cover each tray with a double sheet of newspaper or empty compost bag to exclude the light and put it in a warm place (see illustration, page 146). A minimum of 21°C (70°F) gives the best results – you'll then get germination in five to seven days.

The moment you see any sign of life, remove the covering and expose the whole tray to bright light. You want to move them to a place where the temperature is more like 18°C (65°F), trying to avoid it falling below 13°C (55°F) at night. A covering of fleece on plants standing on a heated blanket will help.

Keep the compost moist at all times, watering from below to avoid the risk of damping off.

Seven keys to success with tomatoes

1 There has been a great rash of catalogues in the last few years listing a hundred different types of tomatoes. I was carried along with this train-spottery enthusiasm, growing two or three plants of ten or fifteen different types over three or four years. I now realize that you're much better off finding three or four superb and easy varieties you like and sticking to them. So many of the oddities I grew – with strange colours, unusual shapes and sizes – just didn't taste very nice, or else didn't ripen well in our cooler climate, so were left to rot on the plant. Now I grow only a few plants of three or four varieties (see page 231), and almost every fruit is eaten.

2 Don't always buy your seedlings from a garden centre. It seems a sensible thing to do to save time, but they have a limited choice, and it's not always the best. If you grow your own from seed, you can select your three or four from a wider crew. Look for variety recommendations in books and ask your tomato-growing friends.

3 Tomatoes are tough and easy plants to grow from seed. You can tell this by the fact that they self-sow. Watch where you've had tomato plants before. You'll see mini seedlings appearing wherever they've grown and they will often appear on the compost heap. The tomato's toughness means that any sowing system you like will do! I sow mine into the large-diameter Jiffy 7, two seeds into each pellet (see page 145), but Matthew Rice, one of my main veg-gardening friends, prefers to chuck the whole pack into one pot in the greenhouse and prick them out from there.

4 Tomatoes do well in containers inside or out, where they will thrive against a sunny wall. As a general rule, large-fruited varieties ripen best in a greenhouse. They need that extra protection to ripen in our grey climate. All other smaller tomatoes, particularly the cherries, will grow outside in a sunny, sheltered spot.

5 Potato blight is a fungus that affects tomatoes, particularly those grown outside. It is bad in a wet summer. Fruit turns black and shrivels on the plant. When I first had blight on my tomatoes, I thought it was all my own fault. It's true that I hadn't been watering them quite enough, but after going away one weekend, I came back to find them looking as if someone had attacked them with a flame torch! Every leaf was curled up, brown or black and almost crispy. Then I looked at the fruit and this was blackened too. Blight presents utter devastation almost overnight, leaving you with not one single fruit to pick. It is rife in my garden – particularly in a damp year – and so I can only grow tomatoes outside with a two-weekly preventative dose of Bordeaux mixture, starting in July. I try to avoid the use of chemicals, so opt to grow my plants with the extra protection they get inside.

6 If you love tomatoes and would like to have them to harvest from July until November, two sowings is a good idea. I sow one lot in late February to crop from July until early October and another lot in May to crop from August until November. If you have a greenhouse, this succession system works well.

7 You can easily save your own tomato seed. Towards the end of the season, pick some fruits, scoop out the seeds and lay them out, gunge and all, on a sheet of paper towel. Leave them to dry there for a week or so and then remove the seeds and store them in an envelope in the fridge for next year.

Left **Comfrey leaves, rotting in water, make the perfect tomato food.** Opposite **Ripe yet firm – tomato 'Costoluto Fiorentino' is perfect just with Maldon salt.**

Below **Growing-bags contain
very few nutrients, so
correct watering and
feeding are crucial.**

Potting on

After the seed leaves appear, true leaves, characteristic
of a tomato plant, will unfurl. As soon as they have
good-sized true leaves, transplant the seedlings into
9cm (3½in) square pots (or bigger).

Plant them deep, sinking them to a depth of 7.5mm
(¼in) below the seed leaves. If you have lanky plants
don't worry. Nip off the seed leaves and bury the plant
to within 2.5cm (1in) of the first pair of true leaves. The
buried section of stem will grow roots.

Planting out

Tomatoes taste better when grown outdoors in a good
summer, which is why they sometimes seem to be a
different fruit when bought in Mediterranean markets of
southern France, Italy and Spain. In Britain, the lower

light levels and greater rainfall cause more of a problem
with potato blight for tomatoes grown outside. Sadly it's
usually safer to grow them indoors (see page 16).

Tomato growing in the greenhouse or polytunnel

Tomatoes do not like a build-up of heat, so ventilate the
greenhouse, day and night, after the plants are three to
four weeks old. There are three different ways you can
grow them:

✿ **In the soil** Plant them into your greenhouse/
polytunnel beds in May, but only when your plants are
15–20cm (6–8in) tall, with the flowers on the first truss
(the lowest side-stem) just opening. Ideally you want to
build up a good root system before they go in.

Make sure the soil is well manured. If you're creating
raised beds, use a soil-based compost like John Innes
No 2, or even better No 3, which is richer in nutrients.
You need the soil content to help retain moisture.
A compost without soil, or a peat-based mixture, will
dry out completely if it's ever not watered in the summer,
and then it's very difficult to get it to hold water again.
Manure is also said to help with flavour.

Rotate your plants round the beds from one year
to the next. Pests and diseases may build up in the soil
if you grow them in the same place over several years.
I have friends who have a beautiful Victorian greenhouse
and they've grown their tomatoes in the same bed for
years. They get round the problem by changing their
soil. Those who are not organic can use a soil sterilant
instead.

When you plant, dig them in as deep as you dare.
Tomatoes are one of the few plants that actually benefit
from a slight change in soil level. It encourages them to
create more feeding roots from the newly buried section
of stem, and this potentially enhances flavour.

✿ **In pots** Fill the pots, which should be large – at least
5 or 7 litres – with a good, fertile compost (as above)
and plant your seedlings when the plants are 15–20cm

(6–8in) tall, with the flowers on the first truss (the lowest side-stem) just opening. These will need feeding weekly (see page 20).

✿ **In a growing-bag** Growing-bags contain very few nutrients, so correct watering and feeding are crucial. They will need watering a couple of times a day to stop them drying out on a hot day and they contain only enough food to keep a tomato plant going for three weeks. After that point, weekly feeding is essential. You can use plastic ring-culture pots in a growing-bag, planting the seedling and feeding it in the central pot and watering into the collar on the outside (see Watering, right).

Tomato growing outside in the garden

You can use any of the same growing techniques outside, but to get the most from your plants, opt for early-ripening varieties. The growing season outside is at least a month shorter than under cover. Tomato 'Marmande', any of the cherries, and the smaller-fruiting variety 'Gardener's Delight' all grow well outside.

Tomatoes hate wind, so choose your most sheltered place to plant. They don't do well with temperature fluctuations either, with hot days and cold nights. This is important at the beginning and end of the season. If you are growing your plants outside, wait to put them out until June. Night-time temperatures plummet less by that stage of the year. Also, if you know it's going to be cold, wrap them with fleece.

Ground preparation

It's a good idea to add organic garden potash to the soil just before planting. This will encourage heavy fruiting. Fresh wood ash also contains potash, and comfrey leaves, chopped up and added to the soil, are another excellent source. We chop our comfrey down to the ground in May and use some to make a feed (see Feeding, page 20) and lay the rest as a thick mulch of leaves around the base of the plants in the greenhouse. This decreases water evaporation and, as the leaves rot

Below **The small-fruiting tomato variety 'Gardener's Delight' grows well outside.**

down slowly, it helps feed the plants with just what they need to fruit well.

Watering

Tomatoes have a dual root system. The top roots are coarse and fibrous, the lower ones fine and long. The top roots are the feeding roots. The lower ones are the water seekers. This dictates how you should water, and the same applies whether you are growing them inside or out.

You need to get water to the deeper, drinking roots. An effective technique is to sink a plastic bottle to three-quarters of its height upside down in the soil beside each plant. With the cap pierced a few times and the bottom sliced off this works as a funnel, taking water down deep where it's needed. The ideal amount per plant is about a litre – a couple of pints – a day in hot weather.

If you water – as most of us do – into the soil surface, some of the water is absorbed by the feeding roots. This dilutes the fruit's flavour. You also want to water after picking fruit, not before. It sounds crazy that it can be absorbed so quickly, but a recent dousing will again lessen the intensity of the tomatoes' flavour.

Whether inside or out, steady watering is important. Tomatoes don't like fluctuations between drought and water-logging. Once the fruit is formed, sporadic and excessive watering will cause the skin to split and scar where the fruit joins the stem. Over-watering also noticeably dilutes the taste. Don't add fertilizer to this water aimed at the drinking roots. It is the feeding roots that you want to nourish.

Feeding

Once the flowers set, and not before, give your plants a liquid feed about once a week, straight on to the soil. With fruiting as opposed to leafy crops you want low-nitrogen and high-potash feed – exactly what you get with comfrey.

Comfrey leaves, rotting in water, make the perfect tomato food. Cut your plant down to the ground when you plant your tomatoes, and put all the leaves in a standard-sized bucket. Fill the bucket with water and leave the whole thing to stew for three to four weeks. Pour off the revolting-smelling liquid and store it in a plastic milk carton to feed any fruiting plant. I dilute it 6 to 1 with water.

If you can't stand the comfrey stink, there is now an organic form of Miracle-gro, and Maxicrop and seaweed-based feeds are also good to use.

Supporting

Nearly all varieties of tomato need some support. With bush varieties it's a good idea to use wire mesh rabbit netting, bent round in a circle for support, about 30cm (12in) high and 45cm (18in) in diameter. Cut the bottom horizontal pieces of wire off, so you're left with vertical prongs that can be stuck into the ground.

Cordons will need taller support. The best system is to use canes or taut twine attached to an overhead frame and then regularly tie in your plants. Twine is a quick and easy system. Whenever you walk past, twiddle the latest top growth around the string and it should stay in place.

Trimming

Side-shoots develop in the axils (angles between the leaves and stems) of each leaf, and in cordons must be removed while they are small. These leafy shoots grow quickly and use up water and nutrients needed by the main stem to produce lots of flowering trusses and large fruit. If this extra foliage is left in place, the plants fruit less well, and produce fewer, smaller tomatoes. It also shades the fruit and reduces ventilation, which can lead to botrytis (a fungal infection that kills the upper stem).

Snap off the small side-shoots between your thumb and forefinger. This is why trimming is often called 'pinching out'. However, if you go away for a few days and the side-shoots become too large, it is better to cut them with a sharp knife than risk bruising the central stem.

You need to stop your plants too – that is, remove the growing point (the tip of the plant) – or they'll keep on growing to the skies. With outside plants, do this two leaves beyond the top truss when five or six trusses (old flower stems) have set fruit.

Under cover, you can leave them to grow to the roof if you want. With heavy croppers like 'Sungold' we encourage them to turn through a right-angle bend when they reach the roof of the polytunnel and train them along horizontal canes. This gives us lots of fruit for harvesting late in the year when all the lower trusses have been eaten. In a good year, 'Sungold' will be left to produce twelve or fifteen trusses and almost all are likely to ripen – with admittedly smaller and smaller fruit.

When the plants are about 1.5m (5ft) tall, remove the lower leaves up to the first truss. This allows light and air into the bottom of the plant and decreases the likelihood of fungal disease.

Below **Cordons need taller support than bush varieties. The best system is to use** **canes or taut twine attached to an overhead frame and then regularly tie in.**

With bigger-fruiting varieties like 'Brandywine', you may need a supporting string for a big truss. You waste the whole lot if it breaks, so support them before it does.

Pests and diseases

Greenfly and whitefly are the main pests of tomatoes. The problem is at its worst as the plants are growing rapidly before they fruit. I dose my plants with an insecticidal soap (this is considered organic), to help prevent virus infections spread by the aphids. There is also a wasp for biological control: *Encarsia formosa* against whitefly and *Aphidius colemani* against aphids.

Companion planting can be an effective form of protection against aphid infestation. Nasturtiums, tagetes, garlic and basil are all good companion plants for tomatoes. Nasturtiums, tagetes and garlic work by repelling the insects with their pungent smell, whereas basil is so beloved by aphids that they will go for that first. You can remove a badly infested basil plant and burn it, with the aphids still stuck to the leaves!

Harvesting

You should be picking tomatoes in July and still harvesting from the cordons indoors until October/ November. Any plants growing outside will not ripen their fruit after September. Pick the whole lot green and ripen them inside on a sunny windowsill. You can ripen tomatoes in the dark if you put a ripe banana in with them. The ethylene gas given off by the banana ripens them, but they won't be as sweet as those ripened in the sun.

21

Peas

Last summer we had vast quantities of peas in the garden. One day in early August, we were about to set off for a family holiday in Scotland and I was packing the car. My daughters Rosie and Molly were bored, so I asked each of them to fill a carrier bag with peas to take with us. We ate some of them straight from the bag on the journey, which were delicious, and then ate the rest on our arrival a couple of days later. These were dull and tasteless, more like plump, protein-rich lentils than peas. There was almost no sweetness left. I hadn't realized until then that if you can't eat peas within hours of picking, you might as well have them frozen.

Sowing and growing peas

Preparing the soil

Peas like a sunny spot, with lots of moisture but well-drained soil. To help with this, add plenty of organic material – farmyard manure or home-made compost – before planting. Make sure the ground is completely weed-free. It's difficult to get in between the plants to weed once they're growing.

Sowing direct

If you are sowing direct into the soil, plan on at least two plantings of peas. Do the first one in March for summer picking (unless your soil is heavy – see below) and the second in mid-summer, with at least twelve weeks before the first expected frost, for picking in the autumn.

You can add a third sowing in the autumn for over-wintering outside. This will give you an early harvest in May and June. For this late sowing you need round-seeded peas that are hardy enough to be sown outdoors in October or November (see varieties, page 216). Cover the shoots with cloches for protection until March. To succeed with peas on heavy soil, don't put them straight in the ground till late April or even May – or they won't germinate and you'll end up with a very patchy row. And watch out for late frosts after a spot of warm weather, or it will be the same story – many of your seeds will rot before they germinate.

Spacing

Create a shallow-bottomed trench about 2.5cm (1in) deep and 15cm (6in) wide, clearing the soil with a hoe. Sow three rows of seeds about 4cm (1½in) apart in each direction. Push the seeds lightly into the ground, and then rake the soil back over them, marking the rows at both ends. The distance between rows depends on the height of the variety. As a general rule, allow the height of the plant between each row. This leaves enough room for sunlight to reach the plants. Remember with the dwarf forms to allow enough room for easy picking.

Sowing into guttering for an early harvest

If you love fresh peas as much as I do and want them for eating as early as possible, the guttering method is a very effective technique, allowing you to sow your pea seeds under cover in early March, for putting out in the garden within a month.

Choose a hardy variety like 'Feltham First' or 'Early Onward' and sow them into lengths of plastic guttering instead of pots, and store this inside.

Geoff Hamilton used to show this technique on *Gardener's World* and tells you how to do it in his *Organic Garden Bible*. Fill the pipe with compost – any cheap sort will do – and sow two staggered rows of peas, 5cm (2in) apart. Cover the seeds with 2.5cm (1in) of compost.

The peas germinate quickly and reliably in the greater warmth under cover – a bit of heat helps, but a cold greenhouse will do – and will be ready for planting out in four to six weeks' time, when they're about 8cm (3in) tall.

To prevent the whole lot ending up on the floor, planting out the guttering calls for two people, one at either end of the pipe. Out in the garden, make a trench to mirror the depth and length of the gutter, scooping out the soil with a trowel or draw hoe. The pea seedlings

Opposite **If you love fresh peas as much as I do and want them for eating as early as possible, the guttering method is a very effective technique.**

Four keys to success with peas

1 Peas are ideal for sowing into guttering. This will give you peas to eat from the end of May on heavy soil, a good two months earlier than those direct sown (see page 22).

2 Successional sowing is the way to achieve a regular drip-drip supply. For perfect timing, space your sowings three weeks apart so that as one crop fades out it is replaced immediately by the next.

3 Mangetouts and sugar-snap peas are both prolific croppers, so take care not to sow great avenues of these. If you don't pick them regularly, they will falter with

their supply. The productivity of these two groups makes them ideal for growing to crop as pea tips (see Picking, below right).

4 Peas like steady temperatures, so make sure it's not too hot or too cold when you sow. Soil temperatures need to have reached 10°C (50°F) for reliable germination outside. Even if you've got this temperature and your sowing is followed immediately by a cold spell, many of your seeds will rot away before they germinate. Peas also dislike hot weather, so avoid sowing in a heatwave.

can then be slid from the gutter pipe into the U trench, in a series of sections about 45cm (18in) long. Slide one section in and then push the next forward to the mouth of the pipe. Then slide that one in, and so on. With each instalment, firm them in well and water.

If it's cold, with frost likely at night, protect the pea seedlings under a mini plastic tunnel or a cloche. You could be harvesting your peas as early as late May.

Growing in containers

Peas are ideal for growing in containers, which is useful if you don't have much space. Sow early dwarf varieties like 'Little Marvel' and 'Lincoln' successionally through the spring. Use large containers with at least 30cm (12in) of loam-based compost below the roots, feeding with liquid manure or seaweed to maintain fertility. Provide support as the plants grow, keeping them weed-free and watered.

Supporting

When the plants are 2.5–5cm (1–2in) tall, you need to stake them. Don't leave them longer to trail along the ground, or they'll be eaten by slugs and snails. Also, yields are higher when plants are supported.

Use netting supported on canes, or pea sticks cut from the top growth of hazel, hornbeam or birch. These are available at good garden centres and wood product outlets. Create a framework from the canes or sticks on either side of your line, 10cm (4in) from the edge, about 15cm (6in) high above the seedlings, and then push in some larger sticks or twiggy branches over the top for the peas to grow on to later.

Aftercare

Hoe between rows to keep your soil weed-free. It's a good idea to mulch with home-made compost, or grit if it's heavy soil, once the seeds have germinated. This helps suppress weeds and prevents the soil drying out. Water in dry spells if the plants are in flower or fruiting. One good watering when the flowers are just finishing will improve yields substantially. The peas themselves age and toughen more quickly when it's dry.

Picking

There are three rules of picking to ensure that you get the best. Always pick peas young; leave picking as late as you can before you eat, to maximize the sweetness; and pick regularly, ideally two or three times a week, to promote the formation of more pods.

You can get one pea tip (see page 64) from each plant to eat in a salad. Pinching the top as the first peas set makes the plant bush out and increases the total yield.

Clearing

It's time to cut the plants down when there are too few new pods being formed to make the rows worth picking. Leave the roots in the ground. After the growing season, pea roots are rich with nitrogen-fixing nodules, which will add fertility to the ground for the following crops.

Below **When the plants are 2.5–5cm (1–2in) tall, you need to stake them. Don't leave them longer to trail** along the ground, or they'll be eaten by slugs and snails. Yields are higher when plants are supported. Overleaf **The vegetable bank in early spring with hardy cut-and-come-again salad and herbs.**

Pests and diseases

Peas are usually a very healthy crop, but it's good to be aware of a few hazards.

Birds Seeds and seedlings may be eaten or dislodged from the soil by birds. Cover the line of seed with a home-made, wire-netting cloche, or with hazel arranged so that the birds can't get at the seed.

Mice As mice love pea seeds they may be a problem in your garden. If they are, try a useful allotment technique. Douse a rag in paraffin and roll the peas around in the rag. This should deter any rodents from feasting on your seeds. Another technique is to soak the seeds in a seaweed fertilizer for about an hour before sowing. This won't harm the seeds, but will discourage pests.

Powdery and downy mildew These are the commonest problems with peas, hitting them particularly in the autumn, so watch this with your summer-sown crop. Sow resistant varieties (see page 216).

Pea moth The adult moth lays her eggs on the flower buds, and the resulting caterpillars may devastate your whole crop. To prevent this, cover your row with fleece when the flower buds start to form. The pea moth pupates close to where the peas are grown, so sow as far away as possible from where you had peas last year. If pea moth is a problem in your garden, avoid sowing in March/April for a June/July cropping, as this is their main egg-laying period. Sow peas either before or after this time.

Sweetcorn

Most of us cook the hell out of sweetcorn and, to be honest, if you buy it that's not much of a loss. The best corn on the cob is picked less than half an hour – some would say ten minutes – before you eat it, and thrown into a pan of boiling water for no more than five minutes. This just heats through every kernel and leaves it sweet and fantastically crunchy. Leave the husk on when you cook it, and use unsalted water. Then eat it stripped bare, with a scrunch of Maldon salt, lots of black pepper and a knob of butter. There's almost nothing better the garden can produce.

For flavour, varieties are the key. I have grown many old varieties of sweetcorn, which sound great in the catalogue but are tough and tasteless. Sweetcorn has improved in taste and productivity in recent years and it's one of the cases where modern varieties seem to be reliably the best. I like F1 'Sweet Nugget' and 'Swift'. These are both so-called supersweet varieties and, if you choose them, you must then grow only supersweet varieties nearby, or they will cross-pollinate and the sweet effect of the F1 is lost. Whichever variety you grow, however, it's still vital to eat them freshly picked.

We also eat lots of sweetcorn on picnics and barbecues. I cook it for its five minutes before we go and then chuck it on to a griddle or barbecue and cook it until slightly charred on all sides. This process intensifies the sweetness till it's almost syrupy, and it's one of Rosie and Molly's favourite things.

Rosie also has a passion for popcorn and has an American pan with a paddle in the bottom to prevent the kernels burning as they pop. We've grown some good varieties, such as 'Strawberry Corn', which pops brilliantly and looks decorative growing in the garden.

As with pumpkins and squash, corn is not just about delicious meals. With its tall, grassy appearance and architectural form, sweetcorn can be mixed into your borders if you run out of space in your veg garden. There are some ornamental varieties in amazing colours – pink, slatey-grey and multi-coloured grains – with stripes in the leaves of brilliant pink and green.

Sweetcorn is a great plant to have in the garden and invaluable for decorating the house when things are lean. To create some annual highlights, grow some of these non-edible forms as well.

Sowing and growing sweetcorn
Sowing

I sow sweetcorn under cover in late April at a temperature of 13°C (55°F), straight into 8cm (3in) pots. Their large seeds are ideal for this system. These fast-growing plants resent root disturbance and checking, so we use biodegradable coir pots that can be planted straight into the ground – plant, pot and all.

Planting

Once the frosts are over, sweetcorn can be planted into the garden. Dig a hole twice the size of your pot to enable you to plant the seedlings deeper than they are in the pots. The buried stems grow more adventitious roots, which help support the plants and usually avoid the need for staking. Earth them up if you see signs of wind rock, or if you can see the roots.

Plant in blocks, not lines. Sweetcorn is wind pollinated and neat rows make pollination less likely. Blocks allow pollination whichever way the wind is blowing. You'll see the male flowers – which look like miscanthus blooms – at the top of the plant in the summer. These drop their pollen down on to the female flowers called 'silks' – the bunch of tassels that pour out of the end of corn. Bald areas of poor kernel formation indicate that poor pollination has taken place.

Space your plants at 40cm (15in) intervals in each direction. A block 1.2m (4ft) square will then contain sixteen plants.

Aftercare

Water well at all times, especially during dry weather, and harvest in late summer as you want to eat them. The greatest threat to a good harvest can be mice. If they find your sweetcorn they can strip every cob!

Potatoes

Is there any point in growing your own potatoes? After all, if you go into your local greengrocer or farm shop, you'll almost certainly find three or four good varieties on offer. 'Maris Piper', 'Cara', 'Wilja', 'Désirée' and 'King Edward' are all widely available. In the spring and summer, add the famous, waxy 'Jersey Royal' (or 'International Kidney'), and if you visit one of the large supermarkets, you'll probably get tasty 'Charlotte' as well. Most of these varieties are grown organically on a large scale, so you won't even have to worry about any chemicals that might have been used to combat blight, scab and other diseases. So, with this selection on offer, why bother to grow your own?

You only have to taste one home-grown 'International Kidney' (which is in fact the 'Jersey Royal') eaten with a few shreds of mint, or a cold 'Pink Fir Apple' mixed with mayonnaise, capers and red onions in a potato salad, and you've got the answer. You will occasionally find 'Pink Fir Apple' at a farmer's market, but I've yet to see them in a shop. In June and July, my husband Adam and I sometimes eat a plate of new potatoes with a bowl of salad for lunch and that's it. There are not many things I'd rather eat: simple and utterly delicious.

You can have some fun with home-grown potatoes too, going for a few weird and wacky varieties like 'Highland Burgundy Red' and 'Salad Blue'. These have deep-red and purple-blue flesh respectively. They are best cooked in their skin and they cause quite a stir as chips (see picture on page 10).

The pleasure of digging up the crop would be enough for me, even if I didn't like eating them. It's the veg gardener's lucky dip, with more and more potatoes emerging as you delve. Growing and eating your own potatoes is like sleeping under a goose-down duvet: once you've experienced it, you won't go back!

Which to grow

Potatoes are either floury or waxy in consistency. I am more a waxy person than a floury, but you may want some of both types as they fulfil different culinary roles. Waxy potatoes have a low water content, which means they hold up well to boiling and chopping once cooked. This makes them ideal as new potatoes, cooked with mint and served hot or in salads, as well as sautéd and dauphinoise.

Floury potatoes have a higher water content, which means the flesh 'collapses' when it's cooked, creating a rough surface that crisps up well in oil, while the inside becomes fluffy. These are the ones for roasting, baking, mash and chips.

In an ideal world, you would grow at least three different types (see pages 218–19):

✿ At least one 'first early' like 'International Kidney' for eating in June and July.

✿ A 'second early' or 'early maincrop' like 'Ratte' (or 'Belle de Fontenay') to follow on for July and August.

✿ One later maincrop like 'Pink Fir Apple' for storing, to give you your own delicious potatoes to eat right the way through until next spring.

Growing potatoes

Chitting

Chitting ensures a quicker, larger harvest. With early varieties it gets them off to a flying start, but I do it for maincrop potatoes too. It makes them grow faster and form larger tubers once they are planted out.

Chitting means sprouting the tuber – putting it, with most of its eyes facing upwards (see left-hand picture on page 33), in a light, cool, but frost-free place, at about 10°C (50°F). I put half of mine in the porch by the window and half in the greenhouse. A garage or porch, slightly warmed by the house, is an ideal place. Light is important. Don't put them in the airing cupboard!

If you have only a few to chit, line them up in egg cartons. If you're doing lots, put the tubers in shallow, open boxes, like the slatted-bottomed ones you can get

Opposite, clockwise from top left **'International Kidney'**, **'Highland Burgundy Red'**, **'Belle de Fontenay'** and **'Salad Blue'**.

from greengrocers. Use folded newspaper to divide these into sections and keep the tubers upright.

Wait for short but strong green shoots about 2cm (¾in) long to appear from the eyes of each tuber. You don't want the white, spaghetti-like things that you get when potatoes are kept in the dark.

If the tubers have lots of sprouts, rub off all but three or four at the top end. If you leave them all intact, there's too much competition – you'll end up with lots of potatoes, but they'll all be small.

Soil preparation

Add lots of well-rotted manure to your patch the previous autumn. Potatoes like a lot of organic material in the soil, but make sure it's not fresh. This will give you all tops and no potatoes, and lots of trouble with slugs. The manure also helps create an ideal water-retentive soil. A good water content helps prevent scab.

Planting

Always plant with the sprouting, or rose, end up.

Start planting first earlies at the beginning of March. Plant this first lot beneath earthed-up soil, an insulating mulch, or black polythene sheeting or cloches. Lay the sheeting over the area to be planted, burying the edges or securing them with bricks.

Cut slits in the plastic in rows 60cm (2ft) apart, with 30cm (12in) between each tuber, and dig a hole 15cm (6in) deep with a hand trowel or potato planter for each one. The top of the tuber should be about 8cm (3in) below the top level of the soil.

Later in March, get a second lot in. This time dig a trench 10–13cm (4–5in) deep, lining it with garden compost or the contents of old growing-bags, spreading about 2.5cm (1in) of soil on top. It gives the potatoes that grow from the seed tuber as soft an area to grow in as possible. Use the same planting distances as above.

Plant your second earlies in April and your maincrops in late April/May. Maincrops make bigger

plants, and wider spacing helps air circulation and so avoids blight. They need more room between the rows. Go for 75cm (2ft 6in) between lines, with 45cm (18in) between tubers, again planted about 15cm (6in) deep. Wider spacing makes for larger potatoes. For tiny potatoes, plant them closer at about 25cm (10in).

My current favourite tool is a potato planter – a circular cutter on a spade handle – and I use this to plant all my potatoes now. It cuts out a core of soil. You plop the potato in and then, as you cut out the next core, the first one pops out of the tool and can be put back over the potato sitting in its hole.

Earthing up

Earthing up gives protection against late frost, improves cropping, protects the crop from pests and diseases, particularly blight, and ensures that the tubers do not push up and turn green in the light. It also makes lifting the crop easier, with fewer damaged tubers.

Earthing up means drawing up the soil around the stems when the plants have shoots 15–20cm (6–8in) tall. Spread a handful of blood, fish and bone down each metre (3ft) of the row, then earth up by pulling soil from between the rows up to the shoots, leaving a few centimetres still showing.

It is particularly important with the earlies. Once the tops start coming through, earth them up, or cover them with a double layer of fleece as protection against frost. They must remain covered until the frosts finish during May.

A very ornamental alternative to earthing up is to grow your potatoes in vast 'baskets'. These can be made from four woven hurdles 1m (3ft) high and about 1.5m (5ft) long. Secure the hurdles in the ground, making a rectangle. Place your tubers on the ground inside and half fill the basket with compost, molehills and well-rotted manure. As the haulms (the top, leafy parts of the potato plants) grow, don't earth up, but fill the rest of the basket. You can then remove a hurdle on one side and harvest the potatoes easily from there.

Six keys to success with potatoes

1 For potatoes early in the year (May/June) plant a few tubers in pots or black compost bags in the greenhouse in February. The quickest of all is 'Swift', which will be ready to eat in May. Other suitable types are 'La Ratte' and International Kidney, ready in early June. I plant mine into large (at least 5-litre) pots or empty compost bags – filled with one-third molehill soil or John Innes No 2, and two-thirds compost. Molehills give you lovely crumbly loam, in the making of which the moles have done lots of the hard work for you. They create the most delicious, friable, grass-free soil from a depth usually below the worst of the weed seed – and it's free! I use it all the time for my container-grown veg.

2 If you want new potatoes at Christmas, plant some tubers in July. You can buy specially treated 'second-cropping' seed potatoes from suppliers, which will produce a delicious crop of new potatoes only 60–70 days after planting, or you can do your own (see page 218). These will hold well in the ground until they're needed. Once the frosts start, though, cover the bed with a mulch of straw. Suitable types are 'Charlotte' and 'Maris Piper'.

3 Earth up all your potatoes (see page 32), except for long, thin potatoes with widely spreading growth, such as 'Pink Fir Apple'. These are best left unridged because if you earth them up, the long tubers may poke out and turn green. You're better off using a mulch of garden compost between the rows for these, right up to the necks of the plants.

4 Broad beans are an excellent companion plant and nurse crop for first early potatoes. Plant the broad bean seeds between rows as you earth them up. When the potato tops come through again, the broad beans will provide protection from the frost. You can crop and remove the beans before the potatoes need more room.

5 Do not use mushroom compost on your potato bed. This may be high in lime, which encourages scab, and in any case potatoes prefer an acid soil. If you have a soil with a high pH and/or scab problems, try to lower the pH with sulphur and grow only early potatoes. These don't suffer as much from scab, which is more prevalent in the dryer months of summer and autumn.

6 Potatoes are good for planting in very weedy areas. They compete with the weeds – and win. When you dig up your crop, your ground is clean as long as you lift the thistle, dock and bindweed roots with the spuds.

Above **Fresh from the soil, 'Dunluce' taste marvellous.** Left **Chitting means sprouting the tuber in light and cool conditions.**

Harvesting

Earlies Start lifting your early potatoes when they begin to flower. Take only what is needed for eating then, leaving the rest to grow on.

Maincrops Harvest the maincrops only after the tops have completely died back. Pick a fine day for your harvest. Dig from the sides of the ridges, and don't stick the fork in too close, or you'll end up spearing all the best ones at the heart of the plant.

Once the potatoes are above ground, remove as much soil as you can without damaging the skins and allow them to dry for a few hours, turning them once. Leave them on the soil if it's dry, or on a path if wet.

If you do not have a problem with slugs or scab, leave even the maincrops in the ground and harvest when you want to eat them. But you must lift them before the frosts.

Storing maincrops

Potatoes have to be stored in darkness, in a cool, frost-free place, preferably near the kitchen. Make sure the potatoes are dry. Look out for any badly damaged tubers and chuck them.

Store them in heavy-duty paper sacks and stand them on a couple of pallets to let the air in underneath, which discourages rot. You still need to check your stored potatoes once in a while. One bad one will rot the bag if left where it is.

You can buy heavy-duty hessian sacks that will exclude light, yet allow your tubers to breathe, which also helps to prevent rot.

Pests and diseases

To minimize problems with disease, practise a system of plant rotation (see page 166).

Blight A fungal disease that starts as a round mark on the leaves, almost like a cigarette burn. White powdery deposits form. These are the spores. At the first signs cut off the top growth if you don't want to spray. Blight spreads very rapidly. Any diseased plants should be burnt, and the tubers left undisturbed for several weeks.

The spray to use – if any – is Bordeaux mixture, a traditional combination of copper sulphate and lime. Apply from the first week of July and then every fortnight after that. Blight thrives in the damp, so if we have a wet summer some people spray as a protective measure.

Scab This is a common problem on dry soils. The best thing with scab is to prevent it. Add plenty of organic material before planting to help retain moisture, and mulch the patch with anything like lawn clippings as long as the soil is moist when you do it. Do not plant on freshly limed ground. This also encourages scab. Watering is a last resort. Once you start you have to keep it up, and the flavour deteriorates.

Slugs I use the biological slug control Nemaslug to protect my potatoes. This kills above and below ground.

Cutworms These can be a problem on grassland brought into cultivation. I had a problem with them when I first started my garden at Perch Hill in East Sussex, which was created out of pasture. In time, with regular cultivation and turning over to encourage birds to feast, the cutworms were reduced.

Potato cyst eelworm Eelworms, either yellow or white, are the things that form lots of tiny channels straight through the middle of your potato. They are a pain, so try to find resistant varieties. Those resistant to the yellow eelworm are 'Accent', 'Nadine', 'Rocket', 'Cara' and 'Maris Piper'. Varieties resistant to both yellow and white are 'Cromwell' and 'Santé'. The best protection is rotation: maincrops over five years, earlies over three.

Opposite **BF15 has wonderful flavour and very good, firm texture, which makes it an ideal, all-round potato.**

Carrots

These are the vegetables, *par excellence*, that taste most delicious picked and eaten straight out of the ground. They have that characteristic taste, somewhere between parsley and celery, but it is much sweeter, earthier and denser than the taste of shop-bought carrots, which have lost at least half their flavour. They're best eaten raw, after a wash under the tap. My children can be bolshie about eating vegetables, but they'll eat bowls of carrots, preferring them raw to cooked.

Sowing and growing carrots
Preparing the soil

If you garden on heavy clay, you will need to improve the drainage. On my heavy soil, I add sharp sand to the sowing position of carrots to encourage good germination. They like hot, dry, well-drained ground. I add a shovelful of washed inland sharp sand to every metre or so of line, and fork it into the top 5–8cm (2–3in) of soil. Sharp sand is the thing for carrots because it's fine. Grit or stony soil can cause them to fork.

Sowing

For early sowing, warm up the soil in mid-February by placing a cloche over it for a couple of weeks before sowing. In early March, create drills 1cm (½in) deep. Sow the seed directly into the ground as thinly as possible. Space rows out at least 30cm (12in) apart.

If you have room, do another sowing in about three weeks. Again, the best method is serial sowing, ideally getting a new batch in every three to four weeks from mid-spring to mid-summer (see page 191). This will keep you in roots until the frosts, and leave you a few to protect and mulch, and then to harvest through the winter.

Thinning

When the seedlings are about 2.5cm (1in) tall, thin them out so they are 5cm (2in) apart. If you want larger maincrop carrots, thin to 10cm (4in). Remove the thinnings from the garden. The smell attracts the carrot fly (see page 38). After thinning, re-cover with fleece.

Aftercare

You must keep the rows weed-free – carrots will not grow well with too much competition around. Start hoeing between rows as soon as the seedlings emerge, hand weeding between the plants to avoid damaging the developing roots.

Always water after weeding, in case you've uprooted or disturbed any carrots. A wilting plant gives off a stronger smell.

Water regularly if it's dry, aiming to keep the ground moist at all times. Sporadic watering causes the roots to split. Apply a seaweed liquid feed every two to three weeks.

Harvesting

The early sowings will be ready from early summer, and the maincrops from autumn onwards. In the south you can leave these in the ground until you want to eat them, as long as you give them the protection of a thick straw mulch. In the north, lift them before the winter.

Opposite **Early picking means early sowing, so warm up the soil in mid-February.**

Below **For later sowing, use the tasty 'Sytan', which has some carrot fly resistance.**

Carrot fly

There is a particular problem with carrots that can make them a pain to grow. You sow your seed. They germinate and grow well, but when you harvest them you find that half the roots are a warren of holes. The entrances of the warrens may be tiny, but they can hide cavities bang in the middle of the root, which leaves you little to eat. The holes also tend to fill with bits of grit, and so, as with a slug-hole-studded potato, you end up with what feels like half the garden in your mouth.

The culprit is the carrot fly, an inconspicuous, tiny fly that lays its eggs in the soil near the crop. The fly lives in sheltered places that have

plenty of cover and a plentiful supply of nectar-rich food – a good description of most people's gardens in summer. It's not a choosy pest, and the maggots feed on carrots and any close relations, such as celery, celeriac, parsnips, parsley, angelica and lovage. A normal vegetable garden will have at least a couple of those, so the flies will have plenty of habitats in which to increase.

The fly is attracted to the smell of carrot, which is detectable all the time, but at its strongest when you thin a line. The smell of crushed foliage, as you pull seedlings out of the ground, is the most delicious thing the carrot fly can think of. Once the eggs are laid and hatching, the maggots crawl downwards and tunnel into the main carrot root. Sometimes the attack makes the leaves of young plants redden and wilt, but you often won't notice any change. So how can you guarantee to grow carrots without all the holes?

Ways to avoid carrot fly

1 Neither the adult flies nor the larvae are around all the time. There are two distinct populations a year – one at the end of May and early in June and another at the end of July and early in August. These are the times when large numbers of flies are looking for places to lay their

eggs, and therefore when carrots are most at risk. Avoid sowing at these times and you can still have a pristine, organic crop, especially if you have a few other protective mechanisms up your sleeve.

2 Never sow carrots on ground that has recently grown carrots, parsnips or any of its umbellifer relations. There may be maggots or pupae still in the soil, waiting to feast on any new crop you sow.

3 Protect your crop physically by using a barrier against the flies. Cover the line in horticultural fleece or very fine mesh netting. Fleece is best for an early crop grown in cool conditions and harvested quickly. At the hotter stage of the year use fine polypropylene netting (called Enviromesh or Insect Barrier Net). It allows more air circulation, and plants underneath are less likely to get mildew or rot. Put on the cover as soon as you sow, allowing plenty of slack at the sides. You can let these out as the crop grows. Leave the cover on into the autumn, removing it only when you finish harvesting. The netting can be annoying when you have to weed or harvest, and it hides slugs and snails, which will thrive in the moist conditions below, but it's a must on my heavy soil. It's the one thing that is guaranteed to

save my crop from carrot fly attack. Another physical defence is to enclose your lines with a screen, standing about 75cm (2ft 6in) high. Carrot flies fly close to the ground and this will prevent them finding your crop.

4 Grow a carrot resistant to the pest. Research over the last twenty years has revealed different fly susceptibilities between varieties. 'Sytan' and 'Flyaway' have shown partial resistance in tests. The roots contain a reduced level of chlorogenic acid, which the larvae need for survival, but results can vary from year to year and site to site.

5 A traditional organic way of protecting your carrots from fly was to try to disguise the smell of the carrots with a stronger smell. Interplanting a line with onions was recommended as a cunning way of confusing the pest and thus keeping it away. In our small trials at Perch Hill, we have had good results from intersowing our carrots with the spring onion North Holland Blood Red (or 'Noordhollandse Bloedrode' – see page 230).

Left **Some particularly nasty specimens, where the roots are a warren of holes.** Opposite **A healthy-looking bunch of 'Sytan', washed and ready to go.**

Hearting lettuce

Having a good, crunchy, sweet hearting lettuce to pick from the garden is fundamental to a perfect salad. There are few other plants that give you that bitey texture, and leaves that you can hear break in half and make lots of noise as you eat – an essential part of many salads.

As their sugars gradually start to turn to starch after picking, lettuce are guaranteed to be tastier when home-grown.

Types of lettuce

Lettuces divide into two groups – hearting lettuce and continental, loose-leaf types. The continentals are cut-and-come-again. You can slice them off a couple of centimetres above the ground, or pick as many leaves as you want for each meal, and they regrow. The root is left in the ground and quickly resprouts bright, baby leaves in a week or so. You sow and harvest them in the same way as salad leaves, so for this reason you'll find them in the salad leaf section (see page 94).

The lettuce we're talking about in this section are the hearting types – the ones that form a juicy centre to fill the palm of your hand. They tend to have a perter, more water-filled crunch. This lot divides into three groups: the Butterhead, Cos and Crisphead types.

Butterheads, like the widely grown 'Tom Thumb', are a bit of a wash-out where crunch is concerned. They tend to be the ones you get in canteen and school salads: rather tasteless, with limp, boring, mid-green leaves and hardly any heart.

Some people, including my husband, love floppy leaves. He says they're more friendly than the perter kinds and that their stems give you quite enough crunch. Their plus points are that the tiny leaves at the heart have a good flavour and they are quicker to mature than the Crispheads and Cos, which is why they are often cheaper as a commercial crop. They also generally tolerate poorer conditions. The downside is that they are the first to bolt.

Crispheads produce large hearts of curled and crisp leaves and are generally more resistant to bolting than the Butterheads. 'Webb's Wonderful' and 'Iceberg' are famous examples of these.

Cos, also known as Romaine, lettuce are easy to recognize by their upright growth habit and oblong head. The leaves are crisp and the flavour is good. They can be a little more difficult to grow than the other two groups,

Four keys to success with lettuce

1 Lettuces hate being moved. Whenever you can, sow seed where the crop is to grow, or sow them under cover in modules for planting out later on. Root disturbance encourages quick bolting.

2 Lettuce is the classic crop where you tend to get too many ready to eat at exactly the same time. If you don't harvest them soon, they bolt and turn bitter, and after that there are no more to harvest for months. Successional sowing is the key (see page 226). It's best to sow little and often, using a mix of varieties to get a continuous supply – every two to three weeks is ideal.

3 During hot weather, sow in the late afternoon or early evening. Lettuce prefers cool growing conditions, and seed germination can be inhibited in hot, dry weather. Sown late in the day, the seed starts to germinate during the coldest part of the night. The soil is coldest early in the morning, but the seed takes a certain amount of time to get its act together, so afternoon sowing makes sense. Water the soil where you are to sow as this cools it down.

4 A constant supply of moisture is vital for success. Lettuces bolt quickly if they are kept dry. Sow or plant into deeply cultivated ground, with lots of manure added to help the soil retain moisture. In a dry spell, water, using a leaky hose or a simple irrigation system. Water in the mornings on sunny days, so that the water on the leaves evaporates quickly, reducing the risk of disease and scorch. Watering at night encourages slugs and snails. Growing lettuces surrounded by black plastic sheeting warms the soil, suppresses weeds and conserves moisture, so again delays bolting. It's a good idea to plant the lettuces close together to hide the ugly plastic.

Below **My early summer lettuce bed planted with, from left to right, 'Merveille des Quatre** **Saisons', 'Black-seeded Simpson', 'Bronze Arrow' and 'Lobjoit's Green Cos'.**

and they take longer to mature, but in return they are slower to bolt. All too often with lettuces from the other two groups, I've been away when they have reached their perfect moment. By the time I'm back and wanting to eat them, they've bolted and then have bitter leaves.

Sowing and growing lettuce

Sowing direct

Lettuces thrive in an open, sunny site on light, moisture-retentive soil with a neutral pH. They struggle on dry or impoverished soil, so dig in plenty of well-rotted organic matter the autumn before sowing, or grow on ground manured for the previous crop. Following on from potatoes is a good idea.

Sow thinly in drills straight into the soil 1–1.5cm (½–⅝in) deep and then cover (see the direct-sowing instructions, page 140).

Thin spring and summer sowings to the final spacing when the plants are large enough to handle. Eat the thinnings: most won't survive transplanting. From an autumn sowing of the hardy types, such

as 'Merveille des Quatre Saisons' and Cos 'Freckles' ('Forellenschluss'), you'll inevitably lose a few plants in the winter, so leave thinning those seedlings to final spacing until the spring, or you may end up with a gappy row.

Thin small lettuces so that the distance between them and between the rows is about 20cm (8in). Butterheads should be planted about 30cm (12in) apart, Crispheads and large Cos about 40cm (15in) apart.

Sowing under cover

For early lettuces, sow under cover in March. They dislike root disturbance, so it's best to sow them into Jiffy 7 pellets, modules or guttering (see page 147), rather than traditional seed trays.

Growing in containers

Compact varieties such as 'Little Gem' are suitable for growing in containers. Use a soil-based compost, mix in a slow-release granular fertilizer and water regularly. Add water-retaining granules for summer pots. It is best to sow *in situ*, straight into the pot.

Asparagus

Asparagus is one of the few vegetables where the older it is, the better. The more established the crowns, the more they produce and the thicker the spears. My mother has had asparagus beds in her garden for decades. The spears erupt from her mounded beds, lined with espalier pears and linked with hoops of clematis, thicker than the base of my thumb. I remember how almost every evening in May we used to go out to the garden with a washing-up bowl and fill it with asparagus, which, having quickly cooked it, we would eat straight away with lots of melted salty butter. Other things have come and gone in my mother's garden, but now asparagus is the only vegetable she grows.

Most of us are put off by the idea that an asparagus bed takes years to produce, gives you food for only a couple of months maximum, and takes up too much permanent room. It's one of the last things on many people's list of priorities, and the same was true of me. It has taken me seven years to put in an asparagus bed at home, but what a mistake! Fresh-picked asparagus eaten by the vast plate-load is the caviar of the productive garden world. I wish I'd created my bed earlier, and every year I try to put in more. It's like the savings account – difficult to pay into it, if you're like me, but brilliant for years later if you have!

Growing asparagus
Soil preparation
Asparagus can be productive for up to twenty years, so choose the site with care. It likes light soil, with good drainage. On my heavy soil, vast quantities of horticultural grit and compost have to be added to the sticky clay. That's the only way the seaside asparagus will grow well for me. Over the whole surface of the beds, I added 5cm (2in) of compost and the same of grit and then mixed it in by rotavating.

Planting
Plant in mid-spring, once the soil is warm. Dig a trench 20cm (8in) deep and roughly 60cm (2ft) wide, with 1m (3ft) between two trenches. Put a handful of sand where each asparagus crown is to be planted. Put the base of the crown on the sand and spread the roots out like an octopus. Cover with 8–10cm (3–4in) of soil. Allow a distance of 40cm (15in) between each crown. Once they start to shoot, earth them up a bit, adding some more soil/mulch to give longer spears.

Harvesting
Harvest with a knife, slicing off a little below ground level to get the tender white part. This should mean that, if picked young, the whole spear from tip to base can be eaten. You can earth up your beds to get white asparagus – very popular on the Continent.

Cooking
Cook asparagus flat in a sauté pan with a lid. Add lots of sea salt. Boil a kettle and pour the water into the pan at the stalk – rather than tip – ends and cover, bringing it rapidly to the boil. Take them out of the pan as soon as the colour of the stems changes to that brilliant green. This takes no longer than five minutes.

Steaming the spears in bunches, spears up and base stem down, in a deep pan is another technique, but it has its problems. Water vapour cooks the asparagus more quickly, and the part of the asparagus in the water vapour is the softer tip. This makes the necks prone to breaking. When you take the lid off, you tend to find the best bits, mushy and over-cooked, at the bottom of the pan.

Pests and diseases
Asparagus beetle Black and yellow adults and small greyish larvae of asparagus beetles appear from May, feeding on the shoots and going on to strip stems and foliage. Pick off light infestations by hand. If it's a serious attack, I use derris dust.

Rust This used to be a problem with old varieties, but some resistance has been bred into newer hybrids.

Six keys to success with asparagus

1 New varieties of asparagus can be seed-grown, but I prefer to buy one-year-old crowns. These are at the best stage for planting. Whatever the seed merchant tells you, with seed-sown plants, you will be waiting several years before you can harvest a decent meal. With one-year-old crowns, you'll be picking several meals the following year. There's no point in buying older plants. If they are moved when they are more mature, it may stunt them.

2 New modern varieties of asparagus tend to be all male. They can produce twice the number of spears as the older, mixed male/female varieties. Self-seeding is a problem with older forms.

3 You must keep your beds weed-free. Weeds compete with the crowns, particularly when they are young, and will decrease your crop.

4 It's also crucial to stop harvesting in late June/July, and allow the ferns to grow. If you keep harvesting every spear after their main cropping season, you will weaken the plants. Don't be tempted to cut the ferns in the autumn either. Wait until they brown. They need to photosynthesize as long as possible, storing lots of food below ground to crop well next year.

5 Asparagus is a perennial, so you can't use successional sowing to prolong your season of picking. But what you can do is to choose successional cropping forms, and I've tried to do this in my bed. I've planted three varieties already, and I'm about to add a fourth. 'Connover's Colossal' is the earliest variety, and the most popular choice in Britain, with its thick stalks and heavy production. I could eat every spear of asparagus given to me, but if you can't keep up with the quantities erupting from the ground, this form is also good for freezing. Next in line is 'Franklim', a mid-season, May producer, which again grows lots of spears once it has settled in after a couple of years. I'm adding 'Dariana', a highly recommended French mid-season form to give me an asparagus mountain for May. My last to crop for the latest harvest, into early June, is an American variety, 'Mary Washington', which produces long spears and lots of them. It is resistant to rust (see fungal infections, page 168), which can be an issue with the later forms.

6 Salt applications to asparagus beds are a traditional but now much-debated subject, and you may well hear about it, so it's worth knowing what it was for. The reason for salt is that weeds dislike it and asparagus – as a seaside plant – tolerates it. It was Victorian paraquat! Also the grit that the salt came mixed with would have been beneficial. You can apply salt, but I think its easier to mulch deeply with grit (heavy soils) or compost (light soils) to control the weeds.

Below **I mulch my asparagus bed on heavy soil with a layer of grit 5–8cm (2–3in) thick.**

If you have your own vegetable patch, you don't need to let the greengrocer or supermarket dictate your diet. There are so many fantastic unusual vegetables, and therefore delicious meals, easy to grow, yet almost never available on the shop shelf. These have got to shoot straight to the top of any priority list when you're deciding what to include in your vegetable garden.

I can't imagine a summer without feasts of just-picked borlotti beans, tomato salad with sweet green garlic, punchy chilli and red-pepper ratatouille, or pea tips on top of a soft and at the same time crunchy mint and pea risotto. In winter I would miss baked 'Red Kuri' pumpkin and salads studded with violas or polyanthus. You occasionally see some of these 'vegetables' at a good farmer's market, but even that's rare. To guarantee getting them, it's best to grow your own.

The unbuyables

Above **'Red Kuri' pumpkin.**
Opposite **Edible heartsease viola flowers in a 'Black-seeded Simpson' salad.**

Colours are fun

I love growing varieties of vegetables with unusual colours – yellow courgettes (see page 194), orange or stripy pink-and-white beetroot (page 79), crimson broad beans (page 72), purple-, blue- or crimson-fleshed potatoes (page 30), yellow and purple French beans (page 47) and purple-podded peas (page 214). I have each of these growing in my garden, not necessarily because they excel in terms of flavour or productivity, but because they look fantastic on a plate mixed up with some of the more conventional kinds. These weird and wonderful vegetables are fun to cook and eat and invaluable for showing off! With their extraordinary colours, they really have to be home-grown.

Small is tasty

I also find that commercial growers too often harvest vegetables at a less-than-perfect size. I love my beetroot and broad beans small and tender. I like mini cucumbers, and at least some of my globe artichokes picked with a girth somewhere between that of a golf ball and a tennis ball. All these vegetables are almost always sold at twice the ideal size – the growers invariably get more for their crop that way. So, again, it's good to grow your own. It's like eating a massive lobster, when we all know that the little ones are twice as tender and sweet, or a hill-hardened hogget in preference to a succulent lamb!

Left **Mini artichokes cooked gently in 50 per cent olive oil, 50 per cent white wine (see recipe on page 84).** Opposite **Primrose-yellow French bean 'Rocquencourt' is wonderful to have in your patch. It's rarely seen for sale.**

Unbuyable beans

I've recently fallen in love with borlotti beans. I've walked past them in Mediterranean markets time and time again, liking the look of their beautiful cream and crimson spotty pods, but not knowing what on earth to do with them. I've now found plenty of wonderful recipes, and borlottis have shot up near the top of my home-grown favourites list. They're best eaten fresh, not dried – straight from the plant. They're softer, quicker to cook and with better flavour than when they've been sitting around.

Mix them with some melted red onion, skinned fresh tomatoes and a good slurp of olive oil, stewing them slowly for half an hour. Once they're cooked, cool them for ten minutes before you stir in a generous handful of chopped coriander. Scatter more coriander over the top and add some slivers of Parmesan (see picture, page 49). This is fantastic as a starter or as a side dish to eat with any meat. For a stronger taste, cook them slowly with onions, lots of garlic and wads of thyme. This is the perfect accompaniment to lamb.

I also love using borlotti to make a tasty bean houmous. Cook them for half an hour and, after cooling, purée them with anchovies, garlic, lemon juice and olive oil to eat with black olives and flat bread.

Adornments for garden and plate

If you want your patch to look good as well as produce, borlottis are one of the most ornamental vegetables. They're ideal for the voluptuous and beautiful Villandry style. Grown on a decent frame, they give height and colour in the garden, and I often pick them to arrange inside, laying them out on a large flat plate in the middle of the table (see the picture on the front cover). Throw some shelled beans in together with some stippled pods. Laid bare, they are a wonderful, pale eau-de-nil, developing crimson splotches as they enlarge and age.

The purple-podded French bean 'Purple Teepee' and primrose-yellow 'Rocquencourt' (both dwarf non-climbers) are another couple of beans wonderful to have in your patch and almost never seen for sale.

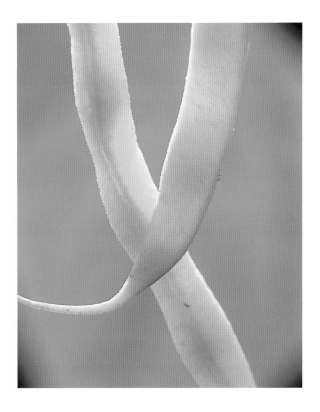

They are both lovely colours sitting on a plate and they have excellent taste and texture. In fact, if I had to name my favourite all-round French bean, it would have to be 'Rocquencourt', when the narrow, young beans are still tinged green. There's no better supper than a mound of these – just picked and lightly steamed – with a good, tasty, well-hung steak and a lake of hollandaise.

If you steam 'Purple Teepee' with a teaspoon of sugar in their water and the lid left off, they keep most of their colour. Cook them till just tender, then plunge them into cold water, and they'll stay bright and firm, not floppy, with the best flavour. If you plunge them for only ten or twenty seconds, enough to give them a quick shake in the cold, then take them out, they'll still be steaming hot, but no longer cooking.

And the great thing about these two bean varieties is that they are hugely prolific. With only a few plants you can have cascades of beans over several weeks.

Below **A green bean tunnel can be a productive and beautiful sight in summer.**

Opposite **Borlotti beans with coriander (see page 47 for recipe).**

Sowing and growing borlotti and French beans

Site

Choose a sunny spot, with shelter from the wind. This is particularly important if you've selected a climbing variety. They are potentially very exposed, growing up and over a 2m (6ft 6in) frame or teepee.

Sowing

French beans in particular are among the most tender veg I grow. Even though my pots have been sitting in the polytunnel, I've lost my early sowings several times when we've had a hard frost in April or May. It kills them dead. So don't get going too early.

In the south of England, you can sow them from early April under cover – leave it longer in the north – but the beauty of French beans is that if you don't get round to sowing them then, it's not too late. For growing outside, sowing any time from mid-spring to late July is fine. A July sowing will give you a crop in the autumn.

If you want to try growing a few inside, sow a couple of weeks earlier. March-sown plants, grown under cover,

should crop in June. A good climbing French bean variety for forcing is 'Cobra'.

If your garden is relatively slug- and snail-free, you can sow direct into the ground from late May, spacing seed in a staggered line over a 15cm (6in) band at 10–13cm (4–5in) intervals. With a trowel dig a 5cm (2in) hole for each seed and cover it. At least one of the seeds is likely to germinate, so you'll get a zig-zag of plants every 20–25cm (8–10in) – an ideal spacing for heavy yields. If all the seeds come up, you'll need to thin. Space rows 60cm (2ft) apart.

Planting out beans sown inside

If you've sown inside, once the plants are at least 5cm (2in) tall and the roots have filled the pot, it's time to plant out your beans.

For the climbers, get your frame in place before you plant. Space them 15cm (6in) apart all the way round; if you're growing them in a long row, space them at the same distance, with 60cm (2ft) between rows.

For the dwarf varieties like 'Rocquencourt', you won't need any structure in place at this stage. Space them 23cm (9in) apart, in staggered rows along a 15cm (6in) band, with 60cm (2ft) between the rows.

Pinch out the growing tips when the plants reach the top of the frame. This encourages the dwarf varieties to start to crop. To keep the pods off the soil, I tend to add some branchy twigs to the line when the plants are mature. The beans are so beautiful, it's sad if half of them are covered in mud!

Watering

French bean plants should be kept well watered when the flowers start to open and the pods swell. The organic material added to the soil before planting will provide enough water at other times. These are wind-pollinated plants, and misting the flowers with water from an atomizer or very fine rose helps displace pollen from one flower on to another and improves 'setting' – flower fertilization – and hence bean production.

Seven keys to success with beans

1 Slugs and snails are a major problem with any of these beans sown straight into the garden. If these pests are a problem in your patch, it's safer to sow two seeds to a 9cm (3½in) pot, or root trainer (a deep plastic pot, ideal for any legume with their characteristic long root run – see page 145), and germinate them under cover in a cool, light place where you can keep them well watered. The seedlings appear quickly, with the large leaves unravelling within days. Once they've got a pair of true leaves, plant them out. At adolescent size they stand a better chance of survival if attacked. If you sow direct, they'll need good protection (see pages 140–1).

2 To guarantee a regular supply of tasty beans, sow two or three times through the spring and summer (see page 181). For dwarf forms like 'Rocquencourt', repeat sow every four weeks from mid-April to the end of July. Plants crop heavily once they're mature, but they don't keep going for long. With climbing varieties like 'Blue Lake' and borlotti 'Lingua di Fuoco 2', sow every two months. They produce more lightly over a longer time.

3 Many climbing beans like 'Purple Podded Climbing' and 'Blue Lake Climbing' are so prolific that, despite the name of the former, it's best not to grow them on a teepee. I did so last year and it was tricky getting into the middle to pick every pod. If you leave beans growing on the plant, energy goes into developing and ripening these, so fewer tasty, mini ones form. Large pods are not as good as small. There's a membrane in the pod which forms a layer on the inside that's tough and unpleasant to eat. It reminds me of toenails! Next year, I'll train the heavy-croppers on to an easy-picking straight line of canes, creating an aisle down a path. You can make this by having two uprights leaning in and joining at the top, with another, horizontal cane up there at right angles, linking one pair with the next and giving strength to the line. Brace against the prevailing wind and don't make the line too long.

4 With borlotti in particular, to keep the foliage from turning a murky yellow as the plants age, and to increase the beans' productivity, plant them with a barrow-load of manure at their roots when they first go in, and then, once they're in flower, feed them regularly with comfrey juice. This is a potash-rich fertilizer, like home-made, organic Tomorite (see page 20). If you're growing climbing beans on a teepee, dig a circular pit and fill it with rotted (or even unrotted) organic material. You can collect up your green kitchen waste or annual weeds and pour them in by the barrow-load. They'll feed the bean roots well.

5 I soak my bean seed for thirty minutes before sowing. They have a tough coat and will germinate more quickly with the coat slightly softened. You can even pre-germinate on a layer of wet kitchen paper.

6 If sowing direct, sow half a dozen extra seeds at the end of the row. If any seeds don't germinate, or the slugs wipe them out, you can use these extra plants as replacements.

7 These beans are legumes – which fix nitrogen in the soil by nodules on their roots and leave it in the soil for the next crop. So when they've finished cropping, don't pull them up. Cut them to the ground instead, leaving the root system intact.

Left **'Purple Podded Climbing' beans climb a post in our veg garden.** Opposite **Borlotti beans and the dwarf French beans 'Rocquencourt' and 'Purple Teepee' are the perfect additions to a leafy summer salad, yet all are difficult or impossible to buy.**

Unusual pumpkins and squash

Pumpkins and squash are one of my favourite vegetable families. They can be supremely delicious and highly ornamental, making some of the best late summer and autumn garden plants if you have plenty of room. You can buy a limited range from a good vegetable shop. Butternut squash are widely available and have good taste and texture, but the other one sold commonly, 'Jack o' Lantern', is boring – it has a mediocre taste and texture, with mean quantities of flesh, and it's one of the first ones to rot. It's hopeless!

Get the right varieties and they taste wonderful, with a dense, waxy flesh and a sweet, comforting taste. They'll also store right the way through the winter to be eaten when there's less around. I don't like the watery, stringy texture of ones like 'Spaghetti Squash'. You need to douse it in mountains of butter to make it interesting, but there are many others that make fantastic eating.

One close to my heart is a deep vermilion red – 'Uchiki Kuri' or 'Red Kuri'. It's one of the best all-rounders, with fantastic texture, taste and unusually high productivity, and it looks marvellous climbing up over statuesque woven willow frames. Then there's 'Marina di Chioggia', whose skin looks like a warty reptile's, hiding the most delicious, creamy-textured, flame-coloured flesh beneath. This produces very little fruit, maybe only two or three pumpkins to a plant in this country, but each one is huge. I also grow the weird, zeppelin-shaped, waxy, orange-fleshed 'Jumbo Pink Banana', the elegant and beautiful, smooth-skinned, primrose-yellow 'Swan White' squash, and the endearing, Shrek-like, knobbly, warted, green-and-cream 'Sweet Dumpling'. All three are delicious.

Large and lasting

From late summer for many months, pumpkins and squash are among the main things we eat. In the school we eat the flowers and we stuff the fruits, roast them – with fennel and cumin seeds – and make delicious soup, risotto and ravioli out of them, mixing the flesh up with sage. If you want lots of small fruit, keep picking the squashes young. If you want to grow large, bumper pumpkins, leave only two or three on the plant and allow them to grow for as long as you can. If you're going for the big ones, it's a good idea to lay the ripening fruit on a floor tile or piece of board to protect them from the soil and prevent rot setting in. If you can, let them ripen on the vine and then pick them with a decent length of stalk. Once you've harvested them, always leave the squashes and pumpkins in the sun, or dry them in a greenhouse for a week or so, before storing them away. This allows the skin to toughen and will prevent rotting.

All the varieties mentioned store well and we're still eating them in January, February and March. Don't put them on a shelf where condensation may collect between the skin and the wood, because this again encourages rot. To keep them edible for as long as possible, hang them in a hammock or a series of string onion bags and you'll be feasting from these until the spring.

Enriching the garden

What I love about this family of vegetables is that it's not just the fruit that's remarkable. They make fantastic garden plants for a new and empty garden. I had a problem area in my own garden this spring, which these quick-growing 'triffids' perfectly solved.

Once the new school greenhouse was finished last winter, we were left with a steeply sloping bank down to the drive, a huge, ugly area that made no sense in the place. It was a made-up section of ground, created thirty years ago from a mix of chalk and hard core – the foundations of an old chalk-floored barn. We had aimed to construct an outside area of decking where everyone could sit when it got too hot in the summer, but every quote was for more than we could afford.

As a temporary measure we decided to plant up the bank with pumpkins and squash to give us time to

Opposite **A spectacular display of ornamental gourds and squash fills the glasshouse.**

Overleaf **The vegetable bank in October as I start bringing in the pumpkins and squash.**

Five keys to success with pumpkins and squash

1 Bear in mind that, with the trailers in particular, these make massive plants. You can train them up over frames to use the space in the air (see picture, page 159), but even so these are not plants for the immaculate small garden.

2 Mice love the seed, so set a trap near your pots.

3 Some pumpkin varieties ('Atlantic Giant' – see picture opposite) have the capacity of putting on over 1kg (2lb) of fresh weight every day. To achieve this they need copious amounts of food and water, particularly at the small seedling stage and when flowers and fruits are forming. On planting, make sure they have rich, deeply dug soil and a sunny position. Dig out a hole at least 30–45cm (12–18in) square and fill with well-rotted manure. Make a mound above this by replacing the soil you've removed and plant in the centre of the mound. The plants also benefit from a general liquid fertilizer every week. You can bury a 9cm (3½in) pot at an angle, pointing at the root of the plant. Fill this with a liquid feed like Miraclegrow or Maxicrop seaweed feed, and let it sink in slowly. This will give the right quantity of food at the right time.

4 If the weather is dry, you'll need to water too. When you plant or sow, mark the plant with a cane. It's important to know where the rootball is amid the jungle of leaves, so that you know where to water. Squash and pumpkin roots are not deep, so with these plants, unusually, frequent watering of the top layer of soil is more useful than really deep soaks. Water in the morning to limit night-time humidity, which can encourage disease. Plants need about 20 litres (4 or 5 gallons) of water each per week.

5 Pumpkins and squash are cucurbits, in the same family as cucumbers, and they suffer from many of the same diseases (see page 89). Drought-stressed plants are particularly susceptible to powdery mildew. Adequate watering is the most effective control. Aphid transfer of cucumber mosaic virus can also be a problem. The leaves are mottled, crinkly and misshapen. Pull out and burn affected plants before the disease spreads to others. Keep a lookout for varieties advertised as having resistance.

Below **A barrow-load of pumpkins and squash is one of the great autumn sights.**

decide. Spacing them about 1.2m (4ft) apart, we dug for each plant a hole about 60cm (2ft) square – the ground was very poor – removing barrow-load after barrow-load of stones and rubble, and back-filling the resulting craters with a mix of home-made compost and manure. Almost instantly, the small potted plants clad the whole area with brilliant green, large and luscious leaves. The foliage looked good, fresh and jungly from May until the middle of September. Then, when mildew struck, creeping in from the hawthorn hedges and oak trees all around, we cut the leaves off and left the fruits beading the slope in all their brilliant different shapes and colours. They sat there looking marvellous until just before our first frost towards the end of October.

Household gourds

As well as many edible squash, I love growing a few purely ornamental varieties – gourds – to pile into bowls to decorate the house and school when flowers are hard to find during the winter. When I was a child we often had these on the kitchen table, and I remember varnishing them to make them last. If you grow the right forms, this isn't necessary. A friend gave me a spectacular watermelon-like gourd last year and told me it would last without varnish – no rotting – for two or three years. So far, she's right. The fruit of this fig-leaved gourd is still pristine. 'Crown of Thorns' is also a good laster. I've got a bowl of these in our kitchen harvested last year. Some are now looking dry and old, but there's still no sign of rot. The creamy-white flying saucer 'Custard White', the 'Swan White' and 'Sweet Dumpling' squash last almost as long, and 'Turk's Turban' will usually keep going for four or five months before collapse.

I also love the vast-fruited 'Atlantic Giant', which looks like a magnificent Buddha's stomach sitting in the middle of the kitchen table. I was sent a wonderful photograph last autumn of a children's boat race taking place in these hollowed-out fruits. My crop from last year lasted right the way through until the summer this year.

Below **The 'Atlantic Giant' pumpkin reminds me of a Buddha's stomach!**

Farmers' markets are a good source of these marvellous vegetables in the autumn, but if you have plenty of space in your own garden, and think of the added bonus of the lush and beautiful plants, you'll want to try growing these unusual and tasty forms.

Sowing and growing pumpkins and squash
Sowing

Squash are half-hardy annuals – they cannot withstand the frost. The only part of England where you can sow them direct with any prospect of success is the south (see page 59).

In most parts of the country, the growing season will be too short for most winter squash varieties to ripen their fruit unless the plants are started indoors. They germinate quickly and their large seeds produce large seedlings. The ample leaf area leads to rapid early growth. Seedlings will be ready to plant out in three weeks – three times quicker than a tomato. You can therefore leave sowing your pumpkins and squash until last, sowing them under cover in April/May, three weeks before the last possible frost in your area.

Sow two seeds to an 8cm (3in) pot, 1cm (½in) deep, placing them vertically straight down. If you sow them flat, the large seeds may rot off before they germinate.

Opposite **Pumpkin
and cumin soup with
pumpkin chips.**

Below **Stuffed butternut
squash, one of my favourite
Sunday lunches.**

Once the plants have their first pair of leaves,
remove the weakest-looking seedling.

They don't like any root disturbance, and sown like
this they won't need pricking out, but potting them on
once is a good idea.

Planting out

When the roots have filled their second pot, and they
have three pairs of leaves, plant them out, but in most
parts of the country you'll need to wait until the
beginning of June. Prolonged low, non-freezing
temperatures will damage seedlings, and the longer
the period of cold, the greater the harm.

Choose a sheltered spot for your seedlings because
the wind can also cause havoc with their huge leaves.

Most varieties are tremendous sprawlers – they will
spread 1m (3ft) or so in each direction. To fruit well,
they need to be planted with lots of room all round.
Space the well-fed holes (see page 56) 1m (3ft) apart,
with the same distance between rows for bush varieties.
For trailers you'll need to make that 1.2m (4ft) apart,
with 1.8m (6ft) between rows.

Direct sowing in the south

The key thing with direct sowing is warm soil. These
plants will not germinate if the soil is below 13˚C (55˚F),
and they prefer it much warmer than this. If you're
sowing straight into the garden, wait until early June.
Sowing this late outside, it's only in the south that you'll
get any chance of fruit at the end of the season.

Dig out a hole at least 30–45cm (12–18in) square,
fill with well-rotted manure and then cloche the soil for
a week before you sow. This will warm it up more
quickly. Follow the rules of spacing above.

Make a mound above the manure and sow two
seeds 2.5cm (1in) deep in the centre of the mound.
Cover the sown seeds again with a cloche or
horticultural fleece. Wait for the seedlings to appear
and remove the weaker-looking plant. After a couple of
weeks, remove the cover.

Training

All trailing forms of squash benefit from training. Nip
out the tips of the main shoots, which will encourage
branching and the formation of a more prolific crop of
smaller fruit. This seems particularly important with
Butternut squash, which has a tendency to grow and
grow at the expense of producing fruit. Once the plants
are well established, pinch them out and fruit formation
will start.

You can train trailing varieties to grow in a circle.
Use wire hoops to hold the runners in position, creating
a spiral of stem and leaf. Some stems will root where
you pin them. This helps to provide additional nutrients
and water to the plant, so it's a good thing.

Trailing types can also be trained over bamboo
teepees, trellis and arches. This looks good and makes
fruit easy to pick. I have a sweet pea tunnel and sometimes grow squashes to follow on from sweet peas for
the late summer and autumn (see picture, pages 158–9).
The small-fruited ones like 'Munchkin' are ideal, but the
stems of the larger fruits – even on the scale of the fig-
leaved gourd – are amazingly strong and will be OK with
the extra support of a loop of string.

The best chillies and sweet peppers

We don't eat huge amounts of chillies or peppers, either in the school or at home, and until recently I wasn't sure it was worth growing our own. I was happy to buy the occasional red pepper from the greengrocer as and when I wanted. I'd tried growing the plants in the past – inside – and felt, when I thought about what they'd given me, that I'd had to lavish too much time and TLC on them. In return for all that watering I was getting about five or at the best ten fruits per plant. Not enough! They joined the list of what not to grow.

I then visited Matthew Rice's vegetable garden and the amazing walled garden at West Dean in Sussex, two gardens and gardeners very keen on their peppers. I did some tastings and realized that a red pepper is not just a red pepper – there are so many different tastes,

which you'd never know if you buy only what's produced commercially. If you've only ever eaten one of those fat, watery Dutch things, that is a bland fraction of what they can be.

Try 'Marconi Rosso', an old Italian variety that looks like a long, wide, red horn. It's sweet, with a strong flavour, ideal for making into slow-cooked, sweet-pepper marmalade perfect for eating with ham or cheese. I also love this cooked with lots of thyme, aubergines, red onions and a couple of chillies for a robust and tasty ratatouille. Or eat 'Hungarian Yellow Wax Hot', mild and perfect for pickling when green, but maturing to eye-watering heat when fully ripened and red. The wonderful thing about this variety is that you'll get both stages on the plant at once. If you're going to grow only one of the hot chilli types, this is it.

I've also now fallen for 'Mini Bell' peppers, the size of a large sweet that you can eat in one or two bites. We have a great duo who teach Japanese and Thai cooking in the school: one English, Philip Paxman, the other Vietnamese, Christine Sanches. Philip grows all the food they use in the demonstrations, and Christine cooks it. 'Mini Bell' are their favourite peppers, with a fantastic, mild, sweet flavour, pretty colour and ideal shape and size. They're perfect for delicous tempura – as they use them – dipped into sweet chilli sauce and eaten all in one go.

These peppers are all marvellous to eat, and they're easy, good performers, each producing baskets and baskets of fruit over three or four months. I was still picking 'Hungarian Yellow Wax Hot' to slice and pep up our salads at Christmas this year. It was growing under glass – frost-free – but with no extra heat. And with all these varieties, if you go away, the fruit just sits there for weeks without going over, waiting for you to pick a bumper harvest when you return. That long, slow, drip-drip production is just what you want from an edible plant. I'm not going for groves of them, but these unusual peppers have now certainly joined my list of unbuyable must-haves.

Opposite **Chilli 'Hungarian Yellow Wax Hot'.**
Below **The rare and very hot, ornamental 'Filius Blue'.**

Sowing and growing chillies and peppers

All these peppers, the sweet and hot chilli varieties, are close relatives and are cultivated in the same way.

Sowing

They are half-hardy annuals, very easy to grow from seed. I use Jiffy 7s or modules (see page 145), with two seeds to each pellet, but Matthew grows them like his tomatoes, scattering a whole pack of seed into a large pot and pricking them out from there (see page 18).

If you're going to grow them in an unheated greenhouse, or outside, sow them under cover in mid-March. If your greenhouse is heated, you can sow them two or three weeks earlier.

Germinate at high temperatures as you would for tomatoes – about 22°C (72°F).

Planting under cover

Pot them on once into 23cm (9in) pots, with a good, fertile compost, and then into large final 4- or 5-litre pots. Or else at this stage put them straight into the soil bed of your greenhouse or polytunnel. This should not be freshly manured. A bed that had a manure dressing the previous autumn is best.

Support

Chillies need some support. A cane by their side will be plenty for most. A wire-mesh cage made from rabbit or sheep netting and standing 30cm (12in) high to hold the fruit off the soil is a good idea for the larger, heavy-fruited varieties like 'Marconi Rosso'.

Harvesting

Start to harvest in August as soon as the fruits are large enough to eat. By picking them young and green, you'll encourage more to form, so regular harvesting is a good idea. There will still be fruits in October with the beginnings of the frosts. You may need to fleece the plants at night, but you can go on picking the fruit.

Four keys to success with chillies and peppers

1 In the south, you don't need a greenhouse to grow any of these peppers – hot or sweet. Their season will be shorter, but with the protection of a bale of straw (see page 114), or a south-facing wall, these plants grow well outside. They may not all ripen fully later in the year, but you can still pick them green.

2 Peppers and chillies do not like to be too hot – buds drop and fruit scorches as temperatures soar above 32°C (90°F). If they're in a greenhouse or polytunnel, good ventilation and possibly some shading may be needed during the heat of the summer.

3 Watering regularly is important. Dry soil again causes the flower buds to drop. When watering, damp down the floor as well as the soil to increase levels of humidity. They like high moisture all around. In a perfect world, once the flowers develop, try to mist with water lightly from a fine rose in the middle of the day to help the fruit set.

4 Once the first fruits are there, feed once a week with a tomato fertilizer, or comfrey slop. You want a low-nitrogen and high-potash feed – exactly what you get with comfrey (see page 20).

Pests and diseases

Peppers and chillies have the same pests and diseases that attack tomatoes. Greenfly and whitefly are the main pests. The problem is at its worst as the plants are growing rapidly before they fruit. I dose my plants with Savona or insecticidal soap to help prevent virus infections spread by the aphids.

Botrytis may be a problem, particularly at the base of plants and on the fruit. Adequate ventilation will help prevent this.

Potato blight may also affect plants, particularly those grown outside (see page 34).

Green garlic

Have you ever tasted 'wet' or 'green' garlic – bulbs lifted in June or July while the leaves are still green? They look marvellous in and out of the ground, huge, plump, curvaceous lumps, with skin as thin as the finest tissue paper. Break a clove off, hold it at the bottom and press. The whole clove erupts from its casing, popping out like an almond, creamy-white and squeaky-clean.

Green garlic tastes wonderful, much sweeter and gentler than the old, stored kind, but still with that multi-layered taste that is difficult to describe. If you plant the vast, milder 'Elephant' form of garlic, and eat it at this stage, you've got something unparalleled in taste. Bake the cloves whole, covered with a drizzle of olive oil, and eat them as a creamy topping to any robust meat or root vegetable. The flavour of garlic is at its strongest if you crush it. Cell damage releases chemicals that give it the pungent taste. Baked whole, the flavour is extra mild and syrupy. Try it mixed up with young, golf-ball-sized beetroot – the garlic and beetroot almost the same size (see picture, page 79).

Use green garlic in salads, making the best ever dressing to put over crunchy Cos lettuce, or grate it – not too much – over your first tomato salad. It has the strength more in the scale of a salad onion and doesn't leave you with that horrid, strong garlic aftertaste.

As well as being delicious, garlic is a good companion plant for the vegetable garden, so it's a worthwhile thing to integrate into your plot. It masks the smell of carrots as you thin, so deterring carrot fly, as well as repelling aphids and other undesirables. Tests in the USA have shown that the health of tomatoes in particular improves dramatically when garlic is grown in the same bed.

Good greengrocers may have 'green' garlic for a short time in the summer, but you have to look hard. With the extra benefits you get from growing it in your garden, it's much better to grow your own.

Four keys to success with garlic

1 Garlic does best if subjected to a cold spell – a month at least with the soil temperature below 10ºC (50ºF). Without this, it may not clove, meaning that the bulb may remain whole instead of dividing into sections. You also want the roots to have time to develop before lots of heavy frosts, so a late summer or autumn planting is the best idea. This will give you armfuls of bulbs to cook for week upon week in the summer. Before then, you'll have garlicky-tasting tops, like chunky chives, to eat right through the winter and spring. Don't pick them all. Remove just the younger, tender leaves, one or two from each bulb, and the swelling clove below won't suffer.

2 Many types of garlic try to flower and set seed, but don't let them. Nip off the central flowering stem to half its height – at 10–13cm (4–5in) – about two to three weeks before lifting. If you allow them to flower, the bulb size will be reduced by about a quarter.

3 Common and 'Elephant' garlic grow best in an open position, in full sun and well-drained soils. They are prone to rotting over winter in wet, heavy clay soils. During the bulbing period in June and July the leaves need as much direct sun as possible. At that time, avoid any shade, including that created by tall-growing veg like peas and beans.

4 Intercrop with quicker-developing crops such as beetroot, carrots, lettuce and radish to maximize your use of space.

Planting and growing garlic
Site

Garlic thrives on a sandy, light, well-drained soil. On a heavy soil like mine, it's a good idea to add a trowelful of sand into the base of the planting hole. It doesn't grow as well on acid soils, so dress the area with lime if you have a low pH. A fertile soil is preferable, but don't grow garlic on soil that has been manured recently. Too much richness and you'll get lots of leaf and small bulbs.

Planting

Plant cloves at a depth of about 8cm (3in). Space them at 15cm (6in) between cloves and 30cm (12in) between rows. If you don't get round to planting in the autumn, there are varieties suited for planting in February or March (see page 199).

Do not split bulbs into individual cloves until just before planting, although 'Elephant' garlic is sometimes sold as cloves, not heads. Break up the bulb and select the cloves with the biggest bases. Cloves at least 1cm (½in) across will give the best results. You can eat the rest, or plant them in pots for a harvest of the leaves as garlic chives. You can also use the smaller cloves for companion planting with tomatoes or carrots (see page 62).

Feeding and watering

Garlic needs water during the period of leafy growth, so a wet spring is ideal. Water occasionally in May and June if it's very dry. Mulching the plants with compost, or protecting with plastic, will help conserve moisture.

Potash, especially in the form of fresh wood ash, is a good thing to add to your soil around garlic. This helps produce a healthy, heavy crop.

Harvesting

On the whole it takes nine months to make good garlic. Autumn-planted garlic will be ready for harvesting in June/July the following summer.

When the outer leaves turn yellow, this is normally a good indication that the bulbs are ready, but to get your garlic green, lift some of the bulbs before that. Scrape the soil from a couple of plants to see if they have bulbed up. Choose a sunny day when the forecast is good for the next few days. Lift the bulbs carefully, trying to keep the stalks intact. You can use these for plaiting.

For green garlic, dig it and use it just as it is. If you want to store some, you need to dry it well before you store it away. Dry the bulbs in the sun, if you have any! Put them in trays lifted off the ground, with plenty of air circulating. If it's wet, put the trays in the greenhouse, or any light, cool place. I have an old meat safe, which I use to dry all my garlic and onions (see picture, page 1). It keeps most of the rain out, but has good air circulation. The drying spell – until the skin on the bulbs is completely dry and papery – may take up to two weeks.

Below **A wet spring is ideal for garlic, as water during the leafy growth period produces plump cloves.**

Storage and plaiting

Once the garlic bulbs are dry, remove any remaining bits of soil and plait the leaves. Moisten the leaves slightly before you plait, and then hang them in a dry, airy place. It should be cool, preferably 5–10°C (41–50°F).

Make sure you eat the short-dormancy varieties first.

Pests and diseases

A slight browning of the leaves in late spring is normal, and probably due to wind burn.

Rust can be a problem with all alliums, but you can ignore it. It doesn't affect the bulbs.

Onion white rot can also be a problem with garlic (see page 168). To help avoid this, use the system of plant rotation (see pages 166–7), and avoid putting garlic, onions or shallots in the same bed for three years. It's worth it, because if you get the rot, you can't grow onions again on that soil for eight years!

Pea tips

We've already talked about peas, which are in my 'fresh-as-a-daisy' category (see page 22). They are definitely worth growing, as they become a less delicious, tasty thing within hours of picking, but I'm also fanatical about pea tips – the top few centimetres of newly emergent stems that cover a pea plant as it grows. They taste like very sweet, fresh peas and have the most succulent flavour of any vegetable I know. They are wonderful scattered over the top of a salad (see page 93), or wilted for a minute over risotto, or pea and pancetta pasta, and they couldn't be easier to grow.

These are now occasionally seen in good greengrocer's, but are expensive and, as ever, have lost half of their sweet taste. It's much better to grow your own, and I now grow these separately, with a different system from normal shelling peas. They are one of the best home-grown things you can create and deserve to be considered on their own.

Sowing and growing pea tips
Sowing
Fill a wooden wine box or polystyrene fish box with compost, making sure there are drainage holes in the container before you start. To cut down the need for watering, use a moisture-retaining John Innes No 2 in the summer. Fill to within about 2.5cm (1in) of the top to allow room for watering without washing compost out all over the bench.

I sow about thirty seeds to each box, pressing each one into the compost down to the first joint in my finger.

Cover the boxes and place them somewhere warm for quick germination.

As soon as shoots appear, place them in a cooler place with maximum all-round light to encourage them to grow well. You should have pea shoots ready to eat – say, 5cm (2in) tall – within about a month.

Harvesting
To get them at their juiciest, keep picking regularly, so that fibrous cells don't have time to form. Pinch out the tips, leaving at least one pair of leaves below where you cut. If you shave them to the ground, the plants will die.

To keep the texture soft and sweet, water regularly.

Three keys to success with pea tips

1 You can harvest pea tips from your normal shelling peas (see page 24), picking the side shoots as they climb, but this curtails the harvest of poddable peas. It's better to think of them as a separate crop, growing boxes jam-packed full of seed, for the pea tips alone. You'll get a few cuts off them, and then, as with cut-and-come-again salads (see page 94), they'll stop sprouting and producing as well. Chuck them out and start again with a new lot.

2 The best varieties of pea to produce tips are the prolific mangetouts or sugarsnap types. If you've grown these to full size, you'll know you have to pick the pods two or three times a week to keep the plants producing well. They are 'triffids', and so ideally suited to the hard treatment of cropping them as tips. Keep cutting them back to a couple of pairs of leaves and they will still be able to regrow.

3 Successional sowing is crucial if you want a seamless supply. I try to sow at least one box every four to six weeks right the way through the year. They are among the few things that are worth sowing even between November and February. With the lower light levels, they don't grow as quickly, but still fast enough for you to crop from your boxes at least once a week.

Right **The best varieties of pea to produce tips are the prolific mangetouts and sugarsnap types.** Opposite **The pea growing tip – succulent and delicious.**

Edible flowers

I've just been gathering elderflowers to make cordial – for which the best recipe is thirty flower-heads, picked in the sunshine for the finest flavour, two sliced lemons, 1.75kg (4lb) sugar and 65g (2½oz) citric acid, all put in a bucket with 1.5 litres (2½ pints) of boiling water, stirred twice a day for five days before you bottle it – and it's made me think about other flowers that are good to eat.

Why is it that these are so difficult to buy? You occasionally see large-flowered pansies for sale in posh food halls, but these are probably the least nice variety to eat. They taste of nothing and are too chunky to be delicious – it's like eating a wad of felt!

There's something uncool about edible flowers. You only have to hear the phrase to think, 'Oh no, Hawaiian weddings with hibiscus, luncheons in Bournemouth, Abigail's party … top-end naffery' – but I don't agree. I love scattering a few petals over the top of a bowl of salad or throwing nasturtiums into mashed potato to add an extra bit of colour and some sharp highlights of taste. It's very rare for me to be patient enough to make crystallized flowers to crown a summer pudding, but it's the work of two minutes to create flowery ice cubes, using either water or olive oil, to float in a bowl of soup.

Growing edible flowers

Many of the edible flowers are annuals, and, as ever with this group of plants, successional sowing is important. Direct sow them in lines, or blocks, straight into the ground any time from mid-spring to late summer. Use the colour to decorate your salad beds. That way they're also handy for picking.

In addition to hardy annuals – marigolds, rocket and nasturtiums – the range of edible flowers also includes biennials, such as violas and sweet rocket, and perennials: anchusa, dianthus, fennel, hollyhocks and fuchsia. I do grow a few marigolds, violas, borage

67

Opposite, left **Garlic chives have characteristic white flowers rather than mauve.**

Opposite, right and below **The small-flowered heartsease violas are good for eating.**

Overleaf *Calendula* 'Indian Prince' and pretty blue borage make a wonderful combination in any bed.

and nasturtiums specifically near the salad, so I can pick the flowers to mix in, but I don't grow the biennials and perennials especially. My advice would be to harvest them from the rest of the garden, where you're probably growing some of them anyway.

Using edible flowers

Raw

Borage
Pull the bright blue flower away from its hairy base.

Calendulas
I like to see the odd calendula – marigold – in a salad or a saffron risotto, but remember to rip the flower apart. If you leave them intact, they are too chunky. You can't expect people to eat the centre and the calyx. Pull off the orange or yellow petals and scatter only them.

Chives
I also like a few of the mauve or white chive flowers, their globes broken up and scattered raw over salad leaves. Their flowers have a mild, oniony taste.

Coriander
Delicious and pretty with delicate, cow parsley-like flowers.

Dandelions
Use like calendulas for a tart, bitter taste.

Dill
Fennel and dill flowers are also tasty and give you a bright acid-green. Scatter these over a crimson-leaved salad of red orach – *Atriplex hortensis* var. *rubra* – and my favourite red-leaved lettuce, the old French 'Merveille des Quatre Saisons'.

Hemerocallis
Some of these have a delicious, peppery flavour.

Nasturtiums
These can also be good used in salad. They have a strong and peppery taste, adding more than prettiness to your bowl.

Rocket
When the summer gets hot, lots of your herbs will start to flower. Salad rocket is usually the first. When the flowers begin to form, the leaves turn very hot. Don't

chuck your plants on the compost heap until you've stripped the lot. These flowers have a flavour similar to that of the leaves, but milder.

Violas
The small-flowered heartsease violas look good, are easy to grow, delicate in flavour and make good eating.

Cooked

Courgette flowers
Stuffed courgette or squash blooms have to be one of the best home-grown meals (see page 112).

Nasturtiums
Try adding nasturtium flowers and buds to mashed potato or, even better, haddock fishcakes, using them

more like a herb than just for decoration. My favourite variety of nasturtium is 'Tip Top Mahogany' (see page 198) with deep crimson flowers, contrasting punchily to their strong-coloured, acid-green leaves. It's a fantastic all-round garden plant and it grows very happily in pots. I prefer the brightness of this to the sultry, fashionable, dark bluey-green-leaved 'Empress of India' with its crimson-orange flowers.

Crystallized flowers

If you're patient by nature, go for crystallizing flowers. Pick primroses and sweet violets in the spring, moving on to sweet rocket – *Hesperis matronalis* – roses, honeysuckle, hollyhock petals, pinks, evening primroses, phlox and even fuchsia bells as the summer arrives. They are all safe and good to eat, although *Primula vulgaris* contains primin, which some people are violently allergic to.

There are two techniques for crystallizing flowers. The simplest is to dip them in egg-white that has been forked through, but not beaten. With fiddly flowers like fuchsias, you may need to use a fine paintbrush to get into the nooks and crannies. Then dust them with caster sugar, back and front, and leave them to dry for a couple of hours on non-stick, grease-proof paper. Like this they stay crunchy for about a week.

If you want them to last longer, you'll need to use a more fiddly technique. This uses gum tragacanth and rosewater, both available from good, old-fashioned chemists. Use one teaspoon of gum tragacanth (also called gum Arabic) and two tablespoons of rosewater. Put the rosewater in a jar, then the tragacanth, shake them up to mix the two together and leave them for twenty-four hours in a warm place. Using a fine brush, coat the flowers, dip them in caster sugar and, again on non-stick paper, leave them to dry. This will preserve the flowers for a few months if you store them in an airtight tin.

Freezing flowers

I like freezing the small edible flowers – anchusas, borage, pansies and violas – in ice or olive oil cubes.

Opposite **Ice cubes, each frozen with an edible flower.** Below **Crystallized flowers – pretty, but fiddly to make.**

Make up different shapes, with some stars as well as rectangles. I know it's going for the mainstream pretty, but they look marvellous floating in gazpacho or a cold cucumber soup. The olive oil turns cloudy when it's frozen, but in the bowl it gradually melts, leaving a good swirl of oil and a scatter of petals near the surface.

More flamboyant is a flower-studded ice bowl. Find a pair of bowls nearly the same size, so one can sit easily inside the other. Fill the larger bowl about a third full of water and then lower the smaller one in, making sure that the water rises right up the sides. Drop in your flowers and edible, tasty leaves of herbs like lemon verbena and mint. After a couple of hours, take the bowl out and, with a chopstick, push any of the flowers that have collected at the surface back down again to the base of the bowl and then put it back in the freezer.

To release the bowl from its mould, put it in a sink of hot water and put some more hot water into the top bowl. They'll loosen in about five minutes. If the surface is frosted, swish the whole thing quickly in a bowl of hot water and both surfaces will be left sparkly and smooth. Fill it with globes of ice cream or sliced fruit. Once you've eaten everything, wash out the bowl with warm water and put it back in the freezer. I've sometimes kept mine going for months.

Broad beans

Whether cooked, or eaten raw straight out of their pods when still small, broad beans are among the most delicious things you can eat. One of my favourite summer suppers would start with a great plateful of these, just picked and uncooked, with a few of the red-beaned variety 'Red Epicure' scattered over the top. The red ones taste just like the grey-green, but they look fantastic as a colourful sprinkling in with the rest. If you have the patience, the beans are at their best if you peel each one as you eat them. Dip them into olive oil and Maldon salt and wrap them in a slither of Pecorino or another strongly flavoured sheep's cheese. Start a June supper like this and things are looking good!

If you grow your own, you can eat more parts of the broad bean plant than you might think. Pick the pods when they are only 2.5–5cm (1–2in) long and try eating them whole like mangetout peas. Broad bean tips – the top section of the young plant – are also tasty. You need to pinch out the tips anyway to prevent blackfly infestation (see point 3 in Keys to success), but as long as they're not already plastered with flies, don't chuck them, eat them! Chop them up and wilt them into a *primavera* risotto, or make a fantastic pasta, with the beans and their tips mixed up with pancetta, summer savory, crème fraîche and grated Parmesan cheese.

If you like the idea of any of these things, you won't be able to get what you need from a visit to the greengrocer. You've got to grow and pick your own.

Sowing and growing broad beans

Broad beans are one of the easiest vegetables to grow, ideal for the beginner or for children. The beans are huge, just smaller than a 10p coin, so sowing is easy. You don't even need to cultivate the ground to produce a fine tilth. These whopper seeds will push their way up through almost anything. They're too chunky to get eaten by birds when in the ground, and they germinate quickly. Most varieties are also hardy and vigorous once they are up.

Five keys to success with broad beans

1 Autumn sowing Broad beans are cold-weather plants that thrive in our climate. Research has shown that the best yields come from early spring and, even better, autumn sowing. For every week that sowing is delayed after the beginning of March, there is a substantial reduction in the crop. So get going with sowing as soon as winter ends. If you sow any later than May, the flowers are unable to set decent pods. The high soil temperatures deter optimum root growth and hot weather encourages the swap from vegetative (leafy) plant growth to flowering. If this happens too early in the plant's development, you get stunted, unproductive plants. Late sowings also suffer from severe attacks of chocolate spot.

2 Successional sowing Studies have shown that successional sowings are best done when the preceding crop reaches 5cm (2in). If you sow in autumn, in February and then a couple of times from early March to early May, you'll be guaranteed to have broad beans to pick right the way through the late spring and summer.

3 Pinching out When the plants are in full flower and the first pod is just forming at the base of the plant, it's important to pinch out the top 10cm (4in). This encourages the pods to form and reduces problems with blackfly (black bean aphid). It is the tasty, fleshy stem tips, full of sweet, sugary sap, that attract the pests. By removing them, you get rid of the most tempting bit. Over-feeding with nitrogen-based fertilizers will also encourage infestation.

4 Don't dig them up In the south try cutting plants back to 5cm (2in) when they finish cropping. Early sowings may regrow to provide a second crop. Broad beans roots 'fix' nitrogen from the atmosphere via the activities of the bacterium *Rhizobium* in their root nodules. These will add some fertility to the ground for your following crops.

5 Companion planting If you're growing broad beans, sow some summer savory (*Satureja hortensis* – see page 202) in among the rows. It discourages blackfly – they're repelled by the smell. It's also a tasty and easy herb to grow, similar in flavour to thyme. I use it raw in tomato salad and on pizzas and pasta, and add it to the water of the beans as they cook.

Site and soil preparation

Broad beans like an open, sunny spot, with lots of moisture, but well-drained soil. Over-wintering crops need shelter from strong winds. In my exposed garden I put in wind-breaks in the autumn to help mine survive until the spring.

Organic material – farmyard manure or compost – added to the soil the previous autumn/winter will help create ideal, moist soil conditions, but broad beans, like all other legumes, make their own nitrogen and require little extra feeding.

Sowing

If you love broad beans as I do and want to have them in the garden for as long as possible, sow a succession of crops straight into the ground in the autumn and from late February to early May.

If you have cold, clammy, poorly drained soil, warm it up with a covering of fleece or cloches for a week or so before sowing. Or, better still, start the first lot off in pots under cover. Sow seed, one per 7cm (2¾in) pot, in a greenhouse or cold frame. Stand them outside for a few days to harden them off, and when they reach 5–8cm (2–3in), plant them out.

For the autumn sowing, sow in October or November and over-winter outdoors for a mid-spring crop. Aim for these seedlings to be 2.5cm (1in) high when colder weather arrives. Aguadulce cultivars (see page 181) are particularly suitable and should crop about a month earlier than spring-sown seeds. The first crops should be ready in late May/June.

Outside, plant seed 5cm (2in) deep, with 20–25cm (8–10in) in both directions between each seed in staggered double rows. The same spacing applies to growing them in blocks. If you sow a pair of double rows, allow 75cm (2ft 6in) between them for easy picking. If the soil is moist, just push each individual seed into the ground. If not, dig individual holes with a hand trowel, or use a draw hoe to create a seed drill.

Sow half a dozen extra seeds at the end of the row.

Unusual size

I try to make room in my garden for vegetables that are not often available at their tastiest size. Commercially, most of these veg are picked and sold far too big.

Broad beans, runner beans and beetroot all taste a hundred times nicer if you eat them young. I think broad beans want eating at about the size of your thumbnail, runner beans should be no longer than your hand, and beetroot only slightly bigger than a golf ball. There are a few dishes that enable you to turn the huge starchy or stringy beans, or the whacking great roots, into something edible, but you need a cunning recipe to make them really good.

Globe artichokes are tasty fully grown, but if you have lots of them, the best home-grown dish ever is baby buds griddled and mixed with mozzarella and chunky slices of tomato. You'll see them this size on every Mediterranean market stall, yet in this country they're incredibly rare, even in the best food store.

Cucumbers are also fine to eat at the normal 30cm (12in) length, but have you tried the mini ones, the size of a Havana cigar? These are wonderful in a mixed plate of crudités, crunchy, sweet and succulent dipped into a plate of houmous or taramasalata. Cut off the stalk end – it can be bitter – and eat the rest. And with this mini size, which means you can eat them all in one go, you don't get left with that dreary yellowing log at the bottom of the fridge.

You can use these as transplants with which to fill gaps if any others don't germinate.

Aftercare

Once the seeds have germinated, or you've planted seedlings out, it's a good idea to mulch with home-made compost, or grit on heavy soil. This helps suppress weeds and prevents the soil drying out. Support is also important to maximize the crop. When the plants are about 60cm (2ft) tall, stake them. They otherwise get flattened in heavy wind and rain and the mice have a field day. Use twine and canes, or a nest of hazel or silver birch pea sticks around the whole clump. The twine should be at a height of about 75cm (2ft 6in).

Below **Broad bean and mint tapenade.** Opposite **Crimson-flowered broad beans,** **fennel and sweet william** **(Dianthus barbatus** **Nigrescens Group).**

Overleaf **An outdoor feast of** **peas and beans straight** **from the garden. These are** **delicious raw with any** **salty cheese, such as feta** **or pecorino.**

Watering

Watering is important, particularly in late spring for broad beans sown in May. They are very susceptible to drought. Over-wintered sowings develop a deep tap root that extracts the water they need, but later plantings and those on a light soil need to be watered. Do so, if it's dry, around the base of the plants during flowering and while the pods are forming. A good soak once a week has been shown to result in a better set and greater yields, and helps to delay the moment when the beans go tough and starchy.

Growing in pots

Dwarf broad beans like 'The Sutton' and 'Stereo' are ideal for growing in containers if you don't have much space. Use large containers. Don't plant in anything smaller than a 10-litre pot, with at least 30cm (12in) of loam-based compost below the roots. For this size of pot, push four seeds in 5cm (2in) deep and 10cm (4in) apart. You do not need to feed the plants, but keep them weed-free and watered in warm weather.

Picking and storing

Pick the lower pods first as they mature, always trying to pick them young, when the beans begin to show in the pods. Open up a pod and check the scar, where the seed is joined to the pod. For the beans to be at their best, it should be white or green, not black. I always find it amazing how quickly broad beans develop from too small to pick to too big to be at their best. If the weather is perfect, this can be within a few days, so keep checking them at the beginning of the picking season in May. Regular picking (ideally two or three times a week) will promote the formation of more pods. When I'm picking in a hurry I also find it all too easy to uproot the whole plant. A good tip is to hold the stem and pull the pod downwards, twisting at the same time. If they don't come easily, use scissors or a knife.

Broad beans freeze well – they are one of the few things I do freeze. Pick them small and then blanch them for one minute only and freeze in polythene bags in single-portion sizes to eat over the winter.

Pests and diseases

The most common problem is the black bean aphid. Control this by pinching off the top when the first beans start to form (see page 72). Ideally, have orange soldier beetles in your garden if you can find some; you won't see an aphid on your beans once you've transferred a few beetles to the bean patch.

Chocolate spot – chocolate-coloured streaks and spots on the leaves and stems – is most likely to occur on over-wintered plants during a wet spring, and on late-sown plants. Pick off and burn the badly affected leaves.

Jays and mice love the fresh and dry beans. If you have lots of jays around, you may need to net your mature crop to stop them pinching the lot. I live in the midst of huge numbers of trees and it's always a race for me to get my beloved broad beans before the jays do. When I first moved to the country I loved these birds and the brilliant blue of their underwing. Not now, though – I'd happily exterminate the lot!

Runner beans

If you're a bean fiend, then runner beans are one of the easiest and most prolific crops you can grow. The secret with these is not to plant too many. Almost all the seeds you sow will germinate and form good strong, bushy plants, so don't get carried away. It is runner beans that are responsible for putting many people off growing veg. They produce so many pods that in many people's minds they epitomize the glut. It's a guilt trip whenever you step outside. You know you should be picking and eating them for supper or, if not, blanching them for freezing and eating in leaner times – but if you're anything like me, you don't do it. I don't particularly like them frozen. There are nicer veg

available growing in the garden in the winter anyway, and I've yet to find a really delicious chutney recipe for runner beans that can compete with tomato or apple.

So sow only a short line of less than ten plants, and then you'll keep on top of picking the beans when they are small and at their tastiest. I find that when I'm eating them and hit a string, gag-worthy memories of grey, over-cooked school beans rush in, so choose an unstringy variety (see page 183) and pick them young, before most of the string has time to form.

Sowing and growing runner beans
Successional sowing

If you love runner beans, do two sowings, one in April and one in June – this will give you a crop from July until October. That's one of the good things about these beans: they produce well for a long stretch of time. I'm a French bean girl myself, so I do only one sowing, and when I do it depends on when I'm going to be around most to eat them. If you tend to take your holidays in August, wait until the second sowing time. You'll then get back to plants just starting to crop nice young beans.

Regular picking

With runner beans more than any other crop, picking regularly is the key to eating the beans at the small and tasty size. Strip the plants at least twice a week to get them at their best. Even if you know you're not going to eat all those beans, and can't persuade your friends to have any more, pick them. Once they're large, they're better off the plant than on. More little pods will then be encouraged to form. There's no such thing as a runner bean too small to pick!

Half-hardy runner beans are grown in the same way as French beans (see page 182). They are, however, insect- rather than wind-pollinated, so you can increase your crop with a beneficial partnering with sweet peas. The scent of the sweet pea flowers draws in more insects and increases pollination, and with it your crop of beans.

Above **'Lady Di', a recent variety bred in the late princess's honour, has an especially bright red flower.**

Opposite **Preparing beetroot and garlic for slow roasting.**

Beetroot

I love beetroot. It has a wonderful flavour – of sweetness and the earth – and the flesh is that extraordinary colour. I grow the magenta-purple variety 'Pronto', as well as the sunny-orange 'Burpee's Golden', and this year I grew an old Italian stripy pink-and-white, 'Chioggia'. This looked brighter and better raw than cooked, but is a good swank, with a clear, home-grown message when you serve it up to your friends. Even the poshest super-markets have yet to cotton on to these lower-yield but unmissable coloured forms.

In each case you must eat the roots young to get them at their best, which means growing your own. When you buy them, they're all too often the size of a fist, with hard black pockets within the flesh. Revolting! Rather than sowing a whole lot and leaving them in the ground to get tough, sow half a packet two or three times a year and eat them quickly.

I love beetroot raw and grated, and I love it hot, roasted in the oven on top of a baking tray of dill or fennel leaves and surrounded with lots of garlic. It's great to eat with roast meat or fish, or you can douse boiled roots in a béchamel or onion sauce. When you're cleaning beetroot, chop or twist the leaves off just above the actual root, and when you cook them, whether baked or boiled, don't peel them. It's quicker and you get a better flavour if you leave them intact and peel them after they're cooked.

Cooked beetroot is also delicious cold, in a salad, particularly good with smoked trout or eel, and it goes perfectly with the peppery flavours of salad leaves like rocket. Beetroot, rocket and feta salad with lemon zest is one of my all-time favourite autumn dishes, and it looks ten times better with weird and wonderfully coloured beets. Mix 'Pronto' with 'Burpee's Golden' or just use the stripy 'Chioggia' to scatter on top of the plate of rocket. In this combination you've got the sweetness of the beetroot, the saltiness of feta, the pepperiness of rocket and the sharpness of lemon. It's a marvellous mix of tastes.

Cut-and-come-again beetroot leaves

If you have beetroot out there in the garden, you mustn't forget to harvest the leaves. When they're small, these make an excellent addition to a mixed leaf salad with a distinctly sweet, beetrooty taste. Or you can wilt the larger leaves like spinach. To bring out the sweetness add a splash of apple juice and olive oil.

I now like eating the leaves so much that I grow a couple of varieties more for these than for their roots. 'Bull's Blood' has superb, shiny, satin leaves in black-crimson – only tasty when tiny – and the more usual 'Globe 2' has dark green leaves and a midrib slash of crimson. This is the variety that fills those so-called 'Bistro' salad bags, but it tastes much sweeter and more strongly of beetroot if you grow your own. Both these leafy varieties are cut-and-come-again. You can cut the tops, and they'll regrow within a week for another harvest.

Sowing and growing beetroot
Sowing

Because most beetroot are cluster-seeded – several seeds together in a lump – they need to be sown widely, at 5cm (2in) intervals. Space lines 30cm (12in) apart.

Early sowings are best made under cover, with one seed to a cell in polystyrene module trays or into guttering (see pages 144 and 147). Modular sown, they will form clumps of seeds. Don't bother to prick them out or thin them; just plant the whole clump widely at 20cm (8in) intervals. Grown like this, they will produce clumps of small but tender beets.

Aftercare

The most important thing with beetroot is to keep them growing well, avoiding any check in growth from the moment that the seedlings first appear. Thinning, watering and weeding are all important to prevent bolting. With those direct sown, thin to 10cm (4in) between plants, remembering to water the remaining seedlings to settle them back in.

Dry soil makes roots hard and woody. You'll see the effect in your rows of beetroot, with the oldest leaves at the base of the plant turning yellow. Water them well, leaving the sprinkler on the line for an hour or so every two weeks until it rains.

Opposite **Beetroot 'Chioggia' with stripy flesh inside.**

Below **Beetroot 'Pronto'. My favourite, straight purple-red.**

Beetroot don't do well with competition from weeds. Hoe and then mulch with a 5cm (2in) layer of compost between the rows as soon as the seedlings appear. Hand weed and then mulch between the actual plants. The beetroots are just below the surface at this young stage and are easily damaged by a hoe.

Harvesting

From about ten weeks on, pick small beetroot, thinning out the row rather than starting at one end and working along it systematically. The roots will then be about the size of a golf ball. The other roots left in the ground will enlarge. If you're picking the leaves for salad, pick only the youngest, 2.5–5cm (1–2in) long. If you're going to eat them cooked, pick the leaf, not the stalk, which takes longer to cook. You can go on using the young leaves – cut-and-come-again – long after the roots that you never got around to eating have become too tough to cook and eat.

Storing

On a light soil, it's best to leave your beetroot in the ground through the winter. Cover the line with a thick layer of straw and dig them up from there. On a heavy soil, they probably won't survive, and even if they do, they have a very muddy taste.

In clay soils, in October, before the first frosts, dig your beetroots up. Cut off the tops without damaging the root flesh. Left on, the tops rot and become a slimy mess through the winter. Clean them gently, but thoroughly, before storing in a cool, reasonably frost-free place in boxes filled with moist (not wet) peat or sand. Take care to ensure they're not touching.

Pests and diseases

Beetroot suffer from few problems. One is mildew, which thrives in periods of drought, with plants becoming dry at the roots. Avoid this by watering. You may also need to protect your seedlings from birds. Use fleece or netting to keep them off.

Five keys to success with beetroot

1 Successional sowing as ever is the key. You can sow a line or two in early May, and do so again every three to four weeks until the end of July. Beetroot is one of the slower crops to develop, but you'll have small ones in the kitchen within eight to ten weeks and some to eat through the late summer and autumn. If you sow enough in July, these can be left in the ground through the winter, protected with a mulch of straw. These large, well-developed roots should survive and start sprouting leaves again in the spring. The roots taste too earthy to be good, but these young, fresh, brilliantly coloured leaves are an invaluable addition to an early spring salad bowl.

2 Do not rush to sow beetroot too early – it's likely there will be some cold periods before May and cold weather makes many varieties of beetroot bolt. They put their energy into forming flowers and setting seed, rather than producing a swollen root. If you want to sow early, use a bolt-resistant form and don't sow direct into the garden, but into guttering. Beetroot is another crop ideally suited to this quick and easy sowing system (see page 144).

3 Other root crops like carrots and potatoes need a deep, cultivated topsoil to do well, but not beetroot. A thin soil is fine for them, and they need it well drained. Freshly manured soil will encourage the roots to split. Choose them a sunny, open position.

4 Soak the beetroot seed in warm water for half an hour before sowing. Some beetroot contain a natural germination inhibitor that slows or prevents germination and you need to wash this off.

5 Pulling is easy. You don't need a spade as most of the root stands above ground level. After pulling them up, water the surrounding plants to resettle the soil around them, or they'll be quick to bolt.

Globe artichokes

When I was a girl we often spent the Easter holidays in a large, creaky house just inside the walls of Asolo, the hill town in the Veneto, west of Venice, looking out across the wide plains of the Po. The smoky, wooden atmosphere of the house, 'La Mura', its rickety balcony covered in dripping, fragrant mauve wisteria, and its entrance row of terracotta pots filled with fruit-laden lemon trees are still a touchstone for me of what a marvellous place can feel like.

Just down the road in Castelfranco or Montebelluno, the twice-weekly markets were a cornucopia of strange and exotic delights for an English child – big, cylindrical olive oil drums, cut in half and filled with dandelion, rocket – which no one in England had heard of at the time – fennel and cress, mostly collected wild; and globe artichokes, plump with leaves or stripped bare, right down to the heart, floating in bowls of water with quartered lemons to prevent the flesh turning brown.

From every market visit we brought back artichokes and ate them with so-called 'Angelica sauce', a roughly chopped mixture of two hard-boiled eggs, a handful of flat-leaved parsley, a good slurp of anchovy paste, red wine vinegar and lots of olive oil. You boil the artichoke whole and then strip the leaves ones by one, dipping the leaf bases and heart into a dollop of the sauce. This remains one of my favourite summer things.

I also love eating my artichokes small, but outside southern France, Spain or Italy these seem impossible to buy. For this very reason, I'm planting up a large bed in my new garden devoted to artichokes alone.

When I'm cooking these very tender, mini ones, I cut off one-third – the tips – of the leaves and the outer layer or two of fronds, and then poach them gently for forty minutes in equal quantities of white wine and olive oil. It's a recipe that was given to me by hotelier Jane Dunn, from Stone House in East Sussex, and it's become one of my top home-grown meals. The artichokes can be eaten still warm, or stored in olive oil for griddling later and mixing up with mozzarella cheese. Jane adds sun-dried tomatoes and a handful of chopped herbs (see picture, page 46).

Sowing and growing globe artichokes

Globe artichokes are delicious to eat and incredibly easy to grow. The best way to introduce them to your garden is to ask for a few offsets from friends who have a good, heavy-fruiting, plump form in their vegetable garden, or grow them from seed.

Sowing

They germinate easily, sown in March or April. I use Jiffy 7s for my sowing, but you can sow them into a seed tray and prick them out from there. I've also sown seed in the summer for planting in the garden in September before the ground gets cold. These will crop well the next year.

Don't over-water your seeds. Artichokes have large seeds that rot easily. Pot them on to a 9cm (3½in) pot and, when the roots have filled that pot, plant them into the garden. Space them widely, leaving at least 60cm (2ft) between plants.

Out of a pack of ten seedlings, perhaps only six or seven will breed true to type. Once they are fully grown and cropping, this is easy to tell. If there are a few substandard plants, you can dig these up and transfer them to the flower garden to use in arrangements when the lovely thistles open.

Left **'Gros Vert de Lâon', an old French form grown for its huge hearts.**
Opposite **Artichokes**

growing with Euphorbia characias **'John Tomlinson', which looks good throughout the spring.**

Six keys to success with globe artichokes

1 Globe artichokes germinate easily and grow quickly, forming substantial plants in a few months. They may well start to crop in their first season. To help them survive our cold, wet winters, remove the buds when they're still small. The young plants must concentrate on developing decent roots, not fruits and seed. Eat them using the recipe on page 84.

2 All the varieties I've tried (see page 177) are reliably hardy with a duvet of straw or mushroom compost over the crown in the winter. In the north, find them as sheltered and sunny a spot as you can.

3 If you're very keen on globe artichokes, as I am, grow a few different varieties with slightly varying flowering times to extend your harvesting season. I grow three. The first to produce is the beautiful, purple-flushed Italian variety 'Violetto di Chioggia', which I start to pick in late May. Then comes 'Gros Vert de Lâon', an old French form, which is my favourite. It has an oddly flat, inelegant shape, with a wide base and a shorter curve of the outer leaves than others.

It reminds me of a lotus flower in oriental paintings, but in green, not pink. The culinary advantage from its squatness is the huge flat disc of heart in the middle of the flower. The last two to crop in my garden are 'Green Globe' and 'Romanesco' (also called 'Purple Globe'), a purple-washed Italian form, invaluable because they both fruit in July. By that time I hope to get a second cropping of the earlier crew to give me rich pickings until early October, when the nights become too cold for much to grow.

4 To keep stocks vigorous and productive, renew the oldest one-third of plants every year. This also extends the cropping season, as mature plants are ready for harvest in late spring to early summer, and young plants in late summer. Do this using offsets from high-yielding plants in mid-spring. Remember to label them when they're cropping well in summer. These offsets should be about 30cm (12in) high with at least two shoots and must have roots attached. Plant the rooted suckers 60cm (2ft) apart with 60–75cm (2–2ft 6in) between each row, trimming the leaves back to 13cm (5in) to help reduce water loss and help the roots settle in.

5 Keep the plants well watered until established. When the weather is dry, water even mature plants thoroughly to increase production.

6 Home-grown artichokes can be thick with earwigs, which can be off-putting once they are boiled and you're about to put them into your mouth! Soak them upside down for a couple of hours in strongly salted water. This should kill and remove any hidden insect life.

Left **Globe artichokes in Jane Dunn's vegetable garden at Stone House in East Sussex.**

Cucumbers

When you buy a cucumber, it's a bit of a lottery. Some are good, but some are bad, with a bland flavour and a cotton-woolly, flaccid texture, chewy, not crisp, and it's impossible to tell which is going to be which. But cucumbers don't have to come as the standard green cylinder. They're often better in odd shapes and sizes. I've grown two unusual varieties this year, a modern F1 miniature-fruiting variety, 'Zeina', and a traditional twentieth-century variety, 'Crystal Apple', and now I want to experiment with more of these weird and wonderful kinds. Both the ones I've tried are peculiarly delicious, and I like the fact that they look different from those uniform, plastic-wrapped ones you get in shops all year.

Round and mini cucumbers are still difficult to buy in the supermarket or greengrocer's – check out Lebanese and Turkish suppliers – so again try to make room for growing at least a couple of plants. They are huge producers, so you won't need many, and if you choose the right varieties, they are happy to be grown outside.

Sowing and growing cucumbers
Sowing

Cucumbers are half-hardy annuals – they can't withstand the frost – but they're easy to grow from seed. If you're going to grow them in an unheated greenhouse, or outside, sow them under cover in March/early April. They'll then be ready to go out when the frosts finish in the middle of May and you'll be eating the fruits by the end of June. I do a second sowing in June to crop well into the autumn.

Cucumbers have large, flat seeds, so sow them individually, vertically, into 8cm (3in) pots. Positioning them on edge – not flat – stops them rotting before they germinate. Using individual pots or Jiffy 7s avoids the need for pricking out.

After sowing, as with most other half-hardy annuals, cover the tray with a double sheet of newspaper or a polystyrene tile to exclude the light, and put it in a warm place. The moment you see any sign of life, remove the covering and expose the whole tray to bright light. Keep the compost moist at all times, watering from below to avoid the risk of damping off.

Planting

The important thing with cucumbers is to keep them growing. Anything that slows down the rate of growth can ultimately kill the plant. They don't like sudden chills or massive rises in temperature. They also prefer to be out of baking heat for part of the day, so plant them next to something that will throw some shade in their direction.

Below **'Burpless Tasty Green' is a particularly** delicious indoor or outdoor cucumber.

As soon as the roots fill their first pot and the frosts are over, plant them out. Cucumbers like a soil that has been deeply dug and has had large quantities of organic material added. They need to grow rapidly and will do this only on a rich soil with plenty of organic material.

Support and aftercare

Cucumbers are climbers. Put a 1.5m (5ft) cane at their side or, with a line of plants, create a netting frame over which they can climb. Do this on planting. If you delay, they'll bend and get a kink in the stem, which may cause them to collapse later on.

Watering regularly is important with cucumbers. Whether inside or out, their soil should be kept moist. If they really dry out, the flower buds drop – but don't over-water. It's a good idea to water in the morning to make sure the base of the stem is dry before the temperature drops at night. I fill a 2-litre pot angled towards the root with water every morning, or at least I try!

Harvest

Start to harvest as soon as the fruits are large enough to eat. You must keep picking the young fruit when they are green, with no signs of yellowing. Once the lower fruits are harvested, more will form higher on the plant. If you leave large fruits growing on the vine, production of new fruit lessens and those left become tough and dry.

Pests and diseases

Cucumbers used to be dogged by infestations and infections. Problems like red spider mite (use the biological control *Phytoseiulus*), mosaic virus and mildew made them difficult to grow without the use of far too many chemicals.

Disease can still be a problem. Cucumbers seem more susceptible than other veg, but it's not as bad as it was ten years ago. If you grow the right ones, with partial resistance to mildew and CMV (cucumber mosaic virus) like 'Zeina' and 'Burpless Tasty Green', you'll have a good crop without having to resort to pesticides.

Opposite **Cucumbers growing on wigwams in amongst the dahlias to save room in the veg garden.**

Below **Cucumber 'Zeina' bought by Molly for her mini patch, and very prolific.**

Four keys to success with cucumbers

1 Germinate cucumbers at unusually high temperatures of at least 21˚C (70˚F) – for quicker germination 24˚C (75˚F). The two varieties I grew this year germinated quickly and easily with my propagator thermostat set at maximum. Seedlings appeared in just over a week.

2 I always thought cucumbers needed to be grown in a greenhouse, but it's not true! I've grown fantastic plants with massive yields out in the garden now for several years. Three years ago my youngest daughter Molly bought a couple of 'Zeina' plants at a garden centre for planting in her mini patch. We were picking fruits from it from July until October, finding it difficult to keep up with the huge production from just two plants. Last year I planted 'Burpless Tasty Green' on a frame of three bamboo canes in the dahlia garden, and these did just as well.

3 Cucumbers are susceptible to root and stem rots, due to bacterial diseases that thrive in warm, wet conditions. If your cucumber plants suddenly wilt, place a mound of soilless potting compost in a pile at the base of the plant and water well. This will encourage new roots to form at the base.

4 It's a good idea to feed cucumbers, but don't use a high-potash tomato feed. It will slow their growth, and it also gives the cucumbers a bitter taste. Once the plants are growing well, three or four weeks after planting, start to feed once a week with a high-nitrogen feed. This encourages good growth. I use one teaspoon of dried blood a week, sprinkled around the base of the plant, not too close to the stem.

My desert island plants

My third and final lot of must-haves – my desert island plants – are included in my garden every year, and for as much of the year as possible. These are things that I would be determined to grow if I were cast off to the middle of nowhere with only limited space and water, and a real requirement to grow my own food. They're the plants that every vegetable patch, however small, should include: the hard-working yet tasty characters, all big producers over a long period of time – not just weeks but months. They're also easy, needing minimal TLC to grow well.

The plants you choose to grow should be not only productive but also versatile in terms of cooking, so that they can be eaten in many different ways. If you're growing only a few things and don't want your diet to be dull, you must have a great range of ways to eat them.

Above **Baby spinach and salad leaves picked minutes before from the garden.**
Opposite **Courgette 'Taxi' looks good in the garden and on the plate.**

Opposite **A mixed leaf salad of Cos 'Lobjoit's Green Cos' with brilliant chenopodium and pea tips.**

There are five vegetables in this category that fill over half the space in my vegetable patch, polytunnel and greenhouse. We love eating them on a daily or almost daily basis. I recommend you to grow as many of these as you can, experimenting with different varieties in each of the groups from one year to the next. That way you will build up your own reliable greengrocer supplying your personal favourites just outside your door, but without the veg patch taking over your life.

First, the cut-and-come-again salad leaves – the most plentiful, most picked and certainly most treasured plants in my garden. It was discovering these – plants such as mizuna, 'Red Giant' mustard, corn salad and the Continental loose-leaf lettuce varieties – that first got me growing my own food. It was amazing to be able to go out into the garden on any day of the year and pick a bowl of the most delicious, varied salad, with a mix of flavours – hot, peppery, sweet, bitter, earthy, mustardy, cabbagy – and also a great variety of textures. There are soft leaves and crunchy leaves and leaves with a succulent, water-filled bite. If you like strong colour contrast, as I do, there are acid-green as well as brilliant pink and crimson-black leaves. And this is true whether it's a baking summer day or freezing cold and wet in the depths of a grey and miserable winter.

Coming a close second to the salad leaves as a mainstay crop are many of the everyday herbs. A handful of parsley, chervil, lovage, tarragon or dill can turn a dull, uncreative meal into something memorable and delicious, and the great thing about these plants is that they can easily be grown in pots or in the smallest garden, where they take up very little room. Supermarkets have extended their range of herbs in the last few years, but many of them are grown hydroponically. This means that the plants sit in water, into which all their nutrients are delivered. This can produce a diluted taste. It's much better to grow your own intense-flavoured herbs which you can pick by the handful time and time again.

The number three plant for my desert island is the courgette. Courgettes are massive producers and one of the most versatile plants you can grow: there are numerous different and delicious ways in which they can be eaten. And the great thing about courgettes is that you can eat the flowers as well.

These three plants or groups of plants are all fashionable with a touch of 'chefy' glamour. They are hardly controversial choices, but I would also select some of the more pedestrian-seeming kale family as my number four, and either chard or perpetual beet as my number five. All three of these leafy greens grow prolifically through the spring and summer, with minimal tendency to bolt – run up to flower – and they'll grow just as well in the autumn and winter too. You may not be able to grow chard uncovered in the north of England, but kale and perpetual beet are as tough as nails. If you harvest the plants regularly, they will produce meal after meal for six months at a stretch. After the first half of the year, you can sow them again to produce for the last half.

With chard (or beet) and kales there is a great range of different ways to cook them. I use the robust flavour of kale to make tasty winter crostini (see picture, page 117); I finely strip the leaves and then deep-fry kale to make Chinese 'seaweed' (see picture, page 115), and it's the invaluable flavour in chunky winter soups like Tuscan *ribollita*, or Scotch broth.

Chard makes one of my favourite simple steamed greens. The Greeks use it as their base for *horta*, a wonderful warm leaf dish doused in lots of lemon juice and olive oil. I love chard, stems and tops, in a Parmesan-rich gratin, and it's invaluable chopped finely for winter risotto. It's fantastic in soup with a tin of coconut milk and makes a superb pastry-free pie, a Provençal mussel dish with nutmeggy chard and a crunchy breadcrumb and Parmesan top in a light béchamel sauce. Adam and I had this as the first course at our wedding.

With these plants in your garden, home-grown, home-cooked food is an easy and achievable thing with little time needed to create it. That suits me.

Cut-and-come-again salad crops

I eat a green salad at least every other day of the year. The best way to construct a salad is to pick a leaf of every salad plant you fancy and roll them up in a tight cigar. Take a few bites. You'll know immediately if it has the right taste for you that day. If you're eating red meat, go for a hot horseradish, mustardy mix. If it's chicken or fish, a fresher, more citrus taste works better. If it's to go with cheese, some of the sweeter leaves are delicious. Whatever you're eating as the main part of your meal, you'll find a brilliant range of flavours from the salad leaves to mix in.

You won't get this flexibility from anything you buy at the supermarket. It's worth knowing that commercial producers, in order to make absolutely sure that you won't come across any bugs as you eat your lunch, will have washed the contents of many of your expensive bought bags of salad in a cocktail of chemicals, including chlorine twenty times as concentrated as that used in a swimming pool. The atmosphere in the bags is also filled with gases, which stops all processes in the leaves and so prevents them bio-degrading for weeks. This means that they can be harvested on the other side of the world and still have a shelf life in our supermarkets. It doesn't appeal to me.

So as a cook, you'll find it's good to grow these plants, but for the gardener they're a gift too. What's miraculous is that they are cut-and-come-again. After harvesting their leaves, every one of them will resprout for picking again. Start at one end of the line of crops and keep picking every few days, until you reach the other end. By that time, the plants you cut ten days or a fortnight ago will have sprouted more. The speed at which they grow back varies according to the time of year. Growth rates and harvest will be limited for half of November and February, as well as all of December and January – nothing grows quickly then – but even in these leaner months, you're still able to pick some leaves. For the rest of the year, you can produce bowls and bowls of varied salads to eat whenever you wish.

The advantages of cut-and-come-again salad leaves

1 With cut-and-come-again salad leaves, you'll pick from the same line, or patch of leaves, again and again. With the majority of the more traditional hearting salad crops, once you've picked them, that's it – you pull up the roots and sow again.

2 They are very quick. You will be harvesting leaves within four to six weeks, whereas it takes three to four months to grow a standard hearted lettuce.

3 They are very easy to grow and, if you're short of space, will do well in a pot. The number of cuts is restricted with a thin layer of soil, but you can even grow them in shallow seed trays. When I gardened with very little space in London, salad leaves were one of the few things I grew in wooden troughs down both sides of the garden path. Six boxes, each 60cm (2ft) long, grew enough for me and Adam to eat salad two or three times a week right the way through the year. I now grow my winter cut-and-come-again salad bang outside my kitchen door in a large metal water trough that I bought at a farm sale for a fiver (see picture, page 98). Even when it's raining and freezing cold, I can pick a tasty salad in a couple of minutes without getting wet!

4 Most of these plants grow well even in poor soil – particularly salad rocket, the cresses and mustards. The oriental greens like mizuna and pak-choi are slightly more demanding, growing best in a reasonably fertile, rich, moisture-retentive soil.

5 Leafy veg are at their most nutritious in terms of vitamin levels at the seedling stage, so you can eat them young.

Sowing direct

From mid-spring to late summer, you can sow your salad leaves straight into the garden (see page 140). They're one of the quickest and easiest crops to grow.

My favourite cut-and-come-again salad leaves and loose-leaf lettuce

There are many different varieties of salad leaves and loose-leaf lettuce (see page 221 for a more complete list), but here is a very limited selection of my favourites in terms of taste, ease, productivity and length of season. Arranged in my order of preference, these *really* are the unmissable crew.

1 Mizuna – all year. This is slow to bolt, easy to grow, tasty and prolific. We should all grow this. It's my number one, the cut-and-come-again salad plant for all seasons.

2 Lettuce 'A Foglia di Quercia' or Oak Leaf – almost all year. Superb, easy, tasty, prolific and pretty loose-leaf lettuce. This is ideal to grow as an edging to a path. In winter it will need to be grown under cover.

3 Salad rocket – autumn, winter and early spring. It has great flavour and is incredibly versatile, delicious in a huge number of different ways. In the summer months it bolts – runs up to flower – and becomes very hot in flavour. When the weather is hot and dry, slower-growing wild rocket is better.

4 Spinach 'Dominant' – all year bar a couple of hot months in the summer. Fantastic flavour and texture and excellent, easy productivity. 'Dominant' is the best of all the spinach varieties I've tried, superb either raw or cooked. When the weather is hot and dry in the summer, however, it will bolt after only a few cuts. 'Trinidad' is a good variety to try growing then. For the winter months, especially if you live in a frost pocket, you will need to choose a really hardy spinach such as 'Winterreuzen' (or Giant of Winter – see page 229).

5 Mustard 'Red Giant' – all year. This has a very peppy flavour and is a fantastically versatile plant, invaluable raw or cooked. Small leaves give you hot, horseradishy flavours in a salad in a wonderful dark crimson. Larger leaves are very hot and can be tough.

These are best cooked. They make one of the best soups and are delicous cut into strips for a stir-fry. When we have lots of it, we also deep-fry it like kale to make Chinese 'seaweed' (see recipe, page 115).

6 Mustard 'Komatsuna' or Spanish brassica – all year. New to me this year, this is one of the best leaves to provide bulk for salad in the winter and through the rest of the year. Its taste is milder than 'Red Giant' but still mustardy, and it has a crunchier, more lettuce-like, water-filled texture. It's as hardy a leaf as any I've tried.

7 Mibuna – all year. A close relative of mizuna, with long, thin, quickly growing leaves. It's as hardy, easy and slow to bolt as mizuna.

8 Lettuce 'Merveille des Quatre Saisons' – early spring to autumn. A wonderful, waxy-looking, green-tinged crimson lettuce which has good flavour and is one of the hardiest lettuces you can grow. In a mild year this will survive and produce small amounts right the way through the winter, but grow it under cover if you can.

Below **Mixed young leaves.**

Opposite **Mango, couscous and mixed leaf salad – a very tasty lunch.**

Wait for the soil to warm up in the spring and go for it – with half of a few packets of seed. You'll know your soil is warm when lots of annual weeds germinate and your tidy garden suddenly looks a mess! This is usually in mid-April in Sussex, where I live. It could be three or four weeks earlier in Cornwall and three or four weeks later in the north.

Don't put the whole lot in at once (see box). That way you will have too much of one thing ready at the same time.

When I sow salad leaves I tend to create stripes rather than lines. Use an 8–10cm (3–4in) hoe to make wide, shallow trenches or drills as close together as possible. The developing seedlings in adjacent drills eventually touch, creating a carpet effect (see picture, page 95). Check the back of the seed packet for the spacing of each one, but allow for the fact that your leaves will not be allowed to reach full size, so you can go closer than the packet says. This looks good and obliterates weeds. Sow in blocks of six or seven rows and then allow room between blocks for a 60cm (2ft) path to make picking easy without a stretch.

Joy Larkcom, the guru of salad-growing, recommends sowing in alternate stripes of red and green to make a productive salad garden look good. You might grow golden purslane for a bright acid-green next to 'Red Giant' mustard, veined and stippled in crimson; or red orach for its deep red leaves. You could develop this theme, thinking about leaf texture and shape, perhaps putting spiky-leaved mizuna next to feathery-leaved dill, and this next to round-leaved lamb's lettuce.

Water the ground if it's dry and then sow your seeds evenly, 5cm (2in) apart, taking them from your palm individually, or in small pinches, and sow as finely as you can into drills. Most of these plants have large enough seed to make individual sowing possible, and this saves both seed and thinning time later on. Press the seed gently into the soil.

You may still need to thin out the seedlings, leaving one good plant every 10cm (4in). If you dig up the roots

Six keys to cutting-and-coming again and again!

1 There's no point doing one sowing of your salad leaves. Successional sowing is vital. Try to sow half a packet every four to six weeks from March until September and every three or four months in the slower-growing season (see page 221).

2 Choose the right plants for the time of year. The ones to sow for summer are, in the main, different from the ones that will produce the best winter crop. There are several that will tolerate almost any climate and condition, but others divide between those that grow best with more light hours than dark and those that prefer it the other way around (see pages 221–9).

3 Watering regularly in the summer months when it is hot and dry helps to prevent quick bolting and stops flavours becoming too strong. Be sure to water in the early morning or late evening – to avoid scorch and wasteful evaporation. A leaky pipe is a good thing to use.

4 On a hot day, it's best to sow cold-temperature plants in the cool of the evening. The hardier varieties such as winter purslane, mizuna and corn salad don't like being sown into warm soil. Purslane in particular won't germinate if you sow too early in the year, when the weather and soil are still warm. Wait until September, or even later in the south. This plant self-sows every year in my polytunnel and germinates naturally in January. If sowing under cover, don't use any heat at the roots.

5 In the summer you must keep brassicas such as mizuna and rocket covered with horticultural fleece right the way through from sowing to harvesting. In a no-sprays organic garden this is the one sure way of preventing infestation by flea beetle, which otherwise will pepper every leaf with holes (see page 168). You don't need to create a frame. Just cover the whole line with fleece – left quite baggy but secured with wire hoops all around the edges – and the plants will push this up as they grow. It's so light that the leaves will not be damaged or even bent.

6 When you sow, think of a 3m or 6m (10ft or 20ft) line in bands, doing up to 1m (3ft) of one type, and then another, and so on. This looks good and produces more interesting and varied meals.

Below **Young leaves growing in a trough outside my back door, for easy winter picking.**

Opposite **Picking a big colander-full of mizuna, mibuna and other winter salad.**

with a trowel, rather than pull them out of the soil, you can transplant them into another row. Most of these plants don't mind root disturbance if still at the seedling stage. Water them in well.

If I have plenty of plants, I tend to eat the thinnings rather than replant them – tiny, delicate, delicious leaves with lots of flavour.

Sowing under cover
Guttering

From late summer until the spring, and when there isn't a chink of space for sowing in the garden, I sow my salad leaves into guttering (see page 144 for more detail). I always sow my first spring crop (February/March) and last autumn crop (September/October) using this system under cover.

I find guttering the most efficient way for sowing shallow-rooting plants in succession. It's very quick: one sweep of the arm with half a packet, then a quick thinning,

and that's all you need to do. There is no need for pricking out, or potting on. What's also fantastic about this system is that you get pre-germinated lines, which are easily grown, to be slotted into the garden when space appears – a guaranteed crop sitting in the wings ready to replace something when previous sowings run to seed. There is also no problem with slow germination on cold, sticky clay soils and none of the dangers of unpredictable weather. And this is true twelve months of the year. If you have somewhere light under cover to keep them, you can sow even between November and February, when almost nothing would germinate if sown directly.

With the plants going out in adolescence, they also stand a much better chance against slugs and snails. I think it's the best system. The only downside to guttering is the need for regular watering in hot weather. You can decrease this by adding water-retaining granules to your compost.

Jiffy 7s

Salad leaves also suit the larger-size (40mm/1½in) Jiffy 7s, with two seeds sown into the dimple in the top of each pellet (see page 145), but sowing takes longer than into gutters. If both seeds germinate, you will need to remove one plant, leaving one to grow on its own.

Planting out

Once the mini plants are about 2.5cm (1in) tall, put them out in the garden. If they were sown into guttering, this will require two of you, one to hold either end of the guttering (see page 22). If they were planted in a Jiffy, remove the net from the pellet, placing them at 10cm (4in) spacings, with 15–20cm (6–8in) between the lines.

Growing in containers

Most of these plants are happy to be grown in pots – a big advantage if you're short of space.

When I lived in London and had a small garden, Adam made up wooden boxes to line my paths and I grew my salad leaves in these. They are all relatively

Opposite **Bringing in the harvest – mixed leaves and flowers always look** **wonderful, and are easy to wash and dry, in this old French wire basket.**

shallow-rooting plants and, if kept fed and watered, are ideally suited to pot growth.

Fill the pots with compost. In the summer, use a loam-based type like John Innes No 2 or else mix water-retaining granules in with potting compost. If you use potting compost on its own, it dries out very quickly and you will have to water at least twice a day in the heat of the summer. With the autumn sowing, any good compost will do.

Water before you sow, so you don't wash everything to the edge of the container, and then broadcast the seed over the compost surface, and crumble or sieve fine soil or compost over the top. Seedlings will appear within a few days.

If you have room for only one or two boxes on a windowsill, the best advice is to choose one of the salad mixes so that you get a bit of everything. The trouble with these is that you must keep on top of the picking. If you leave the plants uncut for more than a couple of weeks, any large, brutish ones that are included, such as borage and Cos lettuce, will outdo and kill the more delicate things like chervil and basil, and you will be left with a boring mix.

Harvesting

As long as you cut or pick them 2.5cm (1in) above the ground, above the first pair of seed leaves, they will sprout again four or five times before they stop producing. By that time, if you've got it right with successional sowing (see box, page 97), you'll have another few lines ready. Take out the tired ones you've been picking for a few months and plant again. With this system, you've got a reliable harvest, from the beginning to the end of the year, without a barren week.

Another way of harvesting salad is what's called 'picking round'. This means cutting some – but not all – the leaves at one time. If there are six leaves, pick three, starting from the outside. The advantage of this system is that the plants tend to form mini trunks at the base. This makes them hardier and more able to withstand

winter wet and cold than the fleshier cut-and-come-again equivalents. I tend to start picking hardy lettuce like this in the autumn and carry on through the winter. This guarantees some large leaves for my salad bowl.

Once picked, your leaves should be soaked in cold water for an hour or two. This is like conditioning flowers, and the leaves absorb water over their whole surface area. They then last better, have a better texture and don't wilt so quickly once the dressing is on in the bowl. Dry them gently before you eat them.

Salads through the winter

For this miraculously productive salad garden to keep going through the winter you don't need a greenhouse or polytunnel if you live in the south of England, as there are exceptionally hardy varieties like mizuna that can withstand temperatures as low as –15°C (5°F) for short periods of time. These will survive under a cloche, or extendable mini polytunnel, almost anywhere in Britain. One of the areas where we grow vegetables at home is a steeply sloping, south-facing bank that is clad with squash in the summer and autumn and then a selection of salad leaves through the winter. They look wonderful in their stripes, tumbling down the slope, and even on a frosty morning can be picked for another delicious lunch. People who come to the school are often amazed that they're eating home-grown winter salad. They look out of the window and there it is. After a really hard frost on some mornings the plants look a bit beaten up (see picture, pages 26–7). The frosted leaves may collapse, but the root ball is fine. You can cut the mushy leaves off and, in a mild spell, more will appear. To guarantee some leaves twelve months of the year you need to know how hardy each variety is and which is suited to winter and which to summer sowing (see pages 221–9). Then you're away.

If I could grow only one edible group of plants it would have to be these. They're easy, prolific and give you a huge range of tastes. With cut-and-come-again salad leaves, home-grown food will never be dull.

Herbs

Opposite, clockwise from top left: **Chervil, 'Bowles' mint, Italian flat-leaved parsley and lemon grass.**

The food I make at home would be much less tasty without having easy access to herbs. I'm a slap-dash cook, who loves chucking a few things together, ready to eat in ten minutes or less, and yet I love good tasty food. Herbs – not the scrappy little handfuls you get in shop-bought sachets but good wads, whole fistfuls of delicious, fresh herbs – are an essential part of this instant, impatient, yet critical style of cooking.

I've worked out a list of the varieties I would miss if I didn't have them out in the garden, the plants I pick at least once a week. There are some I use more, such as parsley, mint and basil, which I pick most days when they're in season. The rest appear in our food less often, but frequently enough for me to want them easily available.

You may have a different list, but whatever appears on it, why not have a go at growing them? Most herbs take up little room – they are a group of plants that thrive in pots – and, with a few tips up your sleeve, are easy to grow.

Sowing and growing herbs

None of these herbs is difficult or time-consuming to grow, but before you start it's good to know which plant group they belong to. Are they annuals – hardy or half-hardy – or herbaceous or woody perennials? Once you know that, you'll have a fair idea how to grow them.

Herbs grown as hardy annuals

True hardy annuals

Coriander	Par-cel
Dill	Summer savory

Biennials grown as hardy annuals because you don't want herbs to flower

Chervil	Parsley

Perennials grown as hardy annuals

Sorrel, buckler-leaved

My favourite herbs

These are herbs I find productive and easy. There is information on a fuller range of herbs on page 200.

1 Flat-leaved parsley Biennial. Grow either this or the curly-leaved English kind. Both are delicious and easy to grow. Parsley, left to its own devices, is slow to germinate. The seeds have a natural germination inhibitor in the seed coat. For quicker germination, wash this off by soaking the seed in a cup of warm water before you sow. Some people sow first and then water the planted seed from a warm kettle. You need a warm temperature and enough moisture to wash them well. Both ways work.

2 Basil Half-hardy annual. Sweet basil has the best flavour, but lemon basil, Greek bush basil and lettuce-leaved basil are all worth growing for their different reasons (see page 203). I now also grow Thai basil for green Thai curries and oriental food. The decorative purple-leaved basil is hardest to grow in this country, as it will rapidly succumb to botrytis (see page 168) in a wet season, but it looks good on the plate.

3 Chervil Biennial. This is the hardiest herb of the lot, brilliant for winter cooking and salads, and it makes a perfect omelette. I find I can grow this easily outside in the winter, where it will self-sow. If you want it for summer eating, sow or plant it in light shade.

4 Lemon grass Tender perennial. The basal stems are the crucial ingredient for Thai fish cakes, curries and soups. At Perch Hill we use the green leafy tips for teas and sorbets. Harvest three or four stems and steep them in boiling water for five minutes. If you have a greenhouse or insulated cold frame, grow your lemon grass there so that you can over-winter the roots from one year to the next. They need a minimum night temperature of 15˚C (60˚F). To maintain this, you may need to bubble-wrap the greenhouse or have a heater on a 1Kw thermostat. From April it needs only night heat.

5 Mint Herbaceous perennial. 'Bowles' mint and spearmint are the varieties I use most. Moroccan mint is good for strong tea. Most mints are rompers, and people tell you to restrict their roots. This may be true in a small, tidy garden, but if you have a wilder area, allow it to romp somewhere out of the way. I've put my 'Bowles' mint on a bank near the polytunnels, so I can pick fistfuls almost every day from April until October. I then dig up a few roots and plant them in a pot to keep under cover for picking through the winter. In good light, if kept frost-free, they grow well inside.

Hardy annuals can be sown direct into the garden, or sown under cover for planting out from guttering, seed trays or Jiffy 7 pellets, exactly as you do the salad leaves (see page 98).

From the middle of April to the end of August, direct sowing is probably the easiest system and the soil will be warm enough for quick germination.

At other times of year sow inside, growing some herbs – parsley, dill and chervil – under cover in a greenhouse or polytunnel if you have room, or on a sheltered window ledge in a city. You can then pick a bunch of these several times a week right the way through the winter.

In my Sussex garden I even pick chervil and parsley in the winter from outside my back door. They grow without any protection against a sheltered south-facing wall.

Half-hardy annual herbs

Basil

Sweet marjoram – *Origanum marjoram*

Half-hardy perennials grown as half-hardy annuals

Lemon grass

For spring and autumn, it's best to sow the half-hardy herbs under cover. They need that extra bit of cosseting to perform as well as they can in our cooler clime. For summer, they're happy outside. Depending on how many plants I want, I use guttering, seed trays or Jiffy 7s for sowing (see page 98) and then plant them out when the seedlings are about 5cm (2in) tall.

Growing herbs in pots and boxes

Like most herbs, these annual and biennial varieties – the hardy and half-hardy types – are very happy to be grown in pots. If you're growing them in containers outside, sow seed direct into a water-retaining compost like John Innes No 2 (as for salad leaves – see page 100).

Some herbs can also be grown in pots inside if you want them all year round. I have adopted a very productive system of herb growing introduced to me by hotelier Jane Dunn. She cooks for all her guests at Stone House in East Sussex and aims to grow a good selection of herbs to use in her cooking every day. She produces fistfuls of chervil, coriander, dill, flat- and curly-leaved parsley, as well as some of the half-hardies – sweet basil, the dark 'Purple Ruffles' basil and Greek bush basil, with its stronger taste, using her brilliantly productive system.

Jane uses empty wooden wine cases to grow all these herbs. The boxes are drilled with drainage holes and then filled with multi-purpose compost and, once a fortnight, whatever the time of year, Jane sows a whole packet of seed into each new case. If she runs out of wooden boxes, she uses polystyrene fish crates, with holes in the bottom banged through with a hammer and nail. These don't look as good but work just as well. And if you can't get hold of them, I've used greengrocers' wooden boxes with a solid base and walls, or else the slatted ones, lined with newspaper.

Five keys to success with hardy annuals

1 Successional sowing is the key to a seamless supply (see page 97).

2 Picking the plants and preventing them running up to flower and setting seed increases their productivity. As soon as you see a flower stem forming, cut it right back and water the plant well.

3 Watering when it's hot and dry also prolongs their season.

4 Growing the right variety – such as coriander 'Leisure' for leaf, not seed, and slow-to-bolt dill like 'Bouquet' – makes a difference to the length of harvest.

5 These are all easy, tolerant plants, with very few pest and disease problems, and will thrive in most soils and situations. Most like full sun, but they will all grow in partial shade. Chervil does better with some shade if sown in the late spring or summer.

Below **Sweet marjoram.**
Overleaf **As you pick
herbs, bind the bunches
separately with elastic**
**bands to avoid creating
a mass of muddled
leaves at the bottom
of your basket.**

Sow your seeds densely in the compost-filled crate and cover the whole thing in cling film to enclose the moisture. Then put them in a greenhouse or cold frame if you have one, on a heated base. Your airing cupboard is fine for this germination stage, but if you grow them in the dark like this, you'll need to check every 24 hours for any signs of green. As soon as the seedlings appear, move them into the light. To improve ventilation and decrease the risk of damping off, take the cling film off at this stage.

Grow them on in a frost-free place that has bright, all-round light. For the winter, you'll need a gently heated greenhouse, cold frame or unheated porch, rather than an over-hot kitchen, but in the summer almost anywhere light will do.

Give them a good watering every day in the summer, but don't drown them. Reduce this to once a week in the winter.

The key to the abundance of the herbs is sowing them closely together, watering, and then harvesting them regularly as soon as they fill out. You must chop them when they've reached about 5cm (2in) in height, before they compete with their neighbours and get wimpy and tall. Generally I cut 2.5cm (1in) above the soil – above the bottom pair of seed leaves – and then the seedlings will quickly regrow.

With your herb boxes regularly sown, you'll be able to slice swathes of herbs – even the half-hardies – any day of the year. Jane even manages to grow basil all through the winter in a heated greenhouse in this way.

Hardy herbaceous perennial herbs

Chives	Horseradish
Fennel	Lovage
French tarragon	Mint
Golden oregano	Winter savory

You can buy your perennial herbs from a herb supplier, or grow them yourself in one of three ways. Some of

Five keys to success with half-hardy annuals

Most of the widely grown half-hardy herbs like basil and sweet marjoram are Mediterranean plants and will grow happily here if you try to mimic their hotter climate as much as you can.

1 Don't plant them outside until cold nights are likely to be over. In Sussex this means early June. Basil will go black outside in mid-September, so pick the lot to make pesto or basil oil before you lose it. A very successful basil grower once taught me that basil is happy outside for the months you're happy to have supper outside.

2 Don't send them to bed wet. Depending on rainfall, plants outside may not need watering; inside, water in the morning not evening. Evening watering encourages botrytis – a potential killer in the cold and wet.

3 In a grey year, you may have problems with damping off, caused by a mixture of soil-borne fungi that wipe out small seedlings. Avoid it by general glasshouse hygiene, which includes cleaning pots and trays, and ensuring good ventilation.

4 Basil in particular likes it hot, but humid and moist, so water liberally if growing inside. The best sweet basil

I ever saw was grown in a polytunnel with a high humidity created by coals, with a tap dripping on to them, as you would get in a steam room. The plants had created a jungle, pickable twice a day! If you're growing it in the garden, basil is very successfully grown from sowing direct in June and July.

5 Take care how you pick basil. If you mow it quickly with scissors, cutting the plant down to half its size, you often leave stem stumps behind. Towards the end of the season particularly, these may attract fungi. I pick basil like an annual flower instead, carefully cutting to immediately above a leaf or lateral bud. This will promote that bud to develop into next week's leaves and leave minimal damaged tissue.

them are easiest to grow from seed, others by division or from semi-ripe (or softwood) cuttings begged from a friend's garden.

Most are prolific and easy, rooting or establishing themselves quickly. Some perennial herbs – mint, horseradish and fennel in particular – are almost too easy and need to be contained, or even banned if it's a small, tidy garden. Fennel self-sows prolifically (see page 205). Mint and horseradish roots romp away, quickly colonizing large areas. Contain their roots or put them somewhere it doesn't matter (see page 103). If you contain them, change the soil regularly or the flavour will vanish.

Perennial herbs to grow from seed	
Chives	Lovage
Fennel	Winter savory

Depending on how many plants I want, I use both seed trays and Jiffy 7s for sowing (see page 98) and then plant them out when the seedlings are about 5cm (2in) tall.

Herbaceous perennial herbs to grow by division	
Chives	Mint
Horseradish	Winter savory
Lovage	

Division is a quick and easy technique suitable for most perennial herbs. In fact tarragon is the only one I find difficult to propagate in this way and is best – but still tricky – from cuttings. I do lovage, horseradish, mint, winter savory and chives like this, with all but chives done in the spring. Chives are best left until late summer/autumn.

If you have a newish clump and don't want to disturb it, leave it in the ground and slice sections off the outside of the plant with a spade or trowel. Pot up each little section of root in compost and grow them on for a few weeks before putting them back into the garden.

With a large old clump, it's best to dig up the whole root and slice it into palm-sized sections. Select from

Three keys to success with hardy herbaceous perennials

1 Most of the perennial herbs thrive in poor soil with good drainage. If you garden on rich, heavy clay, add grit to the planting position and mulch with grit between the plants to keep down the weeds. Mint and horseradish will grow almost anywhere, moist or dry, sunny or shady.

2 It is a good idea to give all these plants a severe haircut towards the end of June. They will resprout quickly and you'll then have plenty to pick right into the autumn. Left to their own devices, they become woody and run to flower and the flavour and the texture of the leaves suffer.

3 I feed potash-rich comfrey juice (see page 20) to lots of our perennial herbs – chives, mint, lovage and lemon balm – to give them an enlivening boost after their haircut in June.

the outside of the rootball, discarding the areas near the centre. This will give renewed vigour to the whole thing. Again, pot each new plant on for a few weeks before putting them back into the garden.

Herbaceous perennial herbs to grow from semi-ripe cuttings	
Golden oregano	Tarragon
Mint	Winter savory

This is a very good way to make lots of cuttings. They may be small to start with, but it's an easy way to create enough plants to line a path. Semi-ripe cuttings are taken from the plants from mid-summer to early autumn – August and September are ideal. What you want is the soft wood at the upper end of the stem and the ripening wood at the base of the current season's growth.

Snip off the top 8cm (3in) of a healthy-looking stem just above a bud. Remove the lower leaves from the bottom 2.5cm (1in) of the cutting, pulling them off downwards for a clean tear.

Push the cuttings into compost with sharp sand added to ensure good drainage. They will root easily without hormone rooting powder. Water them in well and keep the compost moist, trying to avoid getting the leaves wet, and put them somewhere warm and light. Avoid bright sunshine because it dehydrates the rootless cuttings too quickly.

The cuttings should root in a couple of weeks, but some will take longer than others.

Once they are rooted, pot them on into 10cm (4in) pots and put them in an unheated greenhouse or a cold frame until the spring. They'll then be ready for planting out. In the south, we try to take our cuttings earlier so that we can get them into the ground in early autumn.

Woody perennials

Deciduous shrubs
Lemon verbena

Evergreen shrubs
Rosemary	Thyme
Sage	

If you're planting any of these herbs in large numbers, don't buy them; propagate them yourself. Most of them are remarkably easy to do using one of three propagating systems – seed, semi-ripe cuttings or layering.

Growing woody perennials from seed

Seed-grown herbs grow quickly, and you can often find that good, unusual varieties are available from seed catalogues but can be more difficult to buy as plants.

Of the woody perennials that are listed above, the only one that I do not grow from seed is the deciduous lemon verbena. Depending on how many plants I want, I use both seed trays and Jiffy 7s for sowing (see page 98) and then I plant them out when the seedlings are about 5cm (2in) tall in early summer.

Below **Rosmarinus officinalis** Prostratus Group is a creeping or trailing woody, evergreen shrub.

Growing woody perennials from semi-ripe cuttings

This is an easy way to propagate these herbs, which will root within a few weeks if you use a gritty mix of compost and keep it good and moist. Cuttings will quickly grow into decent-sized plants within a year or so.

I take cuttings at almost any time of year, cutting off 8–10cm (3–4in) sprigs, stripping the leaves from half the stem and then poking them into a gritty compost mix. I use one-third grit to two-thirds multi-purpose compost. I stick canes in around the edge of the pot, and create a mini tent by putting a plastic bag over them, secured to the sides of the pot with an elastic band. I stand this on a damp sand tray and leave them to root without any more fuss. They almost always root in a month or two, and I pot them on once before putting them out in the garden. This works well for all but lemon verbena, which needs several months in a cold frame before planting out in the spring.

Growing woody perennials by layering

If you want only a few extra plants, layering is a quick and easy way to propagate. The idea is to make a branch or stem of a plant grow roots while still attached to the main plant.

Look for a healthy shoot or branch close to the ground or one that's easy to bend to ground level. Clear

Below *Rosmarinus officinalis* Prostratus Group is a creeping or trailing woody, evergreen shrub.

Opposite **Self-sown dill is brilliant for both flower arrangements and eating.**

the soil of weeds and leaves. Wound the stem with a few nicks to the bark and push the stem into the soil. Pull up some of the surrounding soil into a mound and secure it with a hoop of wire or a heavy stone. Check the layer every couple of weeks, watering the area if it's dry. In the summer roots may form in a few weeks, or else you can do it in the autumn and wait for it to root in the spring.

Once the roots have formed, cut it from the parent plant, then pot it up or move it elsewhere in the garden.

Storing herbs after picking

With all the annual herbs, it's best to pick them as and when you want them, but you can't pick the soft, non-evergreen herbs like dill all year. When there's plenty in the garden, store them anyway. With dill, wash it, chop it and freeze it in a plastic bag. You can then use it raw and as an excellent flavouring for soups.

I like to make lots of herb-flavoured oils, vinegars and butters to preserve the non-evergreen herb flavours for the winter months. With basil, I whizz up a good bunch of leaves with olive oil in a food processor and let it steep for a couple of weeks before I strain it. Stored in bottles, in cool and dark conditions, it lasts so well that you can make wonderful basil-flavoured dressings throughout the winter.

I also make tarragon wine vinegar, picking three or four stems of tarragon and leaving it sitting in the vinegar for a month. This also makes the most delicious salad dressing, with a sweetish, slightly smoky flavour, and it forms the base of fantastic Béarnaise sauce.

To make herb butters, use any of the soft green herbs. Using butter that's at room temperature and malleable, mix it in a food processor with a bunch of herbs until it has the consistency of Plasticene. Then roll the mixture up like a sausage in cling film and freeze it. You can take out the herb butter roll at any time and, with a warm knife, cut off as much as you want to use that day, putting the rest back in the freezer. This is ideal for eating with steak, or for adding flavour to sauces and soups. Don't put the butter in until right at the end. Apart

Five keys to success with woody perennials

1 Most of these plants thrive in poor soil with good drainage. If you garden on rich, heavy clay, add plenty of grit to the planting position and mulch between the plants to keep down the weeds. Try to replace at least one-third of the volume of soil you've dug out with grit.

2 If you want neat domes – particularly of your sage – you need to keep these evergreen herbs well pruned. Clip each stem back to a bud in mid-spring, taking care not to cut back into old wood, and give them a light clipping after flowering in the summer. With this dual regime, they won't become too woody at the base and will hold their shape better through the winter wind and snow. Don't give them a hard prune in the autumn – this can kill these Mediterranean plants. They need most of their leaves as an insulating blanket to keep them alive through the winter.

3 Rosemary has been suffering from a widespread virus in recent years. Whole sections of a plant die off quickly. Sadly, there isn't much you can do to stop it. Plant your cuttings initially with lots of drainage – grit (see page 109) – to strengthen the plant from the beginning, remove any section of the plant showing signs of illness, and then cross your fingers and hope that it will not spread.

4 Most of these herbs thrive in a sheltered warm spot. Think of where you've seen rosemary growing well. It's surrounded by warm paths and walls. Try to find it somewhere like that in your garden.

5 Because of the transient nature of these herbs, it's a good idea to keep a younger generation coming along. Young, healthy, vigorous plants produce more leaves and are better able to resist disease. Keep propagating new plants every year or two.

from parsley, the softer herbs have highly aromatic oils and lose their flavour quickly on cooking.

If you prefer olive oil to butter, fill an ice tray with the chopped herbs you want to preserve. Cover the herbs with oil and freeze them. You can then knock them out into a plastic box or bag and use them as and when you want them.

Courgettes

Courgettes make it to my desert island because there are so many different ways that you can cook them and they produce copious amounts of fruit and flowers with minimal love and attention. Once you've got the plants in your garden, you'll realize how many flowers you can pick – delicious, glamorous things to eat, yet almost impossible to buy. The flowers don't store or travel well, so most commercial growers don't bother to harvest them. Almost the only thing you need to remember with courgettes is to pick them small, when they are dense-fleshed and tasty. They're often difficult to see, nestling down in the heart of the plant and covered with leaves, but try to remember to check your plants two or three times a week. Once they've reached marrow size, they've lost their charm.

When I say to my students that courgettes are among the most versatile vegetables in terms of cooking, there is always a protest that they have a boring taste. Anyone who thinks that should try small ones – twice finger-size – halved and griddled with chilli and a bit of olive oil. Cook them and then douse them with lemon juice and a scattering of roast pine nuts for one of my favourite instant summer meals. Courgettes are also fantastic for summer-garden tempura, using the flowers and slices of the fruit, which are dipped into batter, deep-fried and then eaten with a soy or red pepper and chilli dipping sauce. You can include the flowers just as they are or stuff them with ricotta, peas, pine nuts and thyme for one of the tastiest summer home-grown first courses your garden can provide.

I also love courgettes as a salad, grated and marinated in good olive oil and lemon juice, or griddled till slightly charred and then baked with goat's cheese. Best of all, try them softened with a chilli, a good handful of tarragon and a pot of crème fraîche. The key here is long cooking, so that the slices fall apart and the flavours intensify. Add the torn-up yellow zap of flowers – just wilted – as you take the pan to the table.

Sowing and growing courgettes
Sowing

Courgettes don't like root disturbance, so it's best to go for two seeds to a small pot, selecting one plant if both seeds germinate. Pot them on once and then put them out.

Sow them vertically downwards, not laid flat. Their large surface area encourages rot if sown flat.

They germinate quickly – within about a week – and have large leaves to do lots of photosynthesis, so they grow quickly.

Resist the temptation to pick off the seed coat if it doesn't shed naturally. You will almost certainly bruise a cell of the leaf and the plant will suffer visibly. I have lost plants that got fungus where I'd taken off the seed case. Mosaic virus and downy mildew (see pages 89 and 168) can also cause major problems with courgettes. 'Defender' has some resistance, so is a good one to grow (see page 194).

Planting out

After giving the roots a good soaking, plant them out with plenty of space – at least 1m (3ft) – between plants. Slugs and snails love small courgette seedlings, so it's worth letting them get to a decent size, potting them on and waiting till the roots fill at least a 9cm (3½in) pot before you plant them out.

Dig a huge hole and fill it with rich organic material. Home-made compost is ideal. Courgettes love it rich and moist, and the compost will help to feed and water the plants. You often see them being grown on compost heaps for exactly this reason. They tolerate the rich conditions and benefit from the warmth emerging from the rotting process of the compost. Just dig a hole in the top of the heap, fill it with molehills or soil-based compost and plant your seedlings.

Opposite **'Tromboncino' courgettes in the veg** **garden – exotic shapes with good flavour and texture.**

Opposite **So-called Chinese 'seaweed' made from shallow-fried 'Red Russian' or 'Redbor' kale.**

Tips for a long courgette season

If you want a long picking season of courgettes, sow a couple of times: once in late March and once in late May/June. The first lot of plants will be fading out by mid-summer, prone to mildew and producing less fruit. You can take these out and the later generation will already be providing perfect mini courgettes to replace them. I plant only six or seven plants each time. This will give you enough for a family to eat for two or three days a week. I usually plant half yellow, half green (see varieties, page 194) so that the dishes look good.

If you want very early courgettes, use a tip given me by my vegetable gardening friend Matthew Rice. In his Norfolk garden he sows his seed at the end of February, plants his seedlings out early – in April – and encloses them inside walls of straw bales, which he covers with fleece or plastic if the nights are cold. The bales create a warm and sheltered microclimate and settle the plants in well. He'll be picking his first courgettes by the middle of May. Matthew sometimes does a late sowing direct into the garden as well. Courgettes are a good crop to fill in the onion bed as you

start to lift the onions in June. Sow two seeds at each station into a large hole filled with compost, spaced at least 1m (3ft) apart. Protect against slugs and snails and you'll have courgettes right into the autumn. In an exposed garden, shield them with a wall of straw bales towards the end of the season.

I visited Raymond Blanc's vegetable garden recently. One of his favourite and most popular dishes is 'Assiette Anne Marie', made from deep-fried courgette flowers. He aims to have plenty of raw materials right the way through

the summer and autumn, and to achieve this endless supply from June until October they do three sowings, which are all grown on under cover. Again, the first crop is sown at the end of February for planting into a polytunnel bed in April. They will crop within about six weeks, but tire quickly, so sowing new stock every four to six weeks is essential to keep up production for as long as you can.

Below left **Courgette 'Nano Verde di Milano'.**
Below right **Summer squash 'Custard White'.**

Kales

I love the kale family. They look fantastic – unbelievably healthy and statuesque – filling the garden with colour and architecture through the winter and spring; and in the summer they have an advantage over other brassicas, in that they mostly don't get eaten by caterpillars or birds. I stood by a large clump of 'Redbor' for half an hour last year, watching large cabbage white butterflies trying to land to lay their eggs. Perhaps because every leaf is so cut and twisted, they didn't seem able to find a satisfactory landing pad. In any case, many kales, unlike cabbages, apparently have a nasty bitter flavour to an insect. Off they go to the unnetted cabbage or nasturtium patch next door.

Kales are huge producers and need almost no attention to keep them going, to churn out basket upon basket of leaves over several months at a stretch. My husband owns three tiny, wild and windswept islands – the Shiants – in the Minch off Harris. They're so exposed that there's hardly a tree on them, yet there are the ruins of a kale yard. This was used to keep the sheep and wind out of an enclosed area filled with kale before the islands were deserted. It's the same throughout the Hebrides and north-west coast of Scotland: kale was the home-grown staple. It's as hardy and reliable as vegetables come.

Cooking with kale

Kale has a wonderful robust and distinctive earthy taste. I used to think of it as nasty school-dinner food. At my primary school we were served kale and cabbage, both disgusting, over-cooked and watery. But I have now found plenty of recipes to make these leaves tasty, with a surprising touch of glamour.

You can eat the small leaves of varieties such as 'Red Russian' raw as salad for a delicious mild cabbagy taste, or you can eat the main leaves, full-sized and cooked. Remove the midrib, wash them and dry carefully. Roll each leaf into a cigar shape, then slice it finely across and deep-fry for less than a minute, not too many at a time, until the leaves noticeably darken to a deep rich green. Drain them on kitchen paper and scatter with salt and sugar. Chinese seaweed!

Kale also forms the backbone of one of my all-time favourite winter vegetable dishes at the great Amsterdam restaurant De Kas, where they grow a large proportion of their own food. It was in November, and what looked to me then like an unpromising mixed bowl of leathery cavolo nero and 'Red Russian' kale was made into the most delicious winter crostini.

You have to try it. As a starter for six people, pick about 400g (14oz) of the inner leaves. Remove the tough stalks and then cook the greens until they're tender in about 2 litres (3½ pints) of water, seasoned with salt and two garlic cloves. After cooking, chop the

Below **'Red Russian' kale with parsley in winter.**
Opposite **Kale crostini with mascarpone (see below).**

garlic and kale together with a large knife until you have a fine texture, but not quite a purée. Add about a tablespoon each of chopped capers, gherkins, shallots, black olives and flat-leaved parsley, and season with salt and pepper. Cut any fresh, good-quality white bread into finger-thick slices and drizzle olive oil over them. Roast the bread on a medium-heated griddle pan until brown and crispy. For a strong taste, lightly rub one side with fresh garlic and sprinkle with salt. Finish the crostini with a dollop of mascarpone, the kale topping and a sprinkle of olive oil. It tastes like a zingy winter *salsa verde*, and you'll find yourself making it again and again.

Sowing and growing kale

Sowing

The kale family could not be easier to grow. You can sow them at almost any time and get fantastic germination. For spring and summer picking, sow in March. For autumn and winter, sow in May or June. You need to do only two sowings a year to get all-year-round pickings.

Brassicas don't like root disturbance, so sow into modular trays or Jiffy pellets for full-sized plants, or guttering for closely planted cut-and-come-again salad leaves (see page 98).

Planting out

Plant seedlings for cut-and-come-again use in salads at 8–10cm (3–4in) intervals. Space your seedlings for fully grown plants at least 40cm (15in) apart. All kales make big plants.

Plant your kale with plenty of well-rotted manure or mushroom compost in the planting hole. These plants love it rich.

Firm soil is also essential to grow good brassicas. They are tall plants with shallow roots, so they need a compact soil to help them stand upright. Bash the soil down with the back of a spade and walk around it again and again. If your trowel bends when planting, the soil is just about firm enough! After you've got your plants in, do the same again, trampling the ground around their roots with your feet.

Pests and diseases

'Red Russian' and cavolo nero both need netting against cabbage white butterflies in the summer, and the net needs to stand slightly above the plants to protect them against egg laying. 'Redbor' and 'Pentland Brig' don't require protection. If the cabbage white numbers get out of hand in my garden, I opt for growing the caterpillar-prone varieties only in autumn, winter and early spring when there are no butterflies about. You can also try dousing the plants, and thus the caterpillars, with heavily salted water. This traditional organic method is worth a go.

You want to avoid clubroot disease (see page 168), which is more likely on acidic soils, so lime the soil before planting, and wait three years before planting brassicas in the same ground again. Move all kales and cabbages around in a rotation (see pages 166–7).

Chard or perpetual beet

I think of chard and kale in the same vegetable-garden group – very tasty, long-producing and remarkably easy plants to grow. It would be rash to leave either plant out of any hard-working vegetable garden. They are both handsome, and essential plants for the ornamental Villandry-style look, and for lining a main path in the winter there are few things that can compete.

I love the way Swiss chard looks – huge, rich, dark, conifer-green, crinkly leaves with a spear of bright white stalk straight through the middle. There are other brilliantly coloured chards. There's the rhubarb, or ruby, red-stemmed variety, as well as 'Rainbow' and 'Bright Lights' – Victorian types that have had a renaissance in the last couple of years. They may be photogenic, and are also good picked very small and added to a mixed leaf salad, but for eating fully grown they aren't a patch on the straight-up, white-stemmed kind. They're also more difficult to grow successfully. They bolt more quickly – the plant puts its energy into flowering and then stops producing substantial bottom leaves. They're not as hardy as the simple white-and-green varieties and less reliable as a winter crop.

Of the white-stemmed chard I've tried, I like 'White Silver' best. It has a strong flavour and a robust texture. It is also disease- and problem-free. If I want an instant meal, I steam it with a splash of olive oil and Maldon sea salt or soy sauce put in the bottom of the pan. I also love it creamed – cooked and added to a nutmeg-flavoured béchamel sauce.

If you want it perfectly cooked – just wilted leaves, with the stems firm but not crunchy – remove the greens from the white midrib before you start. Hold the stem in the left hand and strip the leaf with the other. It's worth the few minutes it takes. The stems take three or four minutes longer to cook and need a good squirt of lemon juice to prevent the ends turning brown. You can cook and eat the stems on their own – they're delicious as a first course with lemon butter or, even better, hollandaise – or you can eat both parts together, but cooked half apart. Cook the sliced stems first and, after three minutes, plonk the leafy part on top. Steam them together in the same pan for another three minutes and you'll have perfectly cooked Swiss chard.

Perpetual spinach beet, the Cinderella leaf

Perpetual spinach beet is a leaf similar to chard, which tends to be scorned by the foodies. It's not as handsome, with dull green stems and slightly darker leaves. It looks as if it might be tough and stringy, with leaves that are bitter like beetroot leaves if they're eaten too big. None of this is true. It's succulent and tasty and one of the easiest winter crops you can grow. It is grown in exactly the same way as Swiss chard. It's 100 per cent hardy and will produce a crop for even longer than chard. If you live at high altitude, or in the north, an autumn frost can cut chard plants to the ground. It will either kill them, or they'll resprout and give you a short picking season in the spring. Spinach beet in comparison will give you guaranteed winter picking wherever you are.

In my garden in the south of England I can pick a basket twice a week from eight to ten weeks after sowing, and if I keep picking, it will continue for over a year at a stretch. If I go away and it runs up to flower, I cut it back on my return and eat every leaf – it's a fallacy that the leaves off the flowering stalks aren't nice – and within a week it will be back as before, happily producing baskets and baskets of juicy, tasty leaves. Don't knock it just because it's easy!

Sowing and growing Swiss chard and perpetual spinach beet

Chard will grow on any soil, but will give its best on a deeply dug, organic-rich loam, so add some farmyard manure if you can.

Sowing

Chards could not be easier to grow. You can sow them at almost any time and get fantastic germination, but it can be slow compared with other leafy greens. Be

Below **Chard 'White Silver' with an ornamental thistle –** *Silybum marianum*.

patient. It may take several weeks to show. For spring and summer picking, sow in March. For autumn and winter, sow in July/August. You need do only two sowings a year to get all-year-round picking.

In March, sow inside into Jiffy pellets for full-sized plants or guttering for closely planted cut-and-come-again salad leaves (see page 98). If you have two seedlings in one Jiffy cell, remove one, leaving the other to grow on alone. Surprisingly, the white-stemmed kind often has pink stems at the small seedling stage. I used to worry I'd got the wrong thing until I realized it grew out of it.

Once the soil has warmed up in spring, Swiss chard can be safely sown straight into the ground. It's a good idea to clump sow – placing three or four seeds closely together 60cm (2ft) apart. With several seeds going in, you're guaranteed a plant at each station. If all the seeds germinate, thin to one. As usual, eat the delicious little thinnings.

Planting

When you plant out your seedlings, space them generously, 60cm (2ft) apart, as these are large plants.

2

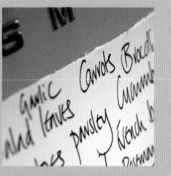

How to grow it

Grow what you eat

Grow lots of vegetables in your garden or allotment and it will become your greengrocer. A short walk can fill your kitchen with food.

In fact it's more than that – from one day to the next, the garden becomes your menu. Half an hour before you eat, you can decide exactly what you want for lunch or supper. What do you feel like today – comfort or adventure? Raw or cooked? Which would you rather have – spicy and strong or calm and mild? It's all there waiting in the garden – not just through the summer, but every month of the year.

It's taken me a while to get it right, to produce from a limited space the correct amount of our favourite vegetables – tomatoes, beans of almost every kind, salad leaves, herbs, carrots and delicacies like globe artichokes – as a regular drip-drip supply. For the first couple of years, there was too much feast and famine, great gluts of some things – runner beans, 'Webb's Wonderful' lettuce and maincrop potatoes – and not nearly enough of other delicious and daily veg.

Page 120 **A delicious handful of dill thinnings.**
Page 121 top **A list of what you eat is the best basis for a list of what to grow (see page 124).**
Page 121 centre **A wine box full of chervil (see page 145).**
Page 121 bottom *Tagetes patula* **'Safari Red'.**
Opposite **The makings of a delicious supper – tomatoes, basil, chard, aubergines and peppers.**

I've now realized that there are a few fundamentals that will help you tailor your vegetable production to your household. The first is to grow what you know you will eat, not what you think you might. The second is having a year-round plan for sowing only a little at a time, but doing so regularly, a short line every three or four weeks – successional sowing – rather than a great one-off swathe from here to beyond. You should also remember to sow and grow not just summer crops, but autumn-, winter- and spring-harvesting food as well.

Know what you eat, grow what you eat

In my first year of growing my own food I found it all too easy to buy seeds because they looked and sounded interesting in the catalogues, rather than for the reason that they were things that we were eating day by day. I spun off in some mad directions. I'd once had a memorable salad from a friend's garden in the depths of winter, with fifteen different hardy herbs and leaves in the bowl, and this set me off determinedly growing every kind of chicory you can think of. My husband hates almost all salad, I'm not very keen on bitter tastes, and my children, not suprisingly, aren't either. We didn't eat more than a couple of plants out of two or three hundred. On to the compost heap they went. What a waste of time! If only I'd spent a few weeks compiling a list of the vegetables, herbs and salad we ate in an average week before buying a single packet of seed.

You may be able to do this off the top of your head. If not, a good idea is to stick a piece of paper on the fridge and, when you remember, write on it which vegetables, herbs and salad you've eaten (see picture, page 122). When you've got enough of a list to create a representative sample of your everyday eating habits, bearing in mind that this is only a cross-section of one season, divide what you buy into four categories.

The first category consists of the veg you buy every week and eat almost every day. For my family this is potatoes, carrots (raw or cooked), tomatoes (raw or cooked), garlic, herbs like parsley, chervil, chives and fennel, and salad, with lettuce or cut-and-come-again salad leaves.

Category 2 includes the things you buy every week, and eat a couple of times – in our case cucumber, broad beans, peas, spinach or chard, courgettes, squash and calabrese.

In category 3 are the things you buy and eat every ten days or so – for us, these include parsnips and celeriac, when they're in season, and aubergines. Finally, category 4 is for the highly seasonal things that have a short harvesting bout, but that you buy if you see them looking tasty and fresh, or if you have a particular recipe in mind. Sweetcorn, globe artichokes, asparagus and purple-sprouting broccoli are in this category for me.

Your growing list and the categories that it's divided into are the important things in judging how much room should be given to each crop. The veg included in category 1 should fill about 50 per cent of your ground. Most of what you eat will come from this. The group in category 2 should take up 30 per cent. I grow very few of our category 3 veg. We eat them rarely, so I tend just to buy them when I want them. You may decide to give these a bit of space and exclude the next category from the garden on account of their short picking season. I love some of the category 4s, so they get my final 20 per cent, but only go for these if you have lots of room.

This pattern is common sense: what you eat dictates how much space to give to each vegetable. It took me a while to get there, but it really helps in producing the right amount of the right vegetables for your household. Give it a try. To sum up, this is how your vegetable plot should be divided:

Category 1 Veg you buy every week and eat almost every day: 50%
Category 2 The things you buy every week, and eat two or three times during a typical week: 30%
Category 3 The things you buy every couple of weeks: 0–20%

Category 4 Limited-season veg – the things that tend not to be around all the time, but that you buy if they look tasty and fresh, or if you have a particular dish in mind: 0–20%

Have a sowing plan
Successional sowing

With your vegetable list achieved, you now need to focus on successional sowing. Some hardy annuals, such as the lettuces and salad leaves, and some of the half-hardies – basil, French beans and borlottis – have a relatively short productive season. You can harvest from one line for only a couple of months at the most.

There are also vegetables you may like to eat in large quantities through many months of the year. With carrots, broad beans, potatoes and peas, for example, we eat so much of them that one sowing or planting will not be enough to give my family a steady supply.

If you sow or plant a little of each of these every few weeks, you'll have a good, regular flow of the veg you want to eat, rather than a daunting glut of one vegetable that will soon bore you and your taste buds to tears. The key is little and often.

Use a storage box for your successional seeds

To help organize my serial sowing I use a special storage box. You could make one by dividing up a shoe box, or use a CD rack. My box has eight labelled compartments – one for every month from March until October, when sowing stops.

When my seeds arrive in the post, I don't organize them alphabetically, but put them in the slot corresponding to the month in which they are best first sown. If the packet has a generous quantity of seeds, I don't sow all of them at once, but after the first sowing of the veg I want to repeat – my carrots, salad and radishes – I return the pack to the box, putting it in a slot a month or two ahead of that first sowing day. As long as I go to my box, I then can't forget that these vegetables need to be sown again.

Storing seed

Seed lasts well if you keep it cool and dry. Don't leave it in the potting shed – the air is too moist. Ideally stash it away it in your storage box in a larder or a cool cupboard, or put it in the fridge in a sealed plastic box. As a rule of thumb, if it's stored correctly, 10 per cent of seed may be lost in terms of germination every year. I find veg seed lasts well, with a few exceptions like parsnips, but not much of it hangs around with me. It tends to get sown, but if I haven't got round to it, I chuck it after three or four years. It takes too much time and effort to sow a line of seed for you to contemplate it not coming up, so if in doubt, I tend to chuck rather than sow.

Timetable for serial sowing

	MARCH	APRIL	MAY	JUNE	JULY	AUGUST	SEPTEMBER	OCTOBER
Beetroot		○		○	○			
Borlotti beans		●		○	○			
Broad beans	○	○						○
Carrots		⊗	⊗	⊗	⊗			
Chervil	●					○ or	●	
Coriander	●		○		○	○	●	
Dill		○		○	○			
Florence fennel		●		○	○			
French beans		●		○	○			
Lettuce	●		○		○	○	●	
Parsley	●					○ or	●	
Peas	●		○		○			●
Radishes	○	○	○	○	○			
Runner beans			○		○			
Salad leaves	●	⊗		⊗		⊗	●	
Sweetcorn		●		○	○			

○ Sow direct into the garden

● Sow under cover and then plant out in the garden a few weeks later

⊗ Sow under fleece because of carrot fly (see page 38) or flea beetle (see page 168); in the summer some salad crops, e.g. mizuna and wild rocket, will need to be sown under fleece as well

Sowing-to-harvest time of my favourite vegetables (see pages 234–5)

Artichokes	60 weeks		**Courgettes**	10–14 weeks
Beans			**Cucumbers**	12 weeks
Borlotti	12 weeks		**Kale**	10 weeks; 4 weeks as salad leaf
Broad	28 weeks (autumn), 16 weeks (spring)		**Leeks**	45 weeks (late varieties)
French	10 weeks		**Lettuce**	10–14 weeks (Cos), 6–8 weeks (Loose-leaf)
Runner	13 weeks		**Onions**	20 weeks
Beetroot	11 weeks (globe varieties)		**Parsnips**	34 weeks
Broccoli	44 weeks (purple)		**Peas**	12–16 weeks (spring)
Brussels sprouts	28 weeks (early), 36 weeks (late)		**Peppers**	18 weeks
Calabrese	12 weeks		**Potatoes**	13 weeks (earlies), 22 weeks (maincrops)
Carrots	12 weeks (earlies), 16 weeks (maincrops)		**Radishes**	4–6 weeks (summer)
Celeriac	30–35 weeks		**Salad leaves**	4–6 weeks

Year-round sowing

When you plan what to sow when, bear in mind when you are going to be away from home. There's no point sowing a packet of French beans in early June if you know you're going away for the whole of August. You won't be there to eat them.

Winter vegetables

Don't forget to include winter veg in your sowing plan either. I never fail to sow my tomatoes in February or March, as I'm dead keen to start picking them as early as possible in the summer, but I often forget to get in my kohlrabi, purple-sprouting broccoli and leeks. These varieties take longer from seed to harvest, somehow feel less glamorous and tempting, and always seem to be a low priority. I regret this every year. Even when the weather's grey and depressing, and the garden is muddy, you can get a real lift from picking a bi-weekly basket of vegetables. Let them sit in the kitchen like a Dutch still life and eat from them for the next few days.

Autumn sowing

For winter eating, remember your autumn sowing of salad and hardy herbs. It's easy to start sowing packets of seed in spring, less so to get going again to the same degree in August and September, and yet you'll benefit to almost the same degree. The garden is full of tomatoes, cucumbers, courgettes and beans and you're overwhelmed with harvesting, but don't give up on sowing quite yet.

How successful you are with growing things outside will depend on where you live and hence your micro-climate, but in the south of England autumn sowing is certainly worth a go. If you have anywhere to grow things under cover, you'll have success with lots of things in the north as well.

French beans sown at the end of July will give you beans to eat in September. Get a few cut-and-come-again salad packets in the ground then, too, for guaranteed pleasure for months at a stretch. I also sow flat-leaved parsley as well as hardy herbs like chervil and winter savory (see pages 103 and 108). This latter has a thyme-like taste and is productive and easy right through the winter. Within the protection of the greenhouse, I've had successes with autumn sowing of dill and coriander too. I pick them lightly through the winter and more heavily from the same plants when light levels increase during March and April. By then the spring-sown plants take over and the older ones can come out.

It's good to sow broad beans and peas in the autumn. The best broad bean for sowing late is 'Superaguadulce Claudia' (see page 181), which has fantastic flavour and pods full of just the right size of bean. The pods are long, often close to 30cm (12in) from stem to tip, but inside there are lots of small, tender beans. Rather than five or six monsters, you usually find eight or nine fingernail-sized lovelies. For a windy spot, I also sow the small-growing, compact 'The Sutton' (see page 181). When I lived in London, I grew it in huge pots outside the kitchen door, but even now I still sow this tough and hardy variety for planting in the ground in a west-facing and exposed bed where little else will thrive.

For peas, I sow two, 'Feltham First' and 'Early Onward'. Both produce tasty peas hardy enough to survive outside all winter in my garden in the south of England. I tend to sow them in a length of guttering inside (see page 22). Once they're 2.5–5cm (1–2in) tall, I put them out with an extendable mini polytunnel to protect them until they've settled in. In a mild spell in the winter, I remove this, but install some sort of wind-break on the windward side. At several centimetres tall, it's not the cold or the wet that will clobber them, but their roots being swivelled around endlessly in the wind.

Further north, if you have a tunnel or greenhouse with some winter room, try growing these peas under cover and you'll be eating your own in May.

Succession with perennials

Successional sowing is obviously not relevant to perennial productive plants, but the differing cropping times of varieties is worth bearing in mind. With both artichokes

Below **Hand-made labels in a friend's garden, stored for spring-time use.**

and asparagus, I grow two or three different forms that crop in succession. I then have a much longer cropping season of these delicious veg (see page 178).

Early emergers

It's also worth planting a few edible perennials that come up early in the spring. In Sussex, I start picking French sorrel and leaf fennel – both bronze and green – in mid-February, and chives aren't far behind. Lovage tends to start sprouting before most other herbaceous plants, and those first leaves are more tender and have a gentler taste than when it's fully grown.

None of these plants will suffer from a regular haircut for putting into a salad or a late-winter *salsa verde*, so

it's good to get them out there in the garden for when there's less around.

Baskets and trugs of veg

With your list created and your sowing plan devised, you can hardly fail to create lots of delicious home-grown meals from your kitchen garden. But having a successful link between the garden and the kitchen is not just about growing the stuff. You've also got to make it enticing to prepare and eat. There is nothing less tempting to a cook than a bucket of mud-clad vegetables plonked outside the back door.

Think instead of a beautiful flat basket laden with ten or fifteen different vegetables, salad leaves and herbs.

Below **Glorious colours of veg picked from the garden.** Overleaf **The view through the cutting garden** to the hut beyond, with beans replacing sweet peas on the arches in late summer and autumn.

It looks wonderful – almost better than a flower arrangement – and, as if from your own Mediterranean market stall, you can choose what to eat for every meal. This is not vegetable growing for economics, or for the sake of earnest self-sufficiency; it's growing to produce fun, tasty and showy things.

Particularly in the winter, I don't go out in the pouring rain for every meal, but harvest two or three times a week. I wash anything that needs it – mainly the roots – and make a vegetable arrangement, which I leave sitting somewhere prominent, but cool. There are a few things that really benefit from picking and eating within hours – notably sweetcorn, new potatoes and peas – but for most produce, particularly in the winter, the flavour doesn't suffer from picking ahead. Even in the summer, I harvest clumps of aubergines, tomatoes, cucumbers, kale, chard, salad leaves, pumpkins and beetroot all in one go.

I also pick with cooking in mind, putting elastic bands on my wrist as I go out into the garden. I cut the herbs or bunch of salad leaves and bind them straight away, a single species at a time. Then they sit separately in the basket rather than falling into one great muddy jumble at the bottom (see picture, pages 106–7). When you go indoors to start cooking, you can fish out the parsley to go with this, the chives with that, without everything being in a chaotic muddle. I often chop them with the elastic band left on the stems – it's easier when they're bunched together.

How to sow and grow

One of the keystones of a vegetable garden's success is getting your soil right and providing a sheltered, sunny spot for most of your plants. There are a few herbs and vegetables that thrive in partial shade – mint, chervil, rhubarb and summer lettuce – but the majority like a sunny place with a rich, free-draining soil.

I'm incredibly impatient by nature, and my instinct is to get stuck in sowing seeds and planting as quickly as possible … but don't do it! Prepare your garden, making it a fantastic growing site, before you get anything into the ground.

Above **Chervil growing in a wine box for an instant supply (see page 104).** Opposite **Spinach 'Dominant' and cauliflower 'All The Year Round' backed by swathes of wallflowers and tulips in the spring veg garden. Woven hazel panels help provide shelter for the growing plants.**

Preparing the garden

Choosing where you actually grow your vegetables, assuming you have that luxury, is an important decision. I made my first garden on a very exposed, west-facing slope and it has not been a success. I'm now moving it 15m (50ft) away to an area with much better shelter from a tall hedge that extends into a wood on the other side of the road. I'm planting the old area with tougher, stronger fruit.

If you live in an exposed place and can't find an area with shelter, think of creating wind-breaks from a hedge, wall or fence. Hedges take time, but provide excellent shelter, as they filter the wind through the gaps in the branches, rather than displacing it up in the air, as a solid barrier does, to cause havoc with back eddies on the other side. Wind-breaks provide shelter to a distance five times their height.

Soil conditioning

My garden has a patchy topsoil, which has needed soil conditioning to lighten and deepen it and ensure that whatever I sow will grow well. What you're aiming for in a successfully productive vegetable garden is a deep topsoil of at least 20cm (8in), but if you can increase this to 30–45cm (12–18in), so much the better. The root crops in particular will not do well on a thinner soil. As well as a decent depth, you also want the soil to be well drained and fertile, with lots of organic material added in, and you're aiming at a fine consistency, with no lumps bigger than a large plum.

Stones, oddly enough, do no actual harm, and if you have stony soil, you might as well leave the stones where they are. Even if you pick them out, more will surface, so don't bother.

Soil depth

If you add lots of organic material, topsoil depth will always increase. On my heavy clay, the addition of huge quantities – tonnes rather than bags – of grit and organic mushroom compost has converted a poor topsoil, only 10–13cm (4–5in) deep in some places, to something twice the depth of my spade (see Soil recipes, opposite).

On very thin topsoil over chalk or sand, this is not as easy. You can't break up any of the subsoil and integrate it. The more you try to do that, the more flints or stones are brought to the surface, and the whole exercise is soul-destroying. Instead, I recommend 'coming up' – making raised beds for your vegetable patch, enclosing them with old railway sleepers or thinner, treated timber boards (see picture opposite). This can also be the easiest technique when growing on seriously vile clay (see opposite).

You may need to import some topsoil to back-fill your newly created beds. If you are going to buy some in, it's a good idea to source it from a different part of the country. If it's locally sourced, you're just adding more of the same problems you had in the first place, so go for a very different soil profile to get the greatest effect.

Creating a fine tilth

To get your tilth to the consistency of damsons or large marbles is what you're aiming for. This won't take years, but is more a question of a few hours with a rotavator or spade by your side and several barrow-loads of well-rotted manure and mushroom or home-made compost, adding some grit if you're on heavy soil.

A 10-tonne load of grit costs me about £150, and 7 tonnes of organic mushroom compost just over £100. This is about a tenth the price you'd pay if you bought it by the bag at the garden centre. Look in your local paper or Yellow Pages. You can add organic material or even clay to sandy or chalky soils.

Soil recipes

Recipe for heavy clay

✿ I think of this as like making apple crumble topping. Heavy clay is like butter, and needs to be cut through with grit (sugar) and bulked up with organic material (flour).

✿ Cover the soil with 2.5cm (1in) of organic material – I use spent organic mushroom compost, which is sterile and free of weed seed, and the same amount of grit.

✿ Rotavate or dig it in.

✿ If large sticky clods are still present in the newly cultivated bed, repeat the process.

✿ Don't try to add 5cm (2in) of each in one go. The rotavator blades won't get down to enough topsoil to mix the three in together, and you'll just get compost and sand on top.

✿ If you keep rotavating time after time, and never dig, you may create a soil pan, so aim to intersperse rotavating with digging every couple of years.

✿ Once the soil is dug, try not to tread on it directly. This is particularly important on heavy soil, as it will compress it and get rid of the air that you've worked hard to add with your digging. To distribute your weight evenly over a large area, stand on a plank. It's worth leaving one or two out in the garden, to be put down whenever you need them.

Recipe for freely drained but poor sandy soils

✿ If I had soil like this I would fork it over on a regular basis, at the same time adding organic material into the soil surface. Any well-rotted farmyard manure, home-made compost or leaf mould is ideal. You certainly don't need more grit.

✿ Every two or three years I would do a deeper dig, integrating lots of rich organic material right down into the soil structure. This is called double-digging. Nitrogen-rich farmyard manure is fine for this and important both for adding fertility and helping to build up a good deep layer of topsoil, which is required for a good veg patch. The manure in this case is buried so deep in the soil, away from the light, that weed-seed germination is not a problem. Even if the seed germinates, the shoots will not survive the long journey into the light.

✿ Add blood, fish and bone to help feed the soil, and mulch the surface to retain moisture.

Below **Autumn-sown broad beans and peas with hazel supports in the spring veg garden. All our new veg beds are raised.**

Sowing

Sowing seed is my favourite gardening pastime. I love the calm of it, the lack of rigmarole. It's the perfect occupation for busy and impatient people like me, as it combines three things that make it both absorbing and relaxing to the right degree. It involves unchallenging repetitive moves, which is therapeutic in a stressful, preoccupied life. It delivers continual and repeated rewards in the form of things working, seedlings emerging and the knowledge that this will provide you with months of fantastic meals. Finally it gives speedy results, with many annual vegetables germinating within a couple of days and then doubling in size within the week.

I often get up very early in the morning, and propagating is the most enriching thing I could think of doing with that extra borrowed time.

Methods of sowing

Most vegetables are raised from seed, and there are two main ways of doing it. You can sow them direct, straight into the garden soil outside, or raise them under cover in your house, greenhouse or cold frame. Both systems are easy with a few keys to success, but it's important to know which veg suit which sowing system. It largely depends on which plant group that vegetable belongs to.

As a general rule, hardy annuals can be safely sown direct into the garden when the soil is warm in the growing season, whereas half-hardies – except in the warmer months of May, June and July – are best sown inside.

Groups and alliances

Annuals are plants that root, form leaves, flower and set seed all within the space of a year. Annuals divide into two groups – hardy and half-hardy – and between them they fill most of the vegetable garden space.

Hardy annuals can withstand the frosts and tend to be easier to grow in our northern climate, where they form the backbone of the vegetable garden. They are happy sown straight into the ground outside from the middle of spring and will germinate and start growing well before

Self-sowers

There are some plants, mainly hardy annuals, that will self-sow in your garden. This is a bonus. If they distribute themselves about the place, that's one less thing for you to sow.

In my garden orach, chenopodium, chervil, coriander, dill, fennel, corn salad, violas and marigolds are all welcome volunteers. Every year I dig up seedlings of these plants when they're about 5cm (2in) tall and plant them in lines or blocks where I want them. If you dig them up when they are small enough, and do it in the evening, not the morning before a hot day, watering them both before and after their move, they won't notice.

the frosts have finished in May. In this group, newly emergent seedlings can survive a few degrees of frost.

If you want an early crop to eat in May, it's a good idea to sow in March, but at this stage of the year, the soil in my garden is too cold and wet for decent rates of germination so it's best to sow them inside, as you would a half-hardy annual (see below).

The hardy annual group includes vegetables like lettuce and salad leaves, peas and broad beans, and some biennials treated as hardy annuals like celeriac, carrots, beetroot, leeks and onions. Some of them – parsnips, cabbages, broccoli, Brussels sprouts, broad beans, leeks and the autumn-sowing varieties of onion – are reliably tough and can survive the winter outside with no protection. Others, such as beetroot, carrots and celeriac, may get frosted if left in the ground in very cold weather. Dig these up or store them, still in the ground, under a winter mulch – a deep duvet of compost or straw.

Half-hardy annuals cannot withstand winter wet and cold and will be killed by the frosts. Sow the seeds and grow the seedlings in a light, frost-free place, protecting them under cover until the frosts are over. You'll then have decent-sized plants ready to put out in the garden at the end of spring. The plants will be zapped by the frosts in the autumn.

Overleaf **Basil growing outside in the middle of summer. In the foreground is sweet basil, then purple,** then 'Mrs Burns's Lemon' basil, garlic chives and curly-leaved parsley.

Tomatoes, cucumber, French beans, runner beans, courgettes, sweetcorn, basil, sweet marjoram, chillies, aubergines, peppers, pumpkins and squash are all examples of this group of plants.

Within the two annual groups, other obvious alliances fall into place:

Roots have a swollen underground root: carrots, beetroot, parsnips, celeriac.

Brassicas are members of the cabbage family: broccoli, cabbages, mizuna, rocket and mustards.

Legumes are nitrogen fixers (see page 73): peas and beans (broad, runner, French and borlotti).

Herbs produce leaves that flavour other things.

Salads produce leaves that are eaten raw.

Perennials are plants that stay in the garden from one year to the next. Compared with the number of annuals, there are few perennials in the vegetable garden, but globe artichokes, aspagarus and herbs such as mint, chives and lovage are in this group.

Shrubs and trees grown in vegetable gardens will mostly be herbs like bay, rosemary, sage and lemon verbena.

Tubers are underground food stores that sprout leaves to produce a plant. I grow ordinary potatoes and occasionally sweet potatoes in this group, which also includes Jerusalem artichokes and ginger.

Common vegetables, herbs and salads classified by plant group

Hardy

Salads	Herbs	Root vegetables	Legumes	Brassicas	Others
Lettuce	Chervil	Beetroot	Broad beans	Broccoli	Chard
Mizuna	Coriander	Carrots	Peas	Brussels sprouts	Leeks
Purslane	Dill	Celeriac		Cabbage	Spinach
Rocket	Parsley	Onions		Cauliflower	
	Summer savory	Parsnips		Mizuna	
				Radishes	
				Rocket	

Half-hardy			**Herbaceous perennials**	**Woody perennials**	**Tubers and rhizomes**
Aubergines	Sweetcorn	Beans/legumes	Asparagus	Herbs	Potatoes
Chillies	Tomatoes	Borlotti	Globe artichokes	Bay	Ginger (rhizome)
Courgettes		French		Rosemary	Jerusalem artichokes
Cucumbers		Runner	Herbs	Sage	
Peppers			Chives	Thyme	
Pumpkins		Herbs	Fennel		
Squash		Basil	Lovage		
		Marjoram	Mint		

137

Sowing direct

Sowing direct into the garden is in many ways the easiest and least time-consuming way to raise your own food. You prepare your soil and then whack in your seeds without any palaver. All it takes is you and perhaps a rake, a watering-can and a packet of seed.

Which plants does this suit?

There are many productive plants, including most of the hardy annuals – salads, roots and spinach, for example – as well as some half-hardies – French beans, sweetcorn and some squash – that will thrive using this simple technique.

You can sow hardy annuals direct into the soil from the middle of spring until autumn. With half-hardy annuals, you need to wait until the frosts are over in spring. There's no point sowing any of these tender plants as late as autumn. They will be zapped by frost before they get to fruiting size. In my part of England, I have to stop sowing these outside by the end of July. After that time, the plants don't get to sufficient fruiting size before the first autumn frost.

Some plants, like radishes, carrots and beetroot, you direct sow into the ground where they are to stay. There are others, like lettuce and leeks, that you sow into a seed bed, closely packed, and transplant later to their final position. Either way, sow them with the following tips up your sleeve.

How to sow direct
Five keys to success

1 Get the timing right

Don't sow too early. Imagine you're a seed sown into cold, damp soil, with more dark hours than light and under grey skies. What happens? You sit there with your thick carapace firmly in place. The most likely thing to happen is that you rot away in the wet, or are eaten by a bird, mouse or squirrel. The result is a very patchy row.

Contrast this to being sown into soil that is beginning to warm up. It has reached about 15°C

(60°F) and has dried out a bit. There are more than twelve hours of daylight and the skies are bright. You germinate quickly and life is on.

It will be clear when this sowing moment has arrived. All over the garden, seedlings are appearing. Many of them will be weeds, from annual seed deposited in the ground last year – chickweed, groundsel, bird's eye speedwell and goose grass – and there will be seedlings from annual flowering plants – poppies, marigolds – as well as some salad leaves popping up like mustard and cress. This is the best sign that sowing conditions for growing these hardy plants straight outside are right. If nature's doing it, you do it too.

In the south of England, I start sowing outside on heavy clay in mid-April and not before. It can be a couple of weeks earlier depending on the soil type, height, exposure and location of your garden. In large cities, with their own microclimates several degrees warmer than the country around, you can sow up to one month earlier. In Cornwall and the south-west, and on a soil that's freely drained and quick to warm up, you could sow at the end of March or the beginning of April. In Scotland and the north, and at high altitudes, delay sowing for a few weeks to guarantee success. My sister gardens in Edinburgh. She can only sow direct successfully, on her allotment, three or four weeks after me. So remember, there's quite a range of sowing times.

Broad beans are an odd exception and need sowing from late February to early May and then again in the autumn (see page 73). It's not worth sowing them after May because you don't get a decent crop in the same year. These are plants whose roots establish much better in cool, moist periods. Without decent-sized rootballs, you don't get a good crop, and your problems will be made worse by the pests and diseases that result from a late sowing. Wait to sow broad beans again until October for next year's harvest.

Wherever you are, you can cheat time and move things forward by a couple of weeks by using fleece or plastic tunnels, or spreading whole sheets of insulating material over your veg beds. This is equivalent to creating mini polytunnels wherever you need them and is a fantastically effective system, without involving much expense. The fabric or plastic protection rapidly warms the soil, and dries it out more quickly. It works very well, but doesn't look great!

I do this where I want to sow carrots and peas, both of which are slow and difficult to germinate early on my cold, clammy soil. If I lived in the north, I'd use this system for almost everything to get my veg patch going in the spring.

Don't sow your seed outside too late in the year either. With soil temperatures and hours of daylight falling significantly, germination and growth rates for most vegetables become poor. They'll just rot in the ground before they germinate. Your location will affect how late to sow at the end of the season, as well as the beginning. In the south-west of Britain, the growing season extends into October. You can carry on sowing the hardy salad leaves and herbs until then (see page 137). In Edinburgh it may end in late August. There will be few plants that will put on any growth after then.

2 Sow into a good, deep, friable soil with a fine tilth

A small soil-lump size is crucial if you want to sow seed direct into the ground, and a fine soil consistency will also help seedlings grown under cover to settle in quickly when they are planted out in the garden.

The importance of soil consistency is easy to understand if you imagine it from the seed's point of view! In the seed itself, there's a small amount of food stored as starch, but there's not much there to keep it going until it gets up into the light, unravels its seed leaves and starts making its own. Once the seed is photosynthesizing, it's almost certainly away, now able to make as much food as it likes to help it grow. And the more it grows, the more leaf it has and the more food it can make.

Whether or not the seed gets the chance to do this depends on the difficulties it's had to face on the way. If the seed has been sown into heavy, sticky soil with clods the size of grapefruits, the journey's going to be

hard. Perhaps the shoot emerging from the seed hits a large clod above its head and can't push its way through. The only way to the light is the long way round, creeping along the bottom of the lump to find the way around the side. It's only half-way up the side of the clod when, still underground, in the dark, it runs out of food. That's it, it's over – the nascent seedling shrivels and dies.

Contrast this to a seed sown into a finer-consistency soil, with small particles, none larger than a damson. If it's lucky, there's lots of organic matter that's easy to push through and, even better, some grit or fine stones that it can creep its way past. Within days of germination, the shoot pushes through the crumbly soil above its head, straight up and out into the light.

A large seed – a beetroot, radish or broad bean – stands a better chance than most. There's more starch in the seed, so it'll survive a longer journey in a coarser terrain. With a carrot, or leek, forget it. They have small seeds, and if the soil's like a building site, they won't stand a chance.

Another advantage of small soil particles is that it is easier for roots to get established. More of the surface area of the roots is in contact with the soil, and therefore with better access to soil nutrients.

3 Sow seed as thinly as you can

Don't pour the seed straight from the packet, or even from the crease in the palm of your hand. This creates a clump of seed in one place, with lots of tiny plants competing for light, food and water, then a bare patch.

And don't just chuck the seed in. The ideal spacing is often about 5cm (2in) apart (see individual spacings on pages 174–233), but this is impossible with tiny seeds. If the seeds are large, like broad beans, take seeds from your palm individually and sow them as finely as you can into shallow drills. The depth of the planting depends on the size of the seed. The bigger it is, the deeper you push it in. With large seed I push it down till the soil reaches my first knuckle, while small seed is almost surface-sown.

141

Below **Pea seedlings just beginning to shoot.**

For small seeds I have a good system to make sure that distribution is as wide and even as it can be. The first thing is to sow quickly. This will give you a thinner distribution of seed than if you're meticulous and slow. The second thing is to concentrate on limiting the number of seeds you have in each pinch. I aim to pinch twenty or thirty seeds in one go – the right number for even distribution of most veg over the length of the stretch of my arm. You can check you've got about this amount by opening the pinch in the palm of your hand. If there are more like seventy or a hundred seeds, put half of them back.

You need to mark in the soil where you got to with a pinch so you don't miss a bit, or go back over the same soil again. I make a line with my finger across the drill.

And don't go back over the line once you've sown, chucking a few more seeds in for good measure. You're just adding more competition and difficulty for the seeds already there.

4 Thinning

Most seeds start to germinate outside after a couple of weeks and small seedlings will appear. When the seedlings are about 2.5cm (1in) tall and have a pair of leaves that look like tiny versions of what you would expect to see on the parent plant, get brutal. Thin them out, checking the back of the seed packet for the exact thinning distance.

At this stage, the seedlings are usually too small to transplant, their root system too basic to be able to settle itself again after being disturbed. Just pull them up by the roots and chuck them, or if it's salads or herbs, eat them.

I used to find this difficult – it feels like infanticide. It's exciting when things appear and it seems such a waste to chuck three-quarters of them away, but it's essential for the seedlings' success. They won't do well with so much competition from close neighbours. Once this stage is complete, firm the soil back around the roots of the plants still in the ground and water to settle them back into the soil.

5 Watering and irrigation

Some varieties of hardy annual veg benefit from watering as they come into flower, and with a good flood, not a sprinkle. This encourages a larger harvest later on.

If the weather is dry I water broad beans, peas and potatoes when they're in flower. Salad leaves, lettuce and leafy greens like spinach also bolt quickly when it's hot and dry, so, in a dry spell, water your salad crops well first thing in the morning. Watering at night encourages feasting by slugs and snails.

Sowing direct: a step-by-step guide for beginners

Preparing the ground

1 In an ideal world, the ground would have been dug over in the autumn or winter to integrate organic material, e.g. well-rotted manure. This is particularly important where you're going to put potatoes. Do this in the autumn if you garden on clay. If you garden on poorly drained clay soil, add grit or washed, inland sharp sand as well, and leave large lumps where they are – the weather will break them down.

2 Get rid of all annual and perennial weeds as you dig. If you think your soil may be thick with non-germinated annual weed seed, cover it with clear plastic for two weeks before sowing. This encourages the first flush of annual weeds to germinate. Then you can hoe them off and compost them.

3 Choose a dry day, following a dry spell, and prepare the ground for sowing. Thump any large lumps of soil with the back of a metal rake. They'll shatter when dry. Work out where your lines are going to be and fine-tune the soil in these places only. Don't try to get every last centimetre of the patch to a perfect consistency. This makes unnecessary work. Rake in one direction, putting to the side any lumps bigger than a plum. Repeat at right angles. This should create a fine soil tilth with the consistency of apple crumble

topping, but only in a narrow band. The lumps at either side will help inhibit weed-seed germination.

4 There are some seeds like dill, chervil and carrots that thrive in a poor, freely drained soil. I garden on heavy clay, so I add a couple of barrowfuls of grit to the areas where I will be sowing these. It makes all the difference to germination.

Sowing

1 Apart from radish, no seed should be sown by scattering widely (broadcasting). Radish seeds seem to thrive from being chucked in, but sow most seeds in long lines or in blocks of shorter lines. With either method, you'll know the seedlings that appear in lines are likely to be the plant you have sown. Those outside the line are likely to be weedlings and should be removed.

2 Mark the line with string, or a bamboo cane laid on the soil. This makes the sowing line clear as the seedlings germinate. Leave the lines *in situ* until the seedlings appear.

3 For a shallow trench for tiny seeds, drag the handle of your rake or trowel along the line, making a drill 1cm (½in) or so deep. There is a general rule that you sow seed at a depth related to its size. The large seeds of broad beans should be pushed in about 2.5cm (1in) with your finger. Tiny

carrots should be almost surface-sown, with only the lightest covering of soil to stop them being displaced by water.

4 Water the trench before sowing. This speeds up germination and means you won't have to water afterwards. Warm soil over the seeds acts like a cloche, so the seed is in the perfect conditions for quick germination – warm, dark and moist.

5 Sow seed as thinly as you can (see page 141).

6 With your hand, replace the displaced soil and, with the palm of your hand, firm it down along the line. This helps displace air pockets and speeds up germination. Don't water again as it will cool the top soil down.

Aftercare

1 If there is no rain, water again twice a week until the seedlings germinate – really wet the ground to a depth of several centimetres. This encourages the roots to follow the water, and the plants will form deep, strong roots. After a couple of weeks, unless there's a prolonged period of drought, I cut down on watering except for broad beans, salads and potatoes.

2 When the seedlings are about 2.5cm (1in) tall, thin them out (see page 142).

3 The seedling bed must be kept weed-free. Weeds will compete for light, food and water and do your plants no good. Regular hoeing in the gaps between lines is the best method to remove annual weeds. Some weeds such as groundsel and bittercress come up to flower very quickly, so you must be vigilant about these. 'One year's seed, seven years' weeds.'

4 If you're using a Dutch hoe, keep it sharp so you can sever the weeds. The best time to hoe is early in the morning on a hot, dry or windy day. The hoed weeds will shrivel up in the sun. You'll need to hand weed between plants as hoeing could damage roots.

5 After hoeing, I use a 2.5–5cm (1–2in) layer of mulch – a thick carpet of any organic material – laid on the soil. You need to wait until the sown seeds have germinated and the lines and groups are clear, and then carpet the soil. I use mulches all year to cut the weeding down. They prevent light reaching weed seed and triggering germination. Even if they do germinate, they run out of stored starch before the shoot gets into the light to start photosynthesis, so they die. Organic mushroom compost is my preferred mulch for my rich, heavy soil. It is perfect for lightening the texture and is easy and nice to use. Also, with my acid pH, its slight liminess helps balance my soil.

Sowing under cover

Sowing direct into the garden is the least time-consuming technique, but it doesn't suit many of the half-hardies – tomatoes, cucumber and some squash. For these plants, you're better off sowing under cover with the protection of glass or plastic in a greenhouse, cold frame or sunny porch. I use a polytunnel, a much cheaper alternative to a greenhouse and thus easier to buy on a larger scale. These are ugly, but provide a wonderful growing environment with, on the whole, better air circulation than greenhouses and so fewer problems with fungal diseases.

It's not just the half-hardies that benefit from sowing inside. If you want an early crop of peas, spinach, lettuce and salad leaves – all hardy annuals – to eat in May, it's a good idea to sow these inside in March.

As a general rule, I prefer sowing things into pots and containers and get better results from this than from direct sowing on my heavy clay. Germination is quicker and more reliable in a protected environment. You can plant out at the correct distance, wasting almost no seed or time with thinning, and you can carry on sowing all year, whatever is happening with the weather outside. It's also nicer to do, sowing standing at a bench, rather than bent over, or scrabbling along on your knees. And that, for me, is the point of it. Having a vegetable garden is about pleasure, not duty.

Sowing systems

We do very little traditional sowing into small rectangular seed trays for the garden here. It's too much of a palaver, with all that pricking out and potting on. Instead we use an assortment of other sowing systems, all less time-consuming, yet effective and easy to do.

Experiment with some of these sowing techniques and work out which one is best for you.

Guttering

I sow loads of things into lengths of guttering from the local builder's yard. When I experimented with peas it was a triumph. They germinated quickly and consistently, all cosy in the warm of my polytunnel, and transplanted

Opposite **Cucumber seedlings growing in their own individual pots.**

outside happily without a hiccup. We were eating sugarsnaps six weeks earlier than in any previous year.

I also tried sowing salad crops and cut-and-come-again herbs like chervil, coriander, parsley and basil into gutters. It worked marvellously. Most of these herbs, and many of the salads, crop well for two to three months, but they need replacing as they start getting tired. Serial sowing every eight weeks, with a new generation coming along elsewhere in the garden, is the ideal, but my vegetable plot is often chock-a-block. Sowing salads and herbs into pipes in the wings is a perfect way of growing these to pick all year. The resulting plants can be slotted in, ready to pick, as the garden lot comes to an end.

They also remind you to sow successionally. As you plant out your guttering, make yourself fill it again and sow another packet of the same seed, or something else that will be thin on the ground in about a month's time.

Modular systems

We also use the modular or cell system of Propapacks (polystyrene trays divided into lots of small cells) or Jiffy 7s (small dehydrated pellets of peat or coir in containing nets, which expand when soaked in water) for lots of our vegetables. Both these are ideally suited to tomatoes, aubergines and chillies, Florence fennel, lettuce, sweetcorn and celeriac – plants that hate having their roots disturbed. Sow two seeds to each cell. If both germinate, remove one and avoid the task of pricking out.

The large – 40mm (1½in) size – Jiffy 7s are the ones to use. With these you don't need to pot the seedlings on before putting them out in the garden. The plants are big enough to survive as they are. Once the roots have filled the net, remove it to allow the roots to run free – leaving the net on really holds them back – and plant them out.

The disadvantage of either of the modular systems is that they easily dry out. If you know you're someone who won't regularly water, this won't suit you. You can try standing them on water-retaining capillary matting. That will help decrease the need for water by up to 50 per cent, but you will still need to water every other day.

Individual pots

I sow larger seeds in small, individual pots. Courgettes, squash, pumpkins, gourds and cucumbers are all difficult to get into a Jiffy 7 and their large seeds with a big surface area rot easily in the compact pellet. Fill the pots with non-peat-based potting compost, water and push the seed in vertically to the depth of your knuckle.

Root trainers

I also use root trainers – long, thin pots – for shrubby herb cuttings, such as rosemary, thyme and sage, and for my early spring broad, French, borlotti and runner beans. (The cardboard tube inside a loo roll also works well for me.) All legumes thrive with a long root run. When the seed first germinates, it puts down one long root. This breaks off when it emerges into the air at the bottom of the pot, and when the tip is pinched out, the root then throws out lots of side shoots so the new root system forms very quickly. If you sow into a short stumpy pot, there is less initial root to branch. Longer root, more branches, quicker, bigger plant!

Boxes of seeds

In the winter, I use one final system for growing many of my annual herbs. Parsley and chervil are hardy in my garden and continue to produce bunches right the way through the winter outside, but dill, coriander and basil are impossible to grow in the garden from October to April. For these, I use empty wooden wine cases, or polystyrene fish boxes with holes in the bottom banged through with a hammer and nail (see Herbs, page 104).

How to sow under cover
Four keys to success

1 Get the timing right

It's not a good idea to start sowing too early. I used to begin with some of my half-hardy annual seed in early February. By then I'm champing at the bit, longing to be out in the polytunnel or greenhouse getting some plants

Opposite **Various herbs
and salad leaves growing
in guttering.**

on the go. There are several reasons why I now wait until the end of February for a few early plants – tomatoes, chillies and aubergines, which need a long growing season before they crop – and the middle of March for almost everything else.

A mid-March sowing gives six weeks from sowing until the frosts are likely to be over at the beginning of May. This is the perfect length of time for quick-growing annuals to form decent-sized plants ready to go out into the garden. Seeds sown this little bit later make healthier, bushier plants. Light levels get brighter through the spring and temperatures fluctuate less between night and day. Both these elements help to produce vigorous, healthy plants, which grow and crop more quickly once they're out in the garden. February-sown seeds make leggy, collapsing things – Nicholas Lyndhurst … when what you want is Mike Tyson!

2 Sow seed as thinly as you can

Whichever sowing system you use, don't overcrowd your seeds. This creates competition for every one of the seeds from the word go.

3 Try to replicate your seedlings' ideal growing environment

To germinate most seeds, you want a warm, moist, dark environment. I place my seed trays on a propagator bench set at 15–20°C (60–68°F). I cover them with empty compost bags to enclose moisture and warmth and keep out the light. I then check, morning and evening, for any signs of germination. After that, the trays must be uncovered and put in a place of maximum light.

Once the seeds have germinated, the ideal environment consists of good light levels, cool air temperatures, but above 5°C (40°F), and warm roots. All-round light is also important in forming strong, bulky plants. If it's too dark and warm, you get seedlings that look like the broad bean bought back from school by one's child. They are about 60cm (2ft) high, with only

The layers on my propagator bench

1 Black plastic
2 Seed trays
3 Capillary matting
4 Horticultural electric blanket attached to a

thermostat on the side of the table
5 Polystyrene insulating sheeting
6 Wooden table

a couple of pairs of leaves on the whole stem – the direct result of being grown in a warm, dimly lit classroom.

A propagator kept in a frost-free greenhouse provides the ideal conditions. If you don't have a propagator, you can germinate your seeds in an airing cupboard, or equivalent warm place, and grow on your seedlings on a cool, but very light windowsill. Water sparingly – the compost should not be saturated, or seedlings may rot or damp off.

4 Do not let your seedlings get pot-bound

Plant them out, or if there is still a danger of frost, pot seedlings on as soon as you see white roots appearing at the holes in the bottom of the pot. A pot-bound plant – one that has over-crammed roots – never quite recovers.

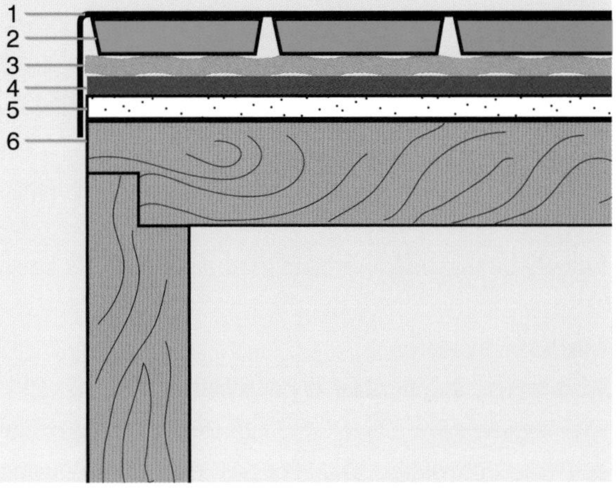

Sowing under cover: a step-by-step guide for beginners

Sowing

1 Soak Jiffy 7s or fill your pots, trays or tray insets with fine, non-lumpy, multi-purpose potting compost and firm down gently to get rid of any large air pockets. The compost level should reach about 1cm (½in) below the top. This allows room for watering without washing every seed away. Water well.

2 Sow as thinly as you can, placing large seed individually where possible. If you're sowing into cells, sow two seeds to each compartment. If both germinate, uproot one. Having two seeds in one increases the chances of every cell producing a plant and prevents wastage of any pellets.

3 If the seed is too small for sowing individually, sow it into traditional seed trays, scattering seed evenly over the compost surface. Pour the seed into your palm and sow a tiny pinch at a time. Don't pour straight from the packet, or from your palm. This creates clumps of seed, and later lots of tiny plants competing with each each other, and bare patches.

4 Label using a soft pencil, not a pen – ink is more easily washed off – and date.

5 Cover the seed with a very thin layer of compost. For tiny seeds, leave them uncovered. There's no need to water again. Cover the tray with newspaper, or an empty compost bag (see illustration, page 146). This excludes light and stores heat and water to help rapid germination.

Aftercare

1 Check morning and night for signs of growth. Remove the cover as soon as the first shoots appear and place in a cool, bright place. If you are unlikely to check for germination every day, leave the trays uncovered.

2 If you've sown into conventional seed trays, you'll need to separate seedlings into individual pots (prick out) when they have two pairs of leaves. This allows them to grow without competition. In one hand, hold the leaves, not the stems or roots. With the other, tease the roots apart with a pencil and plant each one in its own pot. Plant deeply, covering the roots and stem to the level of the seed leaves (the simple pair of leaves that form first). Water them in well.

3 Pot on as soon as you see white roots appearing at the holes in the bottom of the pot. Just turn the plants out and replant them in the next size up.

4 As soon as the frosts have finished, plant the seedlings out in the garden at the distance recommended on the seed packet, or on pages 177–232 of this book.

5 Tomatoes, cucumbers, chillies, aubergines and peppers are happy grown inside and thrive in pots. You can plant these into their final position at an earlier date than you would if growing them outside.

Opposite **Broad beans in root trainers.**
Below **Salad seedlings in Jiffy 7 plugs.**

Growing veg in pots and boxes

A patch just beside your kitchen door is a fantastic thing for instant picking and eating, but we can't all have that. If you don't have a garden, go for an allotment, supplemented by a few pots of things you want to use every day. There are plenty of plants that thrive growing in a pot and will supply you with delicious food. Choose the generous producers with good-looking foliage – parsley, mint, chard, courgettes, or cut-and-come-again lettuce and salad leaves.

As a general rule, use large containers with a drainage layer of crocks or stones in the bottom and at least 30cm (12in) of a rich, water-retaining, loam-based compost below the roots. Feed with liquid manure or seaweed to maintain fertility. I have a perfect container for salad – a large galvanized drinking trough (see page 98). Highly productive cut-and-come-again salad leaves that you harvest over months at a stretch – plants like Oak Leaf lettuce ('A Foglia di Quercia') and mizuna – are ideal, and you can add any of the annual herbs to this category.

My sister lives in Edinburgh without a garden and she is able to pick her own salad and herbs for at least six months of the year from pots on her windowsills. She has the sun lovers – basil, thyme and purslane – on the south side. The shade lovers – rocket, chervil, Oak Leaf lettuce ('A Foglia di Quercia') and mizuna – grow in pots on the north-facing ledges. As long as you grow enough, you can snip away gradually from one end to the other. By then, a bit like the Forth Road Bridge, the first lot will be ready again and you can go back and restart where you began.

Think tall, save space

Productive plants that grow vertically and fill little horizontal space like French, borlotti or runner beans are ideal too. Provide support as the plants grow, making sure they can't be blown over. It's also important to keep them weed-free and watered. If you like to keep picking beans, there are varieties like 'Blue Lake' that are happy in a pot, with a cane structure over which they can climb. They will produce enough for supper for many

weeks and taste delicious. The beans keep a good, firm texture even when they get quite large.

You want plants that look good for a long season. 'Rainbow' and white-stemmed Swiss chard 'White Silver' are both excellent for pots. They have one of the longest productive seasons in my garden and look particularly attractive if you keep picking the plants regularly. The fashionable and tasty cavolo nero is another leafy green with upright growth. If you keep picking its leaves, it looks fantastic for six months at a stretch from early summer till well into the winter, and the same is true of many of the kales.

Courgettes, one to a pot, will also be happy in a container as long as it's big enough and you keep them well fed. Grow at least one green and one yellow variety to give good contrast on the plate.

Dwarf forms and tumblers

You also want to concentrate on dwarf forms of other vegetables like 'The Sutton' broad bean. Go for dwarf varieties of pea, such as 'Little Marvel' and 'Lincoln', and, as in the garden, aim for successional sowing through the spring to give you a regular, reliable crop. Look out for the dwarf French bean 'Rocquencourt' with yellow pods and the purple-black 'Purple Teepee'. These look great with the beans hanging down from a pot.

'Tumbling Tom' cherry tomatoes are also ideal for containers. When I lived in London, I had three plants – two red and one yellow – of 'Tumbling Tom' in a window-box outside my bedroom. I picked them right through the summer, almost every day, and was still eating them in September. They produced so much fruit that we couldn't keep up with them and there was a tomato stain on the pavement below.

Chillies, peppers, aubergines and cucumbers like the mini 'Zeina' are almost tailor-made for pots. I grow most of mine in the polytunnel, but I've also grown them successfully in pots against a sunny, south-facing wall. I think cucumbers in particular are perfect for container growing and are equal to tomatoes in being ideally

Below **Squash are thought to be particularly good at resisting contamination from lead in the soil.**

suited for the small garden. All you need is three plants on three bamboo canes sitting in a sunny corner in the ground, or in a pot, and you'll be picking cucumbers for three months at a stretch.

Other wonderful veg to grow when space is short are lots of new potatoes. If you plant two seed potatoes into a 5-litre pot, you can keep yourself in your own 'Jersey Royal' (or 'International Kidney') from May until September. Surprise people by growing 'Highland Burgundy Red' and 'Salad Blue' – brilliant-coloured potatoes (see picture, page 31). These are currently available as micro-propagated plants, and it's best to plant one to a growing-bag. When the plants have begun to die back, harvest the potatoes straight out of the plastic bag.

Urban veg and lead levels

If you live in a city, the question of lead levels arises – how safe is it to grow your own veg in air that is full of car fumes and pollution? I have friends living with gardens or allotments near to main roads with streaming, continual traffic driving right past the garden, and they all want the answers to the same questions. Are there vegetables that are safe to grow – that sprout so quickly they don't have time to store the lead and other poisons? Is it best to steer clear of roots, which will sit in soil that may have accumulated toxins over many years? Or is it best to avoid a veg and salad patch altogether, and go on buying from the organic shop down the road?

In fact, plants don't absorb large amounts of lead, but they can take up some from contaminated soils, especially if the soil's pH is acidic. Lead loading tends to affect soil near buildings that have flaking, pre-1960s' paint, or in old orchards where lead arsenate was once used as an insecticide – something that is more likely in rural areas. Distributed in these ways, the lead accumulates in the soil and is very slow to disperse. Lead contamination can also be a problem in old soil near major roads, but with lead now no longer added to fuels, this worry is fading.

Vegetables that do not accumulate lead	Vegetables that may accumulate lead
Aubergines and peppers	Carrots, unpeeled
Beans	Herbs
Squash	Lettuce and salad leaves
Sweetcorn	Potatoes, unpeeled
Tomatoes	Swiss chard and leafy greens

If you're worried, import new soil to the area where you want to grow veg. With lead-free petrol, it won't get contaminated again. The alternative is to grow your veg as far away from the road as you can. Choose the back garden, rather than the front, and select varieties that are safe to grow (see above). These tend to be fruiting varieties, rather than leafy or root crops.

Roots can be grown and eaten if you peel them. The lead remains in the outer skin, as do most pollutants, including pesticides and fungicides, in non-organic veg.[*]

* This information was taken from Joseph Heckman, *Lead in Urban Garden Soils* (New Jersey Agricultural Experimental Station, Rutgers University, New Brunswick, USA).

Designing your garden

If you get it right, a productive garden can grow lots of delicious food as well as being one of the most beautiful things in your life.

Fruitfulness and abundance are both optimistic and uplifting. In my own life there's nowhere nicer and few things more wonderful, simply for its oomph, than that prolific growing machine out there, delivering a steady, constant stream of deliciousness into the kitchen.

But how do you combine beauty with this productivity and get around the problem of too many expanses of bare earth?

Above **Tagetes patula 'Safari Red'.**
Opposite **Chillies, sweet basil, aubergines and the crimson Perilla frutescens lining the top path on my vegetable bank.**

How to make a productive place beautiful

Cutting the space up with little lavender hedges is not what you should do. These *petit-point* parterres or mini Villandrys may look great, but they produce very little. The permanent edges seem like a good idea – the garden will look attractive even in the depths of winter – but they add hugely to the amount of work and cut down on the growing space, so that the whole *raison d'être* of the place disappears. The balance tips in the wrong direction and the garden becomes predominantly ornamental, not productive.

I made exactly this mistake when I laid out my first vegetable garden at Perch Hill, creating lots of small diagonal and triangular beds edged in clipped box, rosemary and lavender. I'd seen Rosemary Verey's productive garden at Barnsley in Gloucestershire and

loved it. I came home and copied lots of her ideas, but found it more and more frustrating to maintain. In our garden there wasn't the space for great long lines of carrots and spinach – the things we ate lots of – and the giants like potatoes just didn't fit in.

Perennial weeds also rapidly became my nightmare. Even though the ground was clean to start with, within a couple of years bindweed and couch had crept in and colonized my ornamental edging. I ended up scrapping the whole garden – brick paths and all – and starting again from scratch.

I now have two areas for vegetables which are highly productive and, for much of the year, look good as well. Beyond the practicalities (see pages 166–7) there are a few other things I've borne in mind in the overall design.

Good bone structure

To move beyond purely functional allotment style, it is important to give the garden some bones. I've done this in both my areas in various ways.

Verticals

To me the most important thing is to have lots of verticals and opportunities for climbing plants. The danger with a vegetable plot is that it ends up looking like a miniature child's garden in a tray. You have paths and vegetable beds, all flat in the middle, with little higher than a dahlia, broad bean or pea. The only definite verticals are around the walls and fences on the outside. What you need are plenty of well-made and robust teepees scattered right through the garden, with arches and walkways stretching over one or two of the paths. Suddenly the whole space begins to work, not just as a greengrocer's, but as a lovely place to be – a full garden world.

I've made a hazel walkway that I clad in sweet peas for half the year, followed by climbing beans, nasturtiums or squash. It creates a wonderful coloured wall and uses the air as growing space. The walkway is cheap and easy to make (see below), but needs redoing every two to three years. You can replace wood with metal, but it creates a more formal feel. One advantage of metal is that you can easily pick it up and move it to give the garden a new look.

Making a sweet pea tunnel

The idea is to have poles pushed into the ground along both sides of a path, with thinner sticks bent in a hoop between them.

I made my tunnel from young hazel. It's the ideal material, pliable and easy to use. You can order coppiced hazel from local wood networks and it is sometimes available as pea sticks at good garden centres. Try to find lengths as straight and unbranched as you can, and it's also important for the overall look of the tunnel that they are fairly uniform.

You can use willow, but beware – its roots can become invasive! I made a willow tunnel here three

years ago and have spent the last couple of years trying to control it and dig it out. Silver birch is another option, but it is less flexible and tends to break. Small coppiced chestnut works for the uprights. Chestnut is a hard wood and slow to rot, so is excellent for sinking into the ground and will last well, but it's not bendy enough for the hoops. If you have dogwood in the garden – ornamental and pliable – this also works for the arches.

If you live in a town and all these woods are difficult to find, use bamboo, particularly if you have your own. Thick bamboo canes for the verticals, and thinner, whippy ones – about 1.5cm (⅝in) at the base – for the arches will do fine. Soak the thinner bamboo in the bath overnight and it becomes easier to bend.

Whatever wood you're using, you need some lengths about 4–5cm (1½–2in) thick and 2m (6ft 6in) high. These will be the uprights. For every pair of uprights, you want one thinner stick, approximately 2cm (¾in) thick. This will

Opposite **A view of the top vegetable garden, showing the newly laid brick paths.**

Above **Climbing *Nasturtium* 'Jewel of Africa'.**

Opposite **The sweet pea tunnel looking its best.** Overleaf **Trailing squash climb like triffids over the** **wind-break hawthorn hedge and replace sweet peas on the arches.**

make the hoop over the top and so its length needs to be one and a half times the width of your path.

Position the uprights in groups of four with each upright about 20–30cm (8–12in) from the next. Allow 1–1.2m (3–4ft) between the groups. Using a rubber hammer, sink the sticks at least 20cm (8in) into the ground, so they stand straight and sturdy. The climbers benefit from a strong, robust frame.

Once they're all in the ground, secure the group of four uprights together with a horizontal length, nailed in at the top of the vertical posts, and another half-way up. Mirror this group of four on the other side of the path. Hoop the thinner sticks over to form the 'roof' and tie these on to the uprights. This needs two people. Tarred string lasts a couple of years outside. Flexi-tie or coated wire lasts longer. One of my tunnels has been here for three years, but every year I have to replace a few of the hoops. The curve puts them under strain, and as they age, a few of them ping out of place or break. Just replace the ones as they go, or you can leave the overhoops out altogether!

After you have completed each of the groups, tie in horizontal sticks 4cm (1½in) thick all the way down the tunnel along the apex of the hoops. This unites the structure and strengthens it against the wind.

When you're deciding on size, remember: the longer the tunnel, the better it looks and the more enveloping the experience becomes! It's a magical way of pulling different parts of your garden together. Give it all the space you can spare.

Teepees

Good robust teepees are another brilliant addition to any vegetable patch, but make sure you get them tall. To make them easy to put on the roof of a car, most frames available at garden centres are far too small. To ensure that the structure doesn't blow away, you need the verticals to sink a good 15–20cm (6–8in) into the ground. It should then stand at least 1.8m (6ft), or even better 2.1m (7ft) up in the air. Once any bean, sweet pea

or nasturtium is growing at full tilt it will drown anything smaller. You can buy the right scale of teepee from a good willow supplier, or you can make your own.

You'll need eight straight sticks. I use silver birch or hazel, leaving many of the twigs on the branches. Draw a circle about 1m (3ft) in diameter in the soil with a stick. Poke one of your uprights in, then another about 30cm (12in) away, then the next and so on. You'll then have a circle of wooden uprights. Gather them up at the top and tie them together with twine.

You can plant any of the frames with permanent things like clematis – dark, rich velvety varieties 'Niobe', 'Etoile Violette' and 'Rouge Cardinal' – or highly scented roses. Both of these will take a while to get going, so it's good to go for some annual climbers to give more instant effect. Plant sweet peas 'Matucana' (purple and magenta) and 'Painted Lady' (pale and deeper pink), both hugely scented, small-flowered, old-fashioned types.

Sweet peas are fantastic, but as we all know, they're an early summer thing, so I follow them with morning glories, the wonderful rich purple *Ipomoea purpurea* 'Grandpa Ott' and the dazzlingly brilliant, summer sky-blue, *I. tricolor* 'Heavenly Blue'. Even better is the cup and saucer plant, *Cobaea scandens*. The huge, exotic, glamorous flowers with their spectacular cups sitting on their green calyx saucers are the perfect boats for floating on a child's mini pond. This is my favourite climbing plant.

Cobaeas and ipomoeas are tender perennial climbers, cobaeas not surviving under 0°C (32°F), but ipomoeas a little hardier, thriving in similar circumstances to basil (see page 104). They were Victorian glasshouse hits, but I grow them outside. Sown inside in late winter, they flower by the middle of summer and keep going here in Sussex in a sheltered spot until just before Christmas. If you leave their sowing until the normal annual slot in the middle of March they won't reach flowering size before the frosts cut them down, so get them in early.

Another perfect follow-on crop from sweet peas is beans – French, runner and borlotti, with their beautiful

cream-dappled magenta pods (see page 48). I also plant climbing pumpkins, squashes and ornamental gourds to keep the garden looking good late in the year. I love the pumpkin 'Munchkin', with its delicious little orange fruits that aren't too weighty to climb. We eat these like boiled eggs in our family. Boil them and slice the top off. Scoop out the seeds and then eat them with a knob of butter melted in the flesh.

By early July all the trailing squash are sending off triffid-like arms, ready to climb up and over anything in their path. You can rotate them carefully on their root, picking up the whole plant and turning it like the hands of a clock. I turn every one of mine to be in position to climb up and over the sweet pea arches. The timing is usually perfect. Just as the sweet peas begin to look manky, the squash really take off and cover the whole colonnade in three or four weeks. First you get the downy leaves, then the beautiful exotic fruit forming by September and looking good until the autumn frosts begin.

Growing on the same hoops, posts and teepees that had supported the sweet peas earlier in the year, these exotic autumn vegetables keep the garden alive until the frosts.

Evergreens

I want some evergreens or standard fruit trees to give the garden shape, even in the winter. Box edging can look wonderful, but works best on a large scale. Standard bay trees, laurels (be aware that they are poisonous) and gooseberries all work well, giving the same all-year structure on almost any scale. It will be expensive, but I'm aiming to buy a line of lollipop Portuguese laurels to border the bank. One of the most beautiful vegetable gardens I know is at Hatfield House in Hertfordshire, and I've always coveted the spectacular, well-established avenue of laurels there.

With any of these design distractions integrated into your vegetable garden, you will begin to form a space that not only provides lots of your food but is a marvellous place to be.

Below **It will be expensive, but I plan to plant a line of lollipop Portuguese laurels to border the drive.**

The flesh

Lining your paths

With the bones in place, it's also important to think about the planting – the flesh.

Lining the paths with a uniform planting is a huge help in producing beautiful productive patches. If you have a good sweep of one or two plants all the way down each axis, you can get away with a messy garden in the areas in between. Your eye follows the lines and doesn't concentrate on what's going on behind. Perennials used in this way can become a liability because of the potential weeds, but annual plants work brilliantly, as they are taken in and out regularly, with the soil rotavatable between each individual crop.

I've used this recipe all over my garden and have come up with some good combinations. One of the most successful was a 6m (20ft) ribbon of crimson-leaved

Perilla frutescens var. *purpurascens* interplanted with sweet basil on either side of the path (see picture, page 153). The duo looked good from June until September, when I replaced it with hardy alpine strawberries – the superb large- and tasty-fruited variety 'Mignonette', which is easy to grow from seed. Try planting long-cropping cut-and-come-again lettuce like Oak Leaf ('A Foglia di Quercia') or 'Salad Bowl', flat-leaved or curly-leaved English parsley and trailing nasturtiums like the superb deep crimson-flowered, bright green-leaved 'Tip Top Mahogany'. I also go for swathes of kales – 'Redbor', cavolo nero or 'Red Russian' – in the winter, and ordinary or garlic chives, and globe artichokes with supremely elegant and beautiful flowers and leaves like the deep-crimson-budded 'Violetto di Chioggia' in the summer. My friend Matthew Rice swears by an avenue of sunflowers – the vast 'Mammoth' underplanted with summer savory.

Brilliant plant combinations

Whenever you see a good combination in a productive garden that works in terms of producing food and looking attractive as well, remember and copy it yourself the following year. Having a good smattering of beautiful colour and shape combinations to look at as you walk around the plot will make your garden work in an exciting way.

Spring

One of my favourite plant combinations for early in the year is a mixture of alliums and beans. I have an avenue of the non-edible, but hugely decorative, *Allium hollandicum* 'Purple Sensation', which stays in from one year to the next. It's one of the good things about alliums when compared with tulips. Even on my heavy clay, they reappear better and better each spring.

In early March, I interplant the allium with the crimson-flowered broad bean (see page 213). This is an old-fashioned variety, which isn't a heavy cropper, but the beans are good when eaten small. The silvery-green leaves contrast strongly with the deep crimson flowers,

Below **Alpine strawberry 'Mignonette' lines the path on the veg bank and looks good even in winter with leeks and 'Redbor' kale.**
Opposite '**Red Kuri' pumpkin clambering up a willow teepee.**

and it makes a splendid ornamental and productive plant on its own, but looks even better with the fantastic red-purple allium erupting in between.

As the bean forms its pods and the allium drops its petals, the combination goes on, less colourful, but bold and architectural, with the allium's bead-like seed heads standing out against the lush bean leaves.

Summer

On the go in the summer around a huge, shiny blue pot at the centre of the garden is another duo of plants, again both beautiful and productive. The non-edible chocolate cosmos, *Cosmos atrosanguineus*, is interplanted with the beetroot 'Bull's Blood' in a circular bed. The leaves of the two plants are a good contrast in shape: the big, fleshy roundness of the beetroot, with dark crimson midrib and veins, and the sharply cut elegance of the cosmos. This looks top whack even without the chocolate-scented flowers that stud the bed with black-coffee velvet.

We eat the crimson-and-black, shiny, mildly beetroot-tasting leaves in a mixed leaf salad from mid-spring into the summer. Then the roots have swollen enough to make good eating. I don't want to harvest them all and strip the bed, but I cook a few meals, thinning out the beetroot, pulling plum-sized beets to mix in a delicious salad with wild rocket, feta cheese and lemon juice (see picture, page 81). With chocolate cosmos I also love *Rumex sanguineus*, or the bloody dock, a native plant, but these leaves are edible only when very, very young.

A simple, self-perpetuating combination that recurs in the same area in my garden from one year to the next is dill and orach. Both appear reliably – some would say too much so – from one year to the next (see Self-sowers, page 136) and the two growing together look wonderful. I pick them both for salads and flower arranging.

One of my favourite ornamental edible plant combinations is a bed of the crimson Brussels sprout 'Rubine' mixed thickly with the ever-beautiful honeywort,

Cerinthe major 'Purpurascens'. I've interplanted red cabbage with non-edible cerinthe for a spectacular spring garden combination, but this was better.

The crimson sprout is a compact, neat plant at this stage of the year – huge, silvery-green, elephant's ear leaves with a beautiful, rich crimson-purple midrib and veins. With the lower leaves hanging almost flat and the dripping purple bells of cerinthe cascading down towards them, the mix of colours and shapes is dynamite.

The sprout is sown in early February, the cerinthe at the end of April. The two plants remain of compatible sizes from July until September. The cerinthe then finishes flowering, but if given enough room, a new generation of self-sown babies will follow on behind.

Summer into autumn

A summer combination that lasts right into late autumn is flowering parsnip and the purple leek 'Bleu de Solaise'. Parsnip in flower is almost as good as dill, an elegant, umbellifer bloom in bright golden to greeny yellow. I pick it by the bucket-load for large late spring and summer arrangements. It stands right over my head, and if staked makes a brilliant back-lit curtain in my most westerly bed.

The parsnip is enough on its own, but even better with a few chunky leeks planted in between. To get flowers on leeks or parsnips, you need to sow them in spring one year to flower the next. I try to sow too many of both these plants so that I can harvest some to eat, but leave enough in the ground to over-winter and create their impressive flowers.

I've had one last success story this year – a mix of the elegant, very dark grey-green leaves of cavolo nero with a late sowing of *Chenopodium giganteum*. We use this sparkly, brilliant-pink leaf in bright acid-green salads, and it looks equally good interplanted with the sombre kale. Keep picking both, cutting them right to the ground periodically to make sure they look their best through the autumn.

Practicalities

I grow vegetables on a terraced bank outside the garden and cookery school, and we've just made a new garden to mirror the cut-flower productive patch on the south side of the house. In the new veg plot we've put in the usual wide paths (at least a metre), with wind-breaks to shelter the garden from the strong westerlies. The garden has four main central beds for annual crop rotation (see below) and large outer beds for semi-permanent plantings of things we eat lots of like perennial herbs, rhubarb and globe artichokes. Plants for the sunny, south-facing beds are rosemary, thyme and sage, as well as globe artichokes and teepees of cucumbers and trailing squash. The north-facing beds are ideal for rhubarb, mint and an annual sowing of chervil.

One small area of the north-facing border is a comfrey border. Comfrey is very high in potash (potassium). Potash is needed to produce starch and sugar – it is vital for root crops and fruits. It is therefore well worth creating a small comfrey bed somewhere on your plot. This is a quickly growing plant which, like mint, needs its roots containing to prevent it taking over. You can cut it three times a year and use it to make liquid feed by mixing it with water (see page 20). I use it to feed all my fruit crops and my tomatoes, beans and carrots.

The main vegetable garden is large – 20 x 9m (65 x 30ft). This provides plenty of veg for my family of four, and we also supply the highly productive veg like annual herbs, salad leaves, chard, peas and beans for the cooking courses that take place at home. If you're feeding just two people, you'd be fine with a plot a quarter this size.

Crop rotation

Many problems can be avoided if, instead of growing annual plants in the same place from one year to the next, you move the different types of crop annually from one bed to another. There are three main benefits:

1 If the same crop goes into the same area of soil again and again, you get a build-up of pests and diseases.

Having one year drawn the pest or disease in, you keep providing it every year after that with a host plant on which it will thrive. This does not make good gardening sense. You want to starve the things so that they die out. Crop rotation helps to achieve this.

2 Different types of crop require different amounts of nutrients. By swapping the main groups of vegetables around in a regular order, you can make the most efficient use of the nutrients in the soil. Anyone wanting to grow veg with minimum fertilizer should use this system.

3 Different crops also utilize different trace elements in the soil. If you grow the same thing year after year, your soil will become gradually impoverished in certain trace elements. Herbs are very sensitive to this and appear to lose flavour in 'tired' soil, especially tarragon and mint.

Four beds to provide a four-year crop rotation

If you have four central beds, you can reserve one bed for roots, one for legumes, one for brassicas and one for potatoes or occasionally to be filled with green manure (plants grown and dug back into the soil to improve its fertility) and left fallow. The next year you move the crops on to the neighbouring bed.

Year 1

Bed 1 Potatoes (followed by leeks, lettuce or salad leaves for the winter)

Bed 2 Most of the roots – beetroot, parsnips, onions, garlic, shallots and carrots. (If carrots follow garlic, no carrot fly.) Plus parsley and sweetcorn

Bed 3 Brassicas – kale, cabbage, cauliflower, broccoli (needs netting against cabbage white butterflies and birds) and rocket, mizuna, mustard and radishes (see relevant sections from page 186 onwards)

Bed 4 Legumes – peas, broad beans and French beans – plus courgettes

Year 2			
Bed 1 Legumes		**Bed 2** Potatoes	
Bed 3 Onions and roots		**Bed 4** Brassicas	

Year 3			
Bed 1 Brassicas		**Bed 2** Legumes	
Bed 3 Potatoes		**Bed 4** Onions and roots	

Year 4			
Bed 1 Onions and roots		**Bed 2** Brassicas	
Bed 3 Legumes		**Bed 4** Potatoes	

Note: Even if you cannot rotate your crops, don't grow any allium, such as leeks or shallots, in the same place two years running. This is to avoid problems with rust and various fungal diseases.

The logic behind the plant rotation pattern

If plants are going to move from one part of the garden to another, it makes sense to follow some basic patterns.

✿ Hungry crops, such as potatoes, should go on newly manured ground, and those that don't need high fertility, such as legumes, should follow on from them. In a crop rotation scheme, you need apply manure to only one quarter of the total area – the potato plot – in any one year.

✿ Lettuces, leeks and Florence fennel also thrive on manured ground, because the manure helps to retain moisture and thus slows bolting. Planting them straight after potatoes in the same year is a good idea.

✿ Roots don't like freshly mucked ground – it causes forking – so should not follow straight on from potatoes as their bed will have just been manured.

✿ Peas and beans like freshly limed ground, but potatoes hate it. They are more likely to be scabby if lime has been recently applied. Peas can follow

Below **The brassica bed at Stone House, with its red cabbages, Brussels sprouts and nasturtiums.**

potatoes, but not vice versa. Peas also fix nitrogen in the soil so hungry brassicas follow on well from them.

✿ It's usually convenient to grow related crops together. For example, members of the cabbage family need netting against pests (such as cabbage white butterfly), so they should all be close.

✿ Green vegetables that require regular watering are best kept together and away from root crops that don't need so much water.

Common vegetable garden pests and diseases

Fungal infections

Rust – a problem with all alliums including garlic and leeks, and the herb par-cel

Downy mildew – a problem with squash, cucumbers and calendula. You'll see a white fungus covering the leaves. Try to find resistant varieties.

Blight – a problem with potatoes and tomatoes (see pages 16 and 34).

Clubroot – a problem with all brassicas including cabbages, nasturtiums, mizuna and rocket, particularly on acid soils. Plants can be stunted and have swollen and distorted roots with single, or clusters of, galls. Rotate your plants to prevent this.

White rot – a problem with onions, shallots and garlic. You'll see a white, fluffy fungal growth forming on the base of the bulbs. They're inedible. All infected plants should be removed and burnt. Don't grow any related crop in that position again for eight years. The fungal spores persist in the soil for that long.

Botrytis – a problem with basil. You'll find fungal rot, particularly at the growth tip.

Chocolate spot – chocolate-coloured streaks and spots on the leaves and stems. This particularly affects broad beans.

Pests

Slugs and snails – little subterranean ones damage potatoes, surface ones are a problem with almost anything, but particularly French beans and salads. Use biological control – Nemaslug – or go around the garden early in the morning when the snails are still feeding and haven't yet hidden away, and stand on them! An alternative is to encase every plant in a plastic bottle cloche. This isn't the prettiest system, but it works well if you're only growing a little. Cut the bottom off any plastic bottle and put it over vulnerable plants until they're 20–25cm (8–10in) tall.

Flea beetle – a problem with small brassicas, such as mizuna, rocket, mustard and radish, as well as the larger members of the brassica family. Small black beetles pepper foliage with holes.

Carrot fly – a problem with carrots and rarely with parsnips (see page 38).

Cabbage white butterfly – a problem with all brassicas including cabbages, nasturtiums, mizuna and rocket.

Eelworm – a problem with potatoes (see page 34).

Aphids

- Blackfly invades the growing tips of broad beans.
- Whitefly colonizes glasshouses and polytunnels.
- Greenfly may be a problem with peas, herbs like fennel, and many other things.

Pea moth and maggots – sow peas early or late. Don't sow in March/April for a June/July crop, as this is the main egg-laying season (see page 25).

Keep a plan

To avoid the build-up of these problems, particularly if you get any sign of disease, make sure you remember where the vulnerable crops were planted. Allow at least three years of a 'clean', non-infectable crop so that the problem dies out before you plant the same thing there again. You need eight years with onion white rot!

I keep a simple outline of my garden in thick black felt pen on my wall. Over this I place my planting schemes for each of the seasons for several years on sheets of tracing paper. This ensures that everything is kept together for easy reference.

Left **Evidence of rust on a leek – common among all alliums**.
Below **Beautiful but hungry – the familiar black and yellow stripes of the cabbage white caterpillar.**

Companion planting

When you think about your vegetable garden design, you may want to bear in mind companion planting. The principle of this is to sow one thing next door to another to protect your crop from well-known pests and diseases, or to help with pollination and hence increase your harvest.

There are various mechanisms by which companion planting is thought to work. In many cases it's a matter of smell – the fragrance of the helper plant, nasty or nice, either repelling the pest or masking the scent of the vulnerable crop you're trying to protect. In the second instance, the pest doesn't realize you've got the tasty things in your garden and goes off to infest your neighbour's crop.

Tomatoes and tagetes
Planting tomatoes, chillies, aubergines and peppers inside surrounded by tagetes – French marigolds – is a classic example. The tagetes' pong – a strong, unusual smell, at its most powerful when the plants are in full flower – is repellent to whitefly, and thus keeps it away from your edible crops.

Simpson's Seeds, the tomato and pepper gurus at Horningsham in Wiltshire, have used this plant association as their main means of whitefly control for years, and they swear by it. Their favourite variety of tagetes for looks and efficacy is the deep red *Tagetes patula* 'Safari Red' (see picture, page 121), and they suggest dotting it around at a ratio of one tagetes plant to two or three tomatoes or peppers. Jane Simpson recommends planting some tagetes in hanging baskets, as well as at the base of each tomato, so as to protect the plant tops as well as the bottoms. Her advice is to sow once in March or April and again in a couple of months to give protection later in the year. She also says it's important to remember to dead-head in order to keep the flower going.

Tomatoes and basil
Like tagetes, basil protects many different vegetables grown inside. Whitefly love basil above almost anything else, making it the perfect companion plant to tomatoes

and aubergines, which tend to suffer with the same infestation. They'll go for your pots of basil before plastering your toms!

Carrots and alliums
Another widely used deterrent against one of the scourges of the vegetable garden, the carrot fly, is to interplant onions, garlic or leeks with your carrots. This strategy is also scent-based. Carrot flies are attracted to the line of carrots by their smell, at its strongest when you're thinning. It is thought that the smell of the alliums covers the smell of carrots with a stronger smell, which confuses the pest. Trials have concluded that you need four times as many onions as carrots for the roots to remain completely clean, and that the onions need to be in active growth – before they start bulbing – to be properly repellent.

I did my own mini trial of these two last summer, mixing up a packet of carrot seed with a packet of my favourite, handsome, deep red, sweet and tasty spring onion, North Holland Blood Red (or 'Noordhollandse Bloedrode' – see picture, page 171). I didn't count the number of seeds, but chucked in four or five good pinches of each interspersed. They were sown in a series of lines in a panel about 3m (10ft) long and 1.5m (5ft) wide and harvested from July until November, and my carrots were almost, if not quite 100 per cent, hole-free. Once my soil has warmed and dried out a bit – carrots hate my wet, soggy clay – I'm sowing this combination again. It also looks pretty!

Another ornamental combination worth trying is carrot and coriander. These two together don't just make good soup – the strong coriander scent will protect against carrot fly.

Sweet peas and runner beans
This summer I saw another beneficial plant combination in an ornamental vegetable patch designed and planted by Marilyn Abbot at the intensely beautiful restored walled garden at West Green in Hampshire. They have

teepees covered with a scarlet-flowered runner bean, 'Scarlet Emperor', and a perfectly matching sweet pea, 'Red Ensign'. For those who prefer the more discreet, you could combine a pure white-flowered runner bean with another modern hybrid, a large-flowered, white sweet pea. The small, pretty flowers of the bean, standing upright in mini pagodas, were perfect in contrast to the puckered-petalled, blowzy, prolific pea, and the combination was a gaudy triumph. They look good and the teepees produce more beans per plant than if the two were grown apart. The sweet peas' scent draws in pollinators that help to produce a larger crop from the beans.

I thought this combination would also work with French beans, but it doesn't. Runners are pollinated by insects, French by wind.

Broad beans and early potatoes

This space-efficient combination is not relying on scent, but using one as a nurse crop for the other. If you plant broad beans in the valleys between your earthed-up lines of potatoes, they will protect the tender haulms against late frosts, fix nitrogen in the soil for the hungry potato crop and will have been conveniently harvested and removed before your potatoes are ready.

3

What you need to know

Whatever vegetable, salad and herb families you decide to grow, the varieties you select – the actual named types, the individual hybrids – are crucial. The more I grow vegetables, the more I find this to be true. It's the difference between a red pepper plant dripping with seven or eight tasty fruits at one time ('Marconi Rosso') and one producing the same amount over its whole fruiting season; the difference between a corn on the cob with every kernel sweet, crunchy and delicious ('Sweet Nugget') and one that tastes like a tough, starchy lentil; it's what distinguishes a lettuce that gives you crunchy and delicious leaves, harvestable over several weeks, even months ('Black-seeded Simpson') from one that bolts and turns bitter as soon as it is fully grown ('Tom Thumb'), or a tomato with an intense, almost nicotiney flavour ('Costoluto Fiorentino') from one with practically no taste at all ('Moneymaker'). The whole variety thing is a minefield, a maze to confuse all but the seasoned Mr McGregor. Many seed catalogues have fifteen or twenty different varieties of lettuce, pea and carrot to choose from. How do you know which to buy? The purpose of these information tables is to give you a bit of help by sharing what I know.

Page 172 **Pumpkin 'Munchkin' climbing up a homemade silver birch teepee.**
Page 173 top **Artichoke 'Green Globe'.**
Page 173 centre **French tarragon.**
Page 173 bottom **'Early Butternut' squash.**
Opposite **Radish 'Sparkler' tastes good even when quite large.**

When I started growing vegetables, I found the choice of varieties overwhelming, so I asked anyone I could who had been growing veg for years to tell me which were their favourites. If one type recurred on all their lists, I tried it out myself. There's a modern variety of maincrop carrot called 'Sytan' which has appeared time and again in people's recommendations. Easy to grow, with a lovely, sweet flavour, good colour and texture, it seems to be everyone's favourite. I tried this one as soon as I could and have been growing it ever since. Similarly, the huge, juicy, dark crimson-skinned old variety tomato 'Brandywine' was raved about by almost every foodie tomato grower I met. It's the perfect tomato for salad, with flavour and texture to match the ones you buy in a Mediterranean market. It has large fruits, so ideally should be raised in a greenhouse. If you have one, this is a superb variety to go for.

There is a limited selection of varieties in the tables below. They are my own personal choices, or those that I've seen and tasted that come highly recommended by others. On the whole, I've been strict about this limitation. I don't want the book to be a boring dictionary, and I don't want to give beginners or near-beginners the feeling of being completely bogged down by too much choice. There are more of the herbs and cut-and-come-again salad leaves than of other plants. Their flavours, colours and textures are so different from each other, and they're so easy to grow for harvesting every day of the year, however little space you have, that they deserve more page room than other groups of vegetables. To any beginner, I recommend starting with these.

There is also more space given to tomato and potato varieties than to those of other plants because there are big differences in the characteristics of their many varieties. Two or three types would not give you a true picture of what there is to grow.

By contrast, think of onions. I've tried several well-known traditional varieties and they seem to taste and perform pretty much the same, so I don't give much room to these.

How the varieties were chosen

All the plants included have been chosen first for their flavour, second for their disease resistance and third for their productivity. Many varieties that we find in the shops are selected with these priorities the other way around. Large harvests, appearance and shelf life are the most important things to the retailer, with delicious flavour lower down the list.

It's also useful if you're growing a crop on a domestic scale for the plant to produce a little to pick over a long period of time. Cordon, as opposed to bush, varieties of tomato are a good example of this. You can pick continually from a cordon type like 'Gardener's Delight' or 'Sungold' for four or five months – I have picked these from mid-June to early November from my polytunnel during the course of one year – whereas a bush type will give you a mountain of tomatoes over a six-to-eight-week stretch. Commercial growers often prefer the bounty to come all in a great rush, so they can get in and pick a large quantity at the same time, but for the average domestic grower this is not the case. Varieties here are chosen with this little-for-a-long-time harvesting pattern in mind.

I have given you lots of variety descriptions in the following pages, recommending plants that have excelled at home with me, but do your own asking around. It's always worth listening to local advice. Some forms behave differently on different soil types and sites. My soil is as heavy and rich as it comes, just slabs of grey clay where it's unimproved, and few roots like carrots are happy in it. There are carrots that perform brilliantly on freely drained soil, but on mine only half of them will germinate.

With these tips up your sleeve you should be able to go to your seed catalogues and make an educated choice. Get your seed orders in and you're on your way.

Opposite **Globe artichokes – 'Green Globe' – harvested between golf- and tennis- ball size for cooking in the recipe on page 84.**

US hardiness zones

The zone ratings given for each plant in the A–Z suggest the minimum and maximum temperatures a plant will tolerate. However, this can only be a rough guide as hardiness depends on a great many factors.

Celsius	Zones	Fahrenheit
below -45	1	below -50
-45 to -40	2	-50 to -40
-40 to -34	3	-40 to -30
-34 to -29	4	-30 to -20
-29 to -23	5	-20 to -10
-23 to -18	6	-10 to 0
-18 to -12	7	0 to 10
-12 to -7	8	10 to 20
-7 to -1	9	20 to 30
-1 to 4	10	30 to 40
above 4	11	above 40

Artichokes – Chinese

A plant that produces small root tubers with a sweet, nutty flavour, delicous in salads and to use instead of water chestnuts in oriental cooking – stir-fries and curries. Don't peel them, just scrub and slice. They are native to China and Japan, sometimes called knotroot, and are related to the mint family.

Variety description Chinese artichokes form a bushy plant, with hairy, dark green leaves and produce small, neat, 3cm (1¼in) tubers at their roots, not unlike Jerusalem artichokes.

Propagation Start yourself off with bought-in tubers, then save some from one year to the next, storing them in sand, somewhere cool, dark and not too dry, to replant the following year.

Planting time Plant the tubers inside into individual pots, about 2.5cm (1in) deep on their sides, in mid-spring. Plant them outside when all risk of frost has passed.

Successional sowing Not applicable.

Final planting/thinning distance 40cm (15in) apart.

Special growing requirements They thrive in a freely drained, fertile soil – so add grit on heavy clay – in a sunny position.

Harvesting Begin to harvest the tubers once the plants have finished flowering and are starting to die back. Go on digging them from the garden as and when you want them until frost is forecast. Then, if possible, cloche them where they are. They lose their flavour rapidly on digging up.

US hardiness zone 5.

Artichokes – globe

Globe artichokes are one of my favourite home-grown foods. They thrive in a sunny but sheltered site and a very rich soil. In the autumn, cut the plants back to the ground and mulch. All the varieties I've tried are reliably hardy with me in Sussex with a duvet of straw or mushroom compost over the crown in the winter.

Variety description 'Purple Globe' is hardier than others, with 'Green Globe' (or 'Vert Globe') next, and so they are the most commonly grown forms in the UK. Both have succulent, fleshy scale bases on large, green heads and are widely available. I also grow 'Gros Vert de Lâon' (see picture, page 84), an old French form, with an odd, flat, inelegant shape, with a wide base and a shorter curve of the outer leaves than others. It reminds me of a lotus flower in oriental paintings. The culinary advantage to its squatness is the huge flat disc of heart in the middle of the flower. Both these are mid-season croppers, in early summer, with a second lighter cropping in early autumn. My artichoke season kicks off with 'Violetto di Chioggia', a sensational ornamental and very early, delicious form of globe artichoke, which crops early from mid-spring. It has a tight, neat, upright shape, with dark purple on the exterior of the scales. These are big producers of smaller artichokes, so the ideal form if you like eating baby artichokes in oil (see page 84). The last artichoke to crop in my garden from early summer is 'Purple Globe', also called 'Romanesco'. It has a similar shape to 'Green Globe', with a strong purple wash over every flower bud scale.

Propagation Grow from seed or increase by division.

Division To keep stocks vigorous and productive, renew the oldest one-third of the plants every year. Do this using offsets from high-yielding plants – label the high performers in the previous season – in mid-spring. The offsets should be about 30cm (12in) high with at least two shoots and must have roots attached. You can slice these off with a spade, leaving most of the parent plant in the ground. Plant the rooted suckers 1m (3ft) apart with a similar space between rows, trimming the leaves back to 13cm (5in) to help reduce water loss. Keep the plants well watered until established. Division in this way also extends the cropping season. The mature plants are ready for harvest in late spring to early summer, the new young plants in late summer.

Growing from seed Sow, ideally with some basal heat, at 15°C (60°F) – under cover in late winter. I use Jiffy 7s (see page 145), but you can also sow into a seed tray and prick out from there. The seeds germinate easily and grow quickly, forming substantial plants in a few months. Pot them on once and plant them into the garden when they've reached about 15cm (6in) in late spring. You can also direct sow them once the soil has warmed in mid-spring, and thin during the year, transplanting them into their final position the following spring. Out of a pack of ten seedlings, perhaps only six or seven will breed true to type. This is easy to tell once they are fully grown and cropping. If there are a few substandard plants, you should dig these up. You can always transfer them to the flower garden.

Successional sowing Rather than succession sowing, with perennial edible plants like these you ideally want varieties that crop in sequence. First comes 'Violetto di Chioggia', then 'Green Globe' and 'Gros Vert de Lâon', and finally 'Purple Globe'.

Final planting/thinning distance 1m (3ft) apart.

Special growing requirements Mulch them deeply with organic material in spring to help with feeding and watering and to increase production. Water even mature plants thoroughly when the weather is dry. Most plants will need support, particularly in a windy garden like mine!

Harvesting Cut the flower buds with a short section of stalk when the basal scales are just beginning to open, i.e. flatten out. A well-established plant should yield about twelve flowers a year in early summer, with a second smaller flush in early autumn. From an early spring sowing, plants may well start to crop in their first season. To help them survive our cold, wet winters, remove the buds when still small. The young plants must concentrate on developing decent roots, not flowers and seed.

US hardiness zone 7.

Opposite **Artichoke 'Violetto di Chioggia'.**

Artichokes – Jerusalem

These herbaceous perennial plants look similar to a coarse sunflower, to which they are related. They are hardy plants that produce prolific quantities of tubers at their root tips and will survive in the ground from one year to the next. A delicious, underrated vegetable that you can bake, fry, roast or stew. There's only one problem – they make you fart!

Variety description 'Fuseau' is a good variety, with a much less knobbly shape than usual, so it's easier to clean and peel.

Propagation Save some of your tubers and store them in cool, dark and dry conditions to replant the following year.

Planting time Plant 15cm (6in) deep in rows 1m (3ft) apart, with 45cm (18in) between the tubers in early spring.

Successional sowing Not applicable.

Final planting/thinning distance 45cm (18in) apart.

Special growing requirements Pinch out the tips when the plants reach about 1.5m (5ft). This encourages tuber formation. Jerusalem artichokes will tolerate partial shade, but yields will be greater in the sun. They can provide a useful, quick-growing wind-break in an exposed garden, but take care where you plant them. They can be invasive if left unchecked. Try to remove every fragment of tuber at the end of one season, replanting in the spring for the following year.

Harvesting Dig them up as and when you want them from late summer right the way through the autumn and winter. They will be fine in light frosts, but in colder areas cover them in a mulch of straw.

US hardiness zone 5.

Asparagus

Asparagus gives you one of the most luxurious home-grown meals, and if you have room in your vegetable garden, it's a must. It's unusual in that it produces separate male and female plants. Male plants grow more spears. Female plants have fewer, but bigger, spears and also self-seed, which can be a nuisance. Hybrids are now available that produce only male plants.

Variety description 'Franklim' is a good, chunky, all-male, mid-season Dutch hybrid that crops heavily and has very good flavour, even when frozen. 'Dariana' is a new hybrid from France that I have just started to grow. It is higher yielding than the Dutch hybrids. It's not all male, so some plants may produce berries, but this will not affect the yield.

Propagation From seed. If possible, buy one-year-old crowns – named varieties grown from seed by the supplier the previous year – which will be quicker to crop than seed-grown plants.

Sowing time You can grow asparagus yourself from seed, but you'll have a longer wait for a decent harvest. Your first light crop will be in the third year. Sow in pots under cover in early spring, maintaining a temperature between 21° and 27°C (70–80°F) throughout germination and seedling development. Thin seedlings to 8–10cm (3–4in) apart. Pot them on for planting in their final position the following spring.

Successional sowing As asparagus is a perennial, aim to buy varieties with a succession of cropping times. 'Franklim' is a mid-season variety, cropping from late April to early June. 'Dariana' is an early-cropping form, from mid-April until the end of May.

Aubergines

Final planting/thinning distance Plant crowns 30cm (12in) apart in early April. Leave 1m (3ft) between the rows. Dig a wide trench about 5cm (2in) deep and put a handful of sand where each asparagus crown is to be planted. Put the base of the crown on the sand and spread the roots out like an octopus, and then mound up from soil between the rows to a depth of about 15cm (6in) in total. Once the crowns start to shoot in the early spring, two years after planting, earth them up about 8cm (3in) more to create longer spears.

Special growing requirements Ideally, prepare the bed thoroughly in the autumn, digging in well-rotted manure and removing perennial weeds. Asparagus likes the soil freely drained, so add grit if gardening on heavy clay. It's also important to keep the bed free of annual weeds. They compete with the crowns, so mulch deeply with grit or compost in the early spring. Give a high-nitrogen feed in early summer to encourage the ferns. Cut them to the ground in late autumn when the ferns are brown. Watch out for asparagus beetle, a small yellow and black beetle with a red

head. They and their buff-coloured grubs eat the ferns, sometimes defoliating them completely and so weakening them. Pick these pests off whenever you see them.

Harvesting As a rough guide, ten established plants should yield about 3kg (7lb) of spears, over a six-week period each year for up to twenty years. I have thirty crowns, which produce enough for regular meals for our family of two adults and two children. Do not harvest spears in the first year after planting, and only a few in the following year. After that, you should be able to cut lots of spears. When the crowns stop producing heavily, they are coming to the end of their natural season. Stop harvesting then and allow the ferns to grow.

US hardiness zone 4.

Above right **Aubergine 'Slim Jim'.**
Below **Asparagus 'Franklim'.**

Aubergines can be grown outside in a sheltered spot in the south of England. Elsewhere in the UK, they will need to be grown under glass or polythene. You can create a makeshift cold frame for growing aubergines in your vegetable garden with polythene panels or bales of straw to shelter them from the wind and cold. If frost is forecast, cover the top with clear plastic. Grown like this, they form deep roots and larger plants, which crop more heavily than those pot-grown. Enclose them again if they're still fruiting at the end of the season.

Variety description 'Money Maker No 2', an F1 hybrid, is my favourite all-round aubergine, with prolific production of large fruits with exceptional, non-bitter

flavour. This variety is well suited to our cooler climate. I also grow 'Slim Jim', a long, thin, prolific aubergine variety. Like cherry tomatoes, these small fruits are easier to ripen in our cold, grey climate than those with bigger fruits. There is a beautiful, white aubergine called 'Ova' and many unusual-coloured varieties that look tempting in the catalogues, but are, in my experience, poor producers in our climate, with a greater tendency to fungal disease.

Propagation From seed.

Sowing time Sow in gentle heat, 20°C (68°F), under cover in late winter/early spring. These are one of the first packets of seed that I sow, with two seeds to a Jiffy 7 or cell in a modular

tray. If both seeds germinate, remove one. Pot them on once before planting them into large pots for the greenhouse, or out into the garden.

Successional sowing No.

Final planting/thinning distance 45cm (18in), or their own 5-litre pot.

Special growing requirements They can then be grown in a heated or cold greenhouse, or outside in a sunny, sheltered position. When plants reach about 20cm (8in), pinch out the tips to encourage them to bush out. It's a good idea to mist the flowers regularly with water to encourage a good fruit set, and feed once a week with a potash-rich tomato feed. Aubergines and peppers tend to attract whitefly even more than tomatoes, so try planting tagetes or basil to protect them (see companion planting, page 169).

Harvesting 'Money Maker No 2' will give you an average of eight fruits per plant from late summer through the autumn. You'll get twenty small fruits per plant from 'Slim Jim'.

US hardiness zone 10 (but grown as an annual).

Beans – borlotti

Delicious and beautiful shelling beans, with crimson splotches on flat pods, green, fading to cream, with similar-coloured beans inside. Unlike runner beans, these are not huge producers, but they are one of my favourite home-grown crops, lovely to look at and wonderful to eat.

Variety description 'Borlotto Lingua di Fuoco 2' is the most readily available climbing variety of borlotti, which grows like climbing French beans, with a height of about 2m (6ft 6in). 'Borlotto Lingua di Fuoco Nano' is an equivalent non-climbing form.

Propagation From seed.

Sowing time Early crops can be grown from sowing seeds in pots in the greenhouse in mid-spring for planting out in late spring. I use root trainers, which have the advantage of allowing a long root run (see page 145). You can sow direct outside when the risk of frosts is over.

Successional sowing Yes. Aim to sow every four weeks from mid-spring to mid-summer.

Final planting/thinning distance Sow 5cm (2in) deep, 23cm (9in) apart in the row. Grow two rows 45cm (18in) apart with bamboo canes sloping inwards and tied to a horizontal bar in between.

Special growing requirements They thrive in a hot season. Plant with lots of organic material at the roots and, to increase production, feed two or three times once in flower with a high-potash fertilizer.

Harvesting Late summer until mid-autumn.

US hardiness zone 10 (but grown as an annual).

Right **'Borlotto Lingua di Fuoco 2'.**

Beans – broad

All broad beans are easy, hardy plants to grow and are almost always sold too big to be much of a pleasure to eat. To eat them at their most delicious, grow your own.

Variety description For all-round performance the outstanding broad bean, sown in early autumn or late winter, is 'Aquadulce Claudia', and if you're going for only one variety, it should probably be this. It's a superb-tasting, highly prolific, hardy, long-pod type with plenty of beans inside (see page 73). Pick them young, at the size of your thumbnail. When autumn-sown, 'Superaguadulce' is less susceptible to blackfly than others. I also love 'Stereo', a new variety with plants between dwarf and normal size that can be sown through most of spring. They bear many more small pods containing small, green-white beans than other types. It's my favourite variety in terms of flavour. 'The Sutton' is another worthwhile dwarf variety, which reaches only 45cm (18in) and yet produces a good crop of tasty beans. It's ideal for small, exposed gardens.

'Red Epicure' is an unusual form, with lovely, rich crimson seeds, with good flavour. The colour fades on cooking, so eat them small and raw. I usually grow this one, as I love the colour, but it's not a heavy cropper.

For the ornamental vegetable garden, there's also a beautiful, crimson-flowered broad bean (see page 213).

Propagation From seed.

Sowing time Direct sow in lines, or blocks, straight into the ground from late winter for this year's harvest. Also sow 'Superaguadulce' in autumn for over-wintering and an early and heavier crop next year. 'The Sutton' is another hardy variety that can be sown in the autumn, with protection, or in early spring. If the soil is moist, just push each individual seed 5–8cm (2–3in) into the ground, or dig individual holes with a hand trowel, or use a draw hoe to create a seed drill. Plant seeds in staggered double rows with 50cm (20in) spacing between each pair. Sow a few extra seeds at the end of the row to replace any in the line that don't germinate. The same spacing applies to growing them in blocks. If you sow a pair or double rows, allow 75cm (2ft 6in) between them and 1m (3ft) between one double row and another for easy picking. You can sow broad beans under cover, but these plants are so hardy that it's rarely neccesary.

Successional sowing Yes. Studies have shown that successional sowings are best made when the preceding crop reaches 5cm (2in). If you sow in autumn, in late February and then a couple of times from early March to early May, you'll have broad beans to pick right the way through the late spring and summer – without any danger of glut or famine. There's no point sowing at the end of spring or in the summer. Diseases like chocolate spot are rife and yields are very poor.

Final planting/thinning distance See sowing above.

Special growing requirements When the plants are in full flower and the first four pods are just starting to form at the base of the plant, it's important to pinch out the top 10cm (4in). This encourages the pods to form and reduces problems with bean blackfly. Support tall-growing forms.

Harvesting Late May for about six weeks from lines sown in autumn. About three to four weeks later from those sown in spring. Harvest your beans when they are still small. 'Red Epicure', in particular, become too starchy to make good eating once they are twice thumbnail size. With 'Stereo' and other short-podded varieties you can eat them whole like mangetouts or shell them and eat the beans as usual. When you pinch out the tips of your broad bean plants (see picture, page 4), use these in a salad or risotto too. They're delicious.

US hardiness zone 8.

Above **Broad bean 'Stereo'.** Below **Flageolet 'Marengo'.**

Beans – flageolet (or cannellini)

I love these tasty and tender, greeny-white beans, which are good to eat either fresh or dried, and excellent in robust casserole dishes like cassoulet. However, I've yet to be convinced that, unlike beautiful borlotti, they aren't almost as good from a tin!

Variety description 'Chevrier Vert' is a classic French flageolet dating from 1880. These form small bean plants and are grown just like dwarf French beans. I also like 'Marengo', a yellow-podded bean that you can eat whole, or shell and eat the eau-de-nil coloured beans inside.

Sowing time From late spring straight into the garden. You can sow in mid-spring under cover. Use a long, thin pot or a root trainer and then plant them outside once the frosts are over.

Successional sowing Yes. Sow every four to six weeks to guarantee a regular supply.

Final planting/thinning distance Sow 15cm (6in) apart in blocks or double rows 60cm (2ft) apart.

Special growing requirements Plant with lots of organic material at the roots and feed once in flower with a high-potash fertilizer to prolong cropping.

Harvesting Eat the beans but not the pod, except when very small. To dry the beans, pick the whole plant and hang it upside down.

US hardiness zone 10 (but grown as an annual).

Beans – French

French beans come in two distinct categories, climbing and dwarf – non-climbing. Go for a tall, climbing variety if you're going to grow only one row, as these will produce heavier crops over a longer period of time. Dwarf forms take up less room, so these are the ones to grow if you want to experiment with various different types at the same time, and choose dwarf forms if you want to grow beans in pots, or if you garden on an exposed site. French beans are also available in different colours and the shape of the pod is either round to flat, fat or thin ('filet' type).

Climbing French beans

Variety description 'Blue Lake White Seeded' is my favourite. This climbing variety (see picture, page 48) grows to a height of about 2m (6ft 6in). It produces beans fatter than the 'filet' types, famous for having the best flavour and a tender, stringless texture.

'Purple Podded Climbing' is hugely prolific of fine, purple beans, with good flavour and tender texture if picked young and often. It grows to a height of 2m (6ft 6in).

Propagation From seed.

Sowing time From late spring to mid-summer, straight into the garden. If you want to get going early outside, put a cloche in place two weeks before sowing to warm and dry the soil. Check the temperature of the soil in the early morning about 1.5cm (⅝in) deep. It needs to reach a minimum of 10°C (50°F). You can also sow under cover in mid-spring for planting out four weeks later when the frosts are over.

French beans are ideal as an early and late crop as they do not need insects to pollinate the flowers. Early on under glass,

you need to keep the temperature above 5°C (40°F) at night. Sow them direct into inside soil, or use a long, thin pot or a root trainer and plant them out from there.

Successional sowing Yes. Sow every two months to guarantee a regular supply.

Final planting/thinning distance Sow 5cm (2in) deep, 23cm (9in) apart for climbers. Grow two rows 60cm (2ft) apart with bamboo canes sloping inwards and tied to a horizontal bar in between.

Special growing requirements Plant with lots of organic material at the roots and feed once in flower with a high-potash fertilizer to prolong cropping. If it's dry when the first flowers start to form, water to increase yields.

Harvesting As soon as the pods start to form, keep picking them regularly, twice a week. If seed starts to mature in unpicked pods, flowering will cease. You can also allow the pods to ripen at the end of the season and shell the beans for eating.

US hardiness zone 10 (but grown as an annual).

Above **French bean 'Purple Podded Climbing'.**
Above right **Runner bean 'Polestar'.**

Dwarf French beans

Variety description
'Rocquencourt' (see picture, page 47) is my favourite among the dwarf, non-climbing forms. It is a superb, very productive, yellow-podded bean, with rounded pods and lovely flavour. It makes strong plants, very resistant to cold conditions, so sow this one at the beginning and end of the season. 'Masterpiece Stringless' is an excellent green dwarf French bean type. 'Purple Teepee' is a dwarf variety with pods held well above the foliage, so picking is easier than with most French beans.

Propagation From seed.

Sowing time Dwarf forms are compact enough to grow under cloches, so you can sow these early and late without a greenhouse. Sow from mid- to late spring and into the garden in late July and you'll still get a good harvest of beans the same year. For dwarf beans, sow 5cm (2in) deep, 8cm (3in) apart in rows 30cm (12in) apart, or in blocks with plants 15cm (6in) apart each way.

Successional sowing Yes, every four weeks to maintain a good supply.

Final planting/thinning distance 20cm (8in) apart in staggered double rows.

Special growing requirements Plant with lots of organic material at the roots and feed once in flower with a high-potash fertilizer to prolong cropping. It's a good idea to give them pea sticks as support to stop the plants flopping over.

Harvesting These plants crop heavily for four to six weeks.

US hardiness zone 10 (but grown as an annual).

Beans – runner

Runner beans are hugely prolific, easy plants to grow, and so the only thing to bear in mind is not to sow too many. One plant will produce zillions of beans.

Variety description 'Polestar' is my favourite form, a tasty, stringless runner bean with bright scarlet flowers, which grows to a height of about 2m (6ft 6in). 'Lady Di' is also tender and tasty (see picture, page 78).

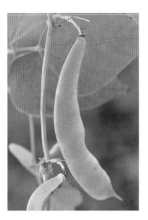

Propagation From seed.

Sowing time Once the frosts have finished, this can be sown straight into the garden. You can start plants off earlier under cover from mid-spring. Use a long, thin pot or a root trainer. Sow 5cm (2in) deep spaced at 23cm (9in). Grow two rows 60cm (2ft) apart with bamboo canes sloping inwards and tied to a horizontal bar in between.

Successional sowing No. One planting will produce plenty of beans over a ten-week period. This is enough for me, but in the south, if you're mad on runner beans, you could do a second sowing in mid-summer for an autumn crop until the frosts. Second sowings often don't do as well.

Final planting/thinning distance As for climbing French beans (see above).

Beans – yard-long (or asparagus beans)

This climbing bean plant produces 45cm (18in) pods, which are thin, stringless and have superb flavour. They are used widely in oriental cooking, in stir-fries, Thai fish cakes and curries, and I also love them steamed like any green bean. Chop them into sections to cook. They thrive in a warmer climate than ours, but in a sheltered spot, or grown inside, they're definitely worth a go.

Propagation From seed.

Sowing time Start these off under cover from mid-spring. They need a bit of extra heat to get going. Use a long, thin pot or a root trainer.

Successional sowing No. One planting will produce plenty of beans over a ten-week period.

Final planting/thinning distance Plant 23cm (9in) apart. Grow them like runner beans, with two rows 60cm (2ft) apart with bamboo canes sloping inwards and tied to a horizontal bar in between.

Special growing requirements These very vigorous plants need plenty of heat to thrive in a greenhouse or polytunnel. Like other beans they are famously hungry and thirsty, so plant them with lots of moisture-retaining organic material at the roots and feed once in flower with a high-potash fertilizer to prolong cropping.

Harvesting Pick your beans when they reach about 45cm (18in) long.

US hardiness zone 10 (but grown as an annual).

Special growing requirements

These are famously hungry and thirsty, so plant them with lots of moisture-retaining organic material at the roots and feed once in flower with a high-potash fertilizer to prolong cropping.

Harvesting Pick your beans young and often. If there are any large beans on the plant, pick these too and discard them. Don't leave them on the plant. At the end of the season, let some mature. The beans inside dry as delicious 'butter' beans in an unusual colour and cook very well.

US hardiness zone 10 (but grown as an annual).

Above **Yard-long beans.** Right **Beetroot 'Boltardy'.** Opposite **Beetroots 'Pronto' and 'Burpee's Golden'.**

Beetroot

Beetroot is at its nicest tender and small, about the size of a golf ball. It's also one of the easiest edible plants you can grow, thriving in almost any soil and situation.

Variety description My favourite purple-coloured beetroot is 'Pronto', a healthy, tasty, bolt-resistant, problem-free variety. It forms perfect, round, smooth-skinned roots, which are lovely small, but remain tender and tasty left in the ground for several months and harvested even at the size of a croquet ball. 'Boltardy' is another excellent, smooth-skinned, bolt-resistant, round and red variety, which will produce an early crop.

I also grow some weird and wonderful-coloured beetroots. 'Chioggia' is a mild, traditional, Italian variety with pink and white stripes through the raw, sliced root. This fades to overall pink when cooked. This form tends to bolt if sown too early, but looks great on the plate. 'Burpee's Golden' is another I sow plenty of every year. It has good bolt resistance and looks fantastic in a salad mixed up with the usual purple kind. It was a popular Victorian variety with a round shape and pinkish-orange skin and sweet, golden-yellow flesh and yellow-veined tops. The roots have the best sweet flavour and texture when eaten young. The tops are also good to eat.

Propagation From seed.

Sowing time From late spring to mid-summer. Don't sow too early, as it tends to make beetroot bolt. If you want to get on with an early sowing in March or April, 'Boltardy' is one unlikely to bolt before the root fills out. Early sowings are best made under cover, with one seed to a cell in polystyrene module trays or into guttering (see page 144).

Because most beetroot are cluster-seeded – several seeds together in a lump – you need to sow them widely spaced, at 15cm (6in) intervals in 2.5cm (1in) drills. Space lines 15cm (6in) apart. You can sow under cover, one seed cluster in a small 8cm (3in) cell at about 1.5cm (⅝in) deep. When the clump of seedlings have devoped the first true leaves, plant them out 15cm (6in) apart. Grown like this, the roots will push each other apart to produce a clump of small but tender beets.

Successional sowing You can sow a line or two in late spring, and do so again every three to four weeks until the end of July.

Final planting/thinning distance If they are sown thinly, don't bother to prick them out or thin them.

Special growing requirements Some beetroot contain a natural germination inhibitor that slows or prevents germination. Soak the beetroot seed in warm water for half an hour to wash this off. Even with this treatment the germination rates of 'Burpee's Golden' are still poor, so double your number of seeds every sowing.

Beetroot does well on most soils, but it's a hungry crop and thrives

best in well-manured ground in full sun. Don't water beetroot unless the soil is very parched. Watering encourages leaf, not root development.

Harvesting Beetroot is one of the slower crops to develop, but you'll have small ones in the kitchen within eight to ten weeks and then beetroot to eat through the late summer and autumn. To harvest, thin out the row, rather than starting at one end and working down systematically. The first roots will then be about the size of a golf ball. The other roots left in the ground will enlarge. You can eat these later in the year or store them for the winter. All the varieties except 'Chioggia' store well.

Also remember to harvest not just the roots but the leaves too, (see 'Globe 2', page 224), picking the youngest about 2.5–5cm (1–2in) long. If you sow enough in July, leave some large, well-developed roots in the ground through the winter. They should survive with a mulch of straw and start sprouting leaves again in the spring. The roots taste too earthy to be good after the winter, but these brilliant-coloured, young, fresh leaves are an invaluable addition to a spring salad bowl.

US hardiness zone 7.

Above **Beet leaf.**
Opposite top **Brussels sprout 'Red Rubine'.**
Opposite bottom **Early purple-sprouting broccoli 'Rudolph'.**

Beet – leaf (or spinach beet)

A fantastic and much under-rated vegetable, grown for its leafy greens, not its roots, which are produced year round from one sowing. One of the slowest plants to run to seed even in dry and shade.

Propagation From seed.

Sowing time April and August, straight into the ground. Cluster sow it, putting a few seeds in at regular stations spaced 60cm (2ft) apart. Then thin out all but one. You can also sow this under cover earlier and later into guttering (see page 144).

Successional sowing Yes, a couple of times a year for year-round picking. One generation of plants will produce for longer than this, but young plants produce nicer-tasting leaves. Also old plants can get fungal diseases that reduce the usable yield.

Final planting/thinning distance Thin to 60cm (2ft) apart in mid-summer.

Special growing requirements Very easy, tolerant, hardy plant that thrives in richly manured ground.

Harvesting Twelve months of the year in the south and all but the winter in the north. If you go away and come back to flowering plants, cut them to within 2.5cm (1in) of the ground, give the line a general fertilizer feed and the roots will quickly resprout to produce for several more months. You can strip and eat the leaves from the flower stalks you've cut.

US hardiness zone 7.

Broccoli

I love purple-sprouting broccoli, which starts cropping in the garden at the leanest time of year. Most of your winter-stored squashes have been eaten, and your leeks and kale are coming to an end. Then broccoli appears and makes the most delicious eating. Eat it as a first course, to dip like asparagus into lemony butter or hollandaise. And cook it with melted anchovies, chilli and garlic for one of the best winter pasta sauces. In contrast to calabrese, sprouting broccoli produces lots of small buds at the ends of side shoots, rather than a few large heads.

Variety description Purple-sprouting broccoli comes in various early- and late-cropping forms, and if you love it you will want to grow both for the longest possible harvesting season. The new F1 hybrids (see below) produce larger crops than the unnamed older varieties, but the seed is more expensive. You can also give the white a try. It looks good mixed up with the purple on the plate.

Propagation From seed.

Sowing time Sow in a seed-bed 1cm (½in) deep in rows 10cm (4in) apart in mid- to late spring. Bear in mind that the plants need plenty of space, so don't sow too many. You can also sow under cover, two seeds to a Jiffy or small pot. If both germinate, remove one.

Successional sowing No; use different varieties instead. Sow early and late purple-sprouting broccoli to extend the harvest. For very early purple try 'Rudolph', which starts cropping after Christmas. Then comes 'Red Arrow', which crops from February, and finally the late 'Claret', which crops in April. For early white try 'White Eye', and for late 'White Star'.

**Final planting/thinning
distance** Transplant to 60cm
(2ft) apart each way in mid-
summer. Until the plants reach
full size, you can grow a catch
crop like lettuce, radish or
annual herbs in between.

Special growing requirements
As a brassica, this plant likes the
soil rich, with plenty of nitrogen.
Add lots of well-rotted organic
material, or top-dress with
bonemeal. An alternative is to
grow broccoli where you last
grew legumes – peas or beans.
The roots of the leguminous
plants use nitrogen in the air and
fix it in the soil as a nutrient.

All brassicas are also at their
best with a high pH, which
makes them less prone to
clubroot, so you may need to
add lime (see page 116).

Firm planting is also important
and you will need to stake.
Purple-sprouting broccoli is a tall
plant, about 1m (3ft) high, and is
best supported with a short cane.

During the late spring and
summer, flea beetle may

become a problem, and almost
all brassicas need protecting
against cabbage white butterflies
(see page 168). These can strip
every one of the leaves down to
a beautiful skeleton of midrib
and veins. A covering of fine
netting, anchored to provide a
complete barrier and not
touching the foliage, should
prevent any butterfly from laying
its eggs.

Pigeons love the young shoots.
Tin foil on canes will help keep
them from eating your crop
before you do.

Harvesting It's important to
keep harvesting regularly to
prolong production. Purple-
sprouting broccoli is a cut-and-
come-again vegetable, so you
can pick small amounts of it over
a period of several weeks or
months. The other thing to bear
in mind is that broccoli occupies
ground in late winter and early
spring that would otherwise be
unproductive.

US hardiness zone 7.

Brussels sprouts

Brussels sprouts are another
useful autumn and winter crop
that will fill the ground at a time
of year when there's little
competition. They do, however,
need to be planted in the spring
and so fill space for many
months before they crop. I have
other plants like purple-sprouting
broccoli that take precedence in
my vegetable garden, but I love
the look of the red-sprouted
Brussels.

Variety description 'Rubine' is
the Brussels sprout I grow. It's
an old variety with a beautiful
crimson colour and a good, nutty
taste. The colour gets better and
better as temperatures cool and
it looks wonderful in the autumn
and winter vegetable garden, but
its yields are low. 'Braveheart' is
a good all-round green.

Propagation From seed.

Sowing time If you want only a
few plants, sow under cover, two
seeds to a Jiffy or small pot. If
both germinate, remove one. If
you want a winter Brussels bed,
sow seeds into a seed-bed 1cm

(½in) deep in rows 15cm (6in)
apart in early to mid-spring. Thin
to spacings of about 15cm (6in).

Successional sowing No.

**Final planting/thinning
distance** Transplant when
seedlings reach 15cm (6in) high,
to 75cm (2ft 6in) apart in early
summer. If you plant them closer,
you get smaller buttons. Until
the plants reach full size, you
can grow a catch crop like
lettuce, radish or annual herbs
in between.

Special growing requirements
As for broccoli.

Harvesting If you like to harvest
your sprouts all in one go, cut off
the leafy head at the top of the
plant in early autumn. This will
encourage the sprouts to ripen
all at once. If you want to pick
little and often, leave the plants
as they are. The leafy tops can
then be harvested as spring
greens. 'Red Rubine' produces
small buttons from late autumn
through to early winter.

US hardiness zone 6.

Cabbages

I don't grow vast amounts of cabbages. They take several months to reach cropable size and fill up too much valuable room in the spring and summer when the garden is bursting at the seams. I tend to buy the odd cabbage then. The one time I love to have them growing is in the winter when there's little competition for space and they look so good – chunky and architectural – at a bleak time of year.

Spring cabbage

You can sow some cabbage in the summer to fill the garden through the lean winter months and harvest when there's little around in the early spring. I do grow a patch of these, as much to make the garden look good and full through the winter as for eating!

Variety description My favourite spring cabbage variety is 'Spring Hero'. It forms handsome, grey-green, chunky hearts quite late in the season, so I harvest the winter cabbage first and then move on to these. I also grow an all-year cabbage, 'Duncan' F1, which looks like a pointed summer cabbage. It produces delicious spring greens early in the year, and, if left to grow on, will heart up too.

Propagation From seed.

Sowing time Sow thinly, aiming for a plant every 5cm (2in) into a seed-bed 1cm (½in) deep in rows 15cm (6in) apart in mid- to late summer.

Successional sowing No.

Final planting/thinning distance Transplant to 15cm (6in) apart in rows 30cm (12in) apart in early to mid-autumn.

Special growing requirements As for winter cabbage.

Harvesting In early spring, start cutting alternate plants for spring greens. Leave the others to form hearts and harvest those in late spring. Cut a cross in each stump left after cutting. You may get a crop of greens from these six weeks later.

US hardiness zone 6.

Winter cabbage

Variety description 'January King' is a very handsome, hardy variety of cabbage that can stand outside all winter. This is a drumhead type, which looks lovely in the garden with the frilly-edged outer leaves tinged with red. You may also want to go for a tasty, crinkle-leaved Savoy such as 'Best of All' or 'Tundra', and I grow 'Red Drumhead', a deep red cabbage with excellent flavour. It looks wonderful growing with cerinthe and calendula in an ornamental vegetable patch as it develops in the summer, followed by *Zinnia* 'Cactus Orange' (see pages 214–16) and kale 'Redbor' (see page 116) later in the year.

Propagation From seed.

Sowing time Sow thinly into a seed-bed 1cm (½in) deep in rows 15cm (6in) apart in late spring.

Successional sowing No.

Final planting/thinning distance Transplant to 45cm (18in) apart in mid-summer. Until the plants reach full size, you can grow a catch crop like lettuce, radish or annual herbs in between.

Special growing requirements As for broccoli (see page 187), but no staking required.

Harvesting Matures from December, and these varieties all stand well right the way through the winter.

US hardiness zone 6.

Above **'Best of All' Savoy cabbage.** Opposite **Calabrese 'Corvet'.**

Calabrese
(or green broccoli)

I love calabrese, or what we call broccoli, and it's one of the vegetables that my children eat happily. You harvest it as a summer-cropping vegetable just when the cabbage white butterflies are at their most active and there are lots of caterpillars about. It's crucial therefore to protect against these if you and your children are not to be put off it for life. You can cut into what looks a pristine head from the outside and find twenty little caterpillars hidden in the tiny florets at the heart. A covering of fine netting, anchored to provide a complete barrier and not touching the foliage, should prevent any butterfly from laying its eggs.

Variety description There are many F1 hybrids like 'Chevalier' and 'Corvet' which produce a good-sized main head and, once you cut that, form lots more side shoots.

Propagation From seed.

Sowing time Calabrese hates root disturbance, so sow *in situ* 1cm (½in) deep in rows 45cm (18in) apart in mid- to late spring. Or sow a bit earlier under cover in Jiffy or modular trays, with two seeds to each cell. If both germinate, remove one.

Successional sowing Yes. Calabrese tends to crop all at once, so do a few sowings spread a few weeks apart if you like eating it.

Final planting/thinning distance Thin to 45cm (18in) apart in mid-summer.

Special growing requirements As for broccoli (see page 187).

Harvesting In summer, cut the heads with a decent section of stalk. To make sure there are no caterpillars lurking, soak for half an hour in very salty water.

US hardiness zone 8.

Cardoons

These look like a giant form of artichoke, to which they are closely related, and because of their huge, jagged silver leaves they are most commonly used ornamentally in the UK. In the Mediterranean countries, where they use them much more to eat, they don't cook the spiky flowers, but the stem bases. They are delicious when tender and can be used in the winter – a lean time of year – as an alternative to celery or fennel.

Propagation For ornamental use you can grow them from seed or division, but if you want to eat them, it's best to treat them as an annual, growing them every year from seed.

Opposite **Short carrot 'Parabell' is ideal for early sowing on heavy soil.**
Above **Cardoon.**
Right **Carrot 'Sytan'.**

This makes them more tender for eating.

Sowing time Sow under cover in early spring or outdoors in mid-spring.

Successional sowing No.

Final planting/thinning distance Space 45cm (18in) apart if grown for eating, 1m (3ft) apart if ornamental.

Special growing requirements Tie up the stems in autumn to blanch them. Use soft string, or enclose the whole stem section in newspaper.

Harvesting Harvest blanched inner stems after about six weeks. They don't store well, quickly becoming floppy, so eat them straight away.

US hardiness zone 7.

Carrots

There are few better things to eat as you walk through the vegetable garden than a young carrot that's just been pulled and washed under the garden tap.

Variety description Both the early varieties 'Amini' and 'Primo' are excellent carrots for eating quickly and young. They have good flavour and are the quickest for growing tasty, small carrots. I try to sow a line of these once a month so I've got plenty to pick when they're still very small. I also sow 'Parabell' or 'Parmex', both short and round carrots, early in the spring. These are good for eating when they're about the size of a golf ball and are ideal for heavy clay soil like mine where a normal long taproot won't get an easy run. I love eating these cooked whole in tempura.

For later sowing, I like 'Sytan', which has a lovely sweet flavour and partial resistance to carrot fly. In my experience, the unusual-looking purple or yellow carrots don't have the sweetness and tastiness of a good modern carrot. They taste more like a swede.

Propagation From seed.

Sowing time Direct sow in lines, straight into the ground, from mid-spring to mid-summer. I also sow an early variety (see above) – in late winter – into guttering. As long as you plant out the seedlings at about 2.5cm (1in), before they get too big, the guttering won't affect the development of the root. When sowing straight into the garden, or into guttering, always sow carrots as thinly as possible to avoid the need for thinning. Aim for a seed every 2.5cm (1in) if you can. The less thinning out you have to do, the less chance of carrot fly.

Successional sowing Yes. If you love carrots, try to sow a few lines every three to four weeks, moving from early varieties like 'Amini', with their greater tolerance of cold soils, to later varieties like 'Sytan'.

Final planting/thinning distance 2.5 (1in) apart for earlies in rows 15cm (6in) apart. If you want larger carrots, thin more drastically, to 5cm (2in) apart. If you've sown thinly in the first place, you can usually avoid the need for thinning. With 2.5–5cm (1–2in) between each root, clumps push themselves apart and you'll get plenty of small, tasty carrots packed in close.

Special growing requirements Deep, fertile and, crucially, freely drained soils are preferred, but fresh manure will cause forking so should be avoided. Beware of carrot fly (see page 38).

Harvesting If you pull your carrots carefully, you can often remove one from a clump of two or three, leaving the others to grow. To settle the soil back, water them once you've picked what you want.

US hardiness zone 7.

Cauliflower

I like to sow not only some of the wonderful-looking, unusual-coloured varieties of cauliflower, but also the winter types, which are lovely for harvesting in late winter and early spring when there is less in the vegetable garden to eat. These are easier to grow as they are much slower to flower in the colder temperatures of winter.

Variety description I love 'Limelight' and 'Romanesco' in lime green. Both mature quite quickly, in early autumn from a late spring sowing. I also like the old winter hardies 'Purple Cape' and 'Red Lion', and the easy-to-grow, large, white 'All The Year Round' (see picture, page 133).

Propagation From seed.

Sowing time Sow in a seed-bed 1cm (½in) deep in rows 15cm (6in) apart in mid- to late spring.

Transplant in early to mid-summer. Or sow in mid-summer for autumn planting and late winter eating.

Successional sowing Yes.

Final planting/thinning distance Transplant to 60cm (2ft) apart in mid-summer or early autumn. Don't leave this later than six weeks after sowing, or the late root disturbance will increase the tendency to bolting. Grow a catch crop between them.

Special growing requirements Cauliflowers bolt easily – the curds opening up into flower – before you pick them. To prevent this, water and feed seedlings well or grow them late in the year. They have the same problems as broccoli (see page 187).

Harvesting The curds should be dense, with individual flower buds indistinguishable.

Celeriac

I love celeriac, a root that's easy to grow and has a subtle mix of celery and fennel flavours. It's invaluable for cropping through the autumn and into the winter, but it does fill space in the garden for many months from planting to eating, so is not ideal for the smaller productive patch. One of my favourite celeriac dishes is remoulade, the French classic, with the root raw, cut into slim fingers and served in a mustardy mayonnaise; I also love it mixed with potatoes in mash to eat with roast duck or venison. For me, growing good celery demands too much TLC – fastidious slug control and lots of watering and feeding – so I use celeriac and par-cel (see page 202) as alternative ingredients for flavourful stocks, soups and stews.

Variety description 'Monarch' is the one I grow. It makes large roots, with firm, white flesh, is slow to form a woolly middle and also slow to bolt.

Propagation From seed.

Sowing time Sow in early spring under cover in gentle heat – 12°C (53°F) or less. The seed needs light to germinate, so scatter it on to the compost surface and don't cover.

Germination may be slow and erratic. Prick out the seeds into modular trays when they are still small – they prefer minimal root disturbance – and plant them out in the garden in late spring when they're about 5cm (2in) tall.

Successional sowing Yes.

Final planting/thinning distance Transplant to 30cm (12in) apart in rows 45cm (18in) apart in late spring/early summer. Good ventilation and hence no overcrowding are the key to a good crop.

Special growing requirements Celeriac loves rich, moist, organic soil and a cool, damp climate, so it's an ideal crop for the UK. Mulch between the plants with a good, deep, 15cm (6in) layer of compost or staw to help conserve moisture and suppress weeds. Remove side shoots and lower leaves to expose the crowns during the summer and help the roots swell.

Harvesting From mid-autumn onwards, right through the winter in milder areas. They have a better flavour if left in the ground, so in the south I pull off all the leaf stalks apart from the innermost tuft, which helps prevent rotting, and mulch mine deeply with straw to protect them outside for the winter. Slugs can be a big problem, so protect against these. If you leave celeriac in the ground, you can use the leaves for celery flavour in soups and stews. In colder places, lift them and store towards the end of autumn.

US hardiness zone 7–9 (depending on variety).

Left **Cauliflower 'Red Lion'**. Above **Celeriac 'Monarch'**. Opposite **Chard 'White Silver'**.

Chard

I am mad keen on Swiss chard, with its huge, crinkly, dark green leaves on broad, creamy-white stems, and it's one of the easiest and most productive vegetables you can grow. The flavour of the white-stemmed variety is superb and many times better than the multi-coloured chard varieties, which are better in salads (see page 221). The thing to realize is that chard is really two vegetables in one: to eat it at its best, strip the green from the white and then cook the two parts separately. They have different cooking times, the green three or four minutes, the white more like six or seven.

Propagation From seed.

Sowing time I sow in mid-spring and late summer straight into the ground to give me year-round pickings in the south of England. Cluster sow it, putting a few seeds in at regular stations spaced 60cm (2ft) apart. Then thin out all but one. You can also sow this under cover both earlier and later into guttering (see page 144). It is slower to germinate than other leafy greens and salad leaves, so don't give up and chuck it away.

Successional sowing Yes, as sowing time.

Final planting/thinning distance If sown in rows, thin to 60cm (2ft) apart in mid-summer.

Special growing requirements Very easy, tolerant, hardy plant that thrives in a richly manured ground.

Harvesting Twelve months of the year in the south and all but the winter in the north.

US hardiness zone 7.

Multi-coloured chard
(see page 221)

Chicory

When I was a medical student at Charing Cross Hospital, I worked as a waitress at the River Café and there learnt how to use chicory. It's fantastic as one of the flavours in a mixed leaf salad, and equally delicious wilted under a grill or on a griddle pan and then mixed with crème fraîche and Parmesan to eat with pasta. And, of course, this is a very ornamental and hardy winter crop that looks wonderful in the autumn and winter garden.

Chicories divide into forcing and non-forcing forms. Forcing means you dig it up and force it in the dark inside. Non-forcing means you leave it where it is and harvest it straight from the garden.

Forcing chicories

Variety description 'Zoom' is the chicory that looks like bullets. This one is the classic for forcing.

Propagation From seed.

Sowing time Late spring, 1cm (½in) deep in a seed-bed.

Successional sowing No.

Final planting/thinning distance Thin to 23cm (9in) apart.

Special growing requirements Dig these up in late autumn, once there has been a frost. This breaks their dormancy and makes them easier to force. Select any unforked roots with a diameter of 2.5–5cm (1–2in) across the top for forcing. Cut all the foliage back to about 2.5cm (1in) and trim the roots to 15–20cm (6–8in). Pack the roots in boxes of sand horizontally and cover them to exclude all light.

To force them, take three or four roots at a time and plant them in 25cm (10in) pots filled with multi-purpose potting compost, so that the crowns are just visible above the soil. Cover them to exclude all light and put them somewhere warm, with a temperature of at least 10°C (50°F). If you can't find a completely light-free cupboard or cellar, enclose them in an upside-down pot with the drainage hole covered or in a hessian bag in a dark place. Both these will exclude light, but not air. Don't enclose them in a black plastic bag. They rot easily in this air-tight atmosphere.

Harvesting After three or four weeks, a chicon will have sprouted. Cut the white, crunchy, mildly bitter bullets when they reach 15cm (6in) long. Leave the roots in the same pot to sprout again.

US hardiness zone 5.

Non-forcing chicories

Variety description 'Rossa di Treviso 2' is a beautiful, deep-red, upright leaf, which is the hardiest chicory I've grown, surviving to −15°C (5°F). You can use this type for forcing, or eat it just blanched by its outer leaves (see Special growing requirements) straight out of the garden in winter and early spring. For wilting, 'Palla Rossa', or the more usual supermarket-style radicchio, is a very hardy non-forcing form of chicory, which forms dense, firm heads with a deep red colour in contrast to bright white stems. It's easy to grow. 'Variegata di Castelfranco' is an easy, traditional variety of chicory, with bright green, speckled-red leaves. You can use these to heart up or crop them regularly for winter and spring cut-and-come-again salad leaves.

Propagation From seed.

Sowing time Late spring, 1cm (½in) deep in a seed-bed.

Successional sowing No, you can sow the whole lot in one go.

Final planting/thinning distance Thin to 23cm (9in) apart if you want to create hearts or 10cm (4in) if growing to crop as a cut-and-come-again.

Special growing requirements Most chicories look the same – rather like chunky dandelions – right through the late spring and summer. It's not until the cold weather that they start to form their characteristic shapes and colours. They are easy to grow – quick to germinate and very hardy – but 'Treviso' in particular can bolt if it gets too hot and dry. With 'Treviso', tie the outer leaves around the heart to blanch them, or cover them with a blanching pot where they grow. This decreases bitterness and makes the heart paler and more crunchy and tender. With 'Palla Rossa' the outer leaves naturally blanch the inside leaves without you having to intervene.

Harvesting Leave these hardy chicories for harvesting in the colder months. Leaf production lasts about four months. The beautiful blue flowers are also edible, but die in the afternoon, so they're no good for decorating your salad for a dinner party.

Courgettes and summer squash

If you have a decent-sized vegetable patch, you have to grow at least one form of courgette. They are easy, prolific and versatile. You can eat the delicious flowers as well as the fruits, and they look good, luscious and jungly. No productive garden is complete without them.

Variety description I grow an early F1 hybrid variety called 'Defender' which has excellent disease resistance (e.g. against CMV, also known as mosaic virus) and produces plenty of lovely, tasty, dark green fruit and lots of flowers. 'Nano Verde di Milano' (see picture, page 144) is also superb and popular with firm, tasty, dark fruits and prolific production of flowers. The erect, open plants of this variety make harvesting easy.

I like 'Taxi' (see picture, page 91), another F1 hybrid, in a brilliant yellow of the 'Gold Rush' type, with high yields and good flavour. I like growing a yellow and dark green to mix together on a plate. 'Tromboncino' (see picture, page 113) is another very worthwhile and unusual form, the fruits of which look like a trombone, with long curves and a swollen end. These can reach a large size and still retain a dense texture that is neither woolly nor watery. They are also healthy and prolific.

I also grow 'Custard White' summer squash (see picture, page 114), a bright green, scalloped-edge, patty-pan type, which is best eaten small and young, at 5–10cm (2–4in) across. You can use it for risottos and pumpkin-style soup later in the year, or keep the creamy-skinned flying saucers for a beautiful arrangement. It lasts many months after the skins have toughened in the autumn and looks wonderful filling a huge bowl for the middle of your dining table right the way through the winter.

Propagation From seed.

Sowing time Sow outdoors at the end of spring, or into pots under cover in mid-spring, with the seeds not flat but on their sides, at a temperature of about 18˚C (65˚F). Don't put them out without protection until early summer. Courgettes are the perfect candidates for the temporary, makeshift cold frame created from straw bales or bamboo canes and polythene sheeting around the plants as they grow (see page 114). For planting, dig a 30cm (12in) hole, fill it with soil mixed with well-rotted manure and plant the seedling into there.

Successional sowing Yes. If you want a long picking season of courgettes, sow a couple of times, once in late March and once in late May/June. The first lot of plants will be fading out by mid-summer, prone to mildew and producing less fruit. You can take these out, and the later generation will already be providing perfect mini courgettes to replace them.

Final planting/thinning distance These are all bush, not trailing, plants except 'Tromboncino', which will trail and climb. All varieties need 1m (3ft). Good spacing and regular watering are the best way to avoid the persistent courgette problem of downy mildew.

Special growing requirements Rich, well-manured ground is required, with copious amounts of watering when it's dry. Mulch deeply to help feed the plants and conserve moisture. Liquid feed once a week with a dilute tomato feed once cutting has started.

Harvesting From mid-summer to autumn. Pick the fruit twice a week and the flowers just as they open, rather than when they have fully splayed out, and remove the stigma. Any fruit you miss will rapidly turn into marrows. If you are going away for a couple of weeks, remove all the flowers and fruits to prolong cropping.

US hardiness zone 10 (but grown as an annual).

Cucumbers

I didn't like cucumbers very much until I started growing them. Freshly picked and very juicy, a newly cut slice beading with water droplets within a minute, they are a very different thing from the green log you get at the supermarket. I love eating long-section slices dipped into aubergine houmous and taramasalata.

Variety description 'Burpless Tasty Green' (see picture, page 87), an F1 hybrid, is the best of all outdoor varieties of cucumber. It is early, with a long productive season, with delicious, non-bitter, crunchy fruit. An ideal form for the smaller garden as it will fit into any mixed border, growing up and over a teepee of bamboo canes (see picture, page 88).

I'm also very keen on mini cucumbers such as 'Zeina', an F1 hybrid, or 'Dina', with fruits about 15cm (6in) long. Both are seedless, with sweet and crisp flesh. They are ideal for eating as crudités, cut into four lengthways. 'Zeina' in particular is a prolific producer. Plants have good disease resistance and are suitable for growing outside or in.

I also grow the unusual 'Crystal Apple', a traditional cucumber variety that looks like a mini melon and is quick-growing and prolific. It has good, sweet flavour and crisp texture, with a definite hint of melon crossed with cucumber.

Propagation From seed.

Sowing time Early spring in an heated greenhouse, or mid-spring for unheated greenhouse or outdoors. These seeds are expensive, so sow individually in 8cm (3in) pots (see picture, page 144). Germinate cucumbers at unusually high temperatures of at least 21°C (70°F) – at 24°C (75°F) you'll get quicker germination. Good seedling development requires similar

temperatures. Pot on to at least 25cm (10in) pots as soon as the first leaves have fully opened.

Successional sowing Yes – maybe one lot in March and another in May.

Final planting/thinning distance Plant 45cm (18in) apart each way in a greenhouse or outside in a sunny, sheltered position if they are to grow up supports. Don't plant them outside until late spring. Dig a hole for each plant 30cm (12in) deep and wide. Fill this with a mixture of soil and well-rotted manure and replace the surplus soil to leave a low mound. Plant into the top of this to help prevent stem rot.

Special growing requirements If grown in a greenhouse, they will need daily watering. Create a mini reservoir for each plant out of a 500-ml (17-fl oz) plastic bottle. Cut off the base and make a small hole in the cap which you leave on. Push the cap end into the soil, then fill with water, which seeps out gradually over a couple of hours. Once the fruits start to swell,

feed once a week with a liquid balanced feed or one teaspoon of dried blood and bone per week (see page 89). Outside, they love rich, well-manured ground and should be kept well watered in dry weather. Give them a watering-canful twice a week in dry weather.

Inside or out, each plant will need support. I just tie mine in to canes, or on to a willow teepee standing about 1.5m (5ft) tall. When the plants reach the top, pinch out the tip to encourage side shoots and more cucumbers.

Harvesting Most cucumber varieties produce about twenty fruits from one plant if it's grown well. You can double that with 'Zeina'.

US hardiness zone 10 (but grown as an annual).

Opposite top **Witloof chicory 'Zoom'.**
Opposite bottom **Courgette 'Defender'.**
Above **Cucumber 'Zeina'.**

Endive

I'm not very keen on endive. Eating the coarse-textured, frizzy-edged leaves suggests to me what it would be like eating leaves from a tree. They have no softness to them, just a very fibrous crunch. They are, however, a healthy-looking, interesting crop to have growing in your salad bed.

Variety description There are two types, frilly and broad-leaved. The frilly endive are best from a summer sowing, for eating in the autumn. I have grown 'Green Curled', 'Pancalieri a Costa Bianca' and 'Wallonne', crunchy, frisée types with abundant, self-blanching growth. You can use this form fully grown, or as a cut-and-come-again crop when young. You can blanch them further by covering them for a less bitter taste. The broad-leaved varieties, or escarole like 'Jeti', are supremely hardy and can be sown in the autumn to supplement your winter salad bowl.

Propagation From seed.

Sowing time Sow 1cm (½in) deep in rows 30cm (12in) apart from mid-spring to early autumn.

Successional sowing Yes, particularly if you're growing them as a hearting crop that you'll harvest all in one go.

Final planting/thinning distance Space 30cm (12in) apart to form hearts, 10cm (4in) if for cut-and-come-again.

Special growing requirements To encourage blanching, cover with a pot or plate to exclude light for a couple of weeks before use. Wait until the hearts are full-sized – about the size of a fist. This removes bitterness. Water in dry spells to prevent bolting.

Harvesting Throughout autumn and winter.

US hardiness zone 4.

Florence fennel

Florence fennel is one of my favourite vegetables, whether raw or cooked. I love hitting chunks of it in a mixed leaf salad, and making a salad of it on its own – very finely sliced – with a yogurty dressing flavoured with fennel tops. It's also one of the most delicous vegetables to eat with chicken, slow-roasted in the oven in a sealed pot, or made into tempura fritters to eat on the side.

Variety description 'Fino' is a good, bolt-resistant variety that I grow. 'Romanesco' is an excellent variety for late sowing, which will produce the biggest bulbs of any I've tried, some reaching up to 1kg (2¼lb) in weight.

Propagation From seed.

Sowing time Sow 1cm (½in) deep in rows 45cm (18in) apart in early summer. You can also sow under cover in mid- to late spring, but Florence fennel does not like root disturbance. Sow a couple of seeds to a Jiffy 7 or small pot. Remove one if both grow. Plant out when the seedlings have two pairs of leaves – no later – before the rootball has started to form.

Successional sowing Yes.

Final planting/thinning distance 10cm (4in) or 15cm (6in) for larger bulbs.

Special growing requirements Florence fennel thrives in a Mediterranean climate, growing best in a warm site in light, well-drained soil. It bolts if it gets too dry or too cold. Don't start sowing until late spring as any check in growth induced by cold nights will cause it to bolt. Work in plenty of organic material to the planting soil, and water in dry weather. Earth up bulbs during the summer to increase tenderness.

Harvesting Throughout summer and autumn. In ideal conditions, it will produce a bulb in ten to twelve weeks. Cut just above soil level, and you may get some smaller bulbs forming as a second crop.

US hardiness zone 5.

Flowers – edible

I like throwing edible flowers over salad and freezing them in water or olive-oil ice cubes for soup. These are the ones I pick most.

Anchusa (or alkanet)

Description An easy, short-lived perennial. I grow *Anchusa azurea* 'Dropmore' in brilliant Moroccan blue, and there is another handsome variety, the deep blue-purple *A. azurea* 'Loddon Royalist'. I prefer this to borage and on my heavy, rich soil it is less invasive and has finer, less coarse and hairy leaves. No noticeable flavour. Excellent in drinks and soups and for making ice bowls (see page 71).

Propagation From seed or root cuttings.

Sowing time Sow in a seed tray in June, or propagate from root cuttings. It will self-sow.

Successional sowing No.

Final planting/thinning distance 45cm (18in).

Special growing requirements Very easy.

Harvesting One year after sowing.

US hardiness zone 4.

Borage

Description A very easy hardy annual. It comes in a blue and a white form, which don't seem to hybridize. It is said to have a mild taste of cucumber, but I'm yet to be convinced.

Left **Florence fennel 'Fino'.** Opposite, clockwise from top left **Salad rocket, borage, chive flowers and** *Anchusa azurea* **'Dropmore'.**

Propagation From seed.

Sowing time Sow outside from April to July.

Successional sowing No. It will self-sow, too much in my view.

Final planting/thinning distance 45cm (18in).

Special growing requirements Will grow in sun or partial shade.

Harvesting Eight weeks from sowing.

US hardiness zone 10 (as a biennial – and can be grown as an annual).

Chives

Description A quick-growing perennial that is easy to grow. Like many alliums, chives are useful for being early to emerge in late winter/early spring. I start picking ordinary chives in the garden in early March, and they start to flower in April/May with pretty, globe-like mauve flowers. I then cut them right back in June. An amazingly quick-growing plant, they'll be back to be harvested again with leaves (see page 206) in ten days, and flowers a couple of weeks after that. You may need to hack them back one more time to make sure of a continual supply. They have a sharp, onion flavour.

I also grow garlic chives (see picture, page 66), with white flowers, which look similar to wild garlic. They come slightly later than purple chives, in June and July. Cut them back as the flowers turn brown and you should get another crop in August/September. They have a mild garlicky flavour.

Propagation From seed or division.

Sowing time Sow outside from late April to August, in rich, moist soil in a sunny position. You can sow into modules or Jiffys or into

guttering at least four to six weeks before that.

Successional sowing No.

Final planting/thinning distance 20cm (8in).

Special growing requirements Divide clumps every year in late summer to keep them vigorous. Like many alliums, chives have a tendency to develop rust (see page 168).

Harvesting Leaves eight to ten weeks from sowing, flowers twelve to fourteen weeks.

US hardiness zone 3.

Calendula

Description A very easy hardy annual. It comes in many different yellow and orange forms. My favourite is 'Indian Prince' with orange petals with a plum reverse and centre to the flower. Don't serve the flower whole. Dismember it, pulling the thin, saffron-like petal strands from the central disc. This part of the flower is too chunky to be good to eat.

Propagation From seed.

Sowing time Sow outside from April to July.

Successional sowing If you want edible flowers for salad or risottos, this is one of the easiest to grow, so you may want to sow it a couple of times. It will self-sow a bit.

Final planting/thinning distance 30cm (12in).

Special growing requirements Will grow in sun or partial shade.

Harvesting Eight weeks from sowing.

US hardiness zone 9 (but grown as an annual).

Nasturtium

Description A half-hardy annual plant that can be non-trailing, trailing or climbing, with brilliant-coloured orange, deep red, yellow or cream flowers. My favourite is 'Tip Top Mahogany' (see picture, page 5) with its dark, rich red-orange flowers, a stark

contrast to its acid-green leaves. This and 'Empress of India' with its crimson-flushed leaves and deep red-orange flowers, are both trailing, not strictly climbing varieties. There is a very exotic new form with almost black flowers called 'Black Velvet' – a compact, non-trailing form. Alaska Series, also non-trailing, has dappled cream spots on the mid-green leaves, and 'Jewel of Africa' is a good climbing form with gold, cream and yellow flowers with brown flecks.

Propagation From seed.

Sowing time Any time from mid-spring until mid-summer.

Successional sowing No. Will self-sow – some say too much!

Final planting/thinning distance 30cm (12in).

Special growing requirements These are very easy to grow, but they flower best in poor soil. In rich soils, they tend to form lots of lush leaves and not much flower. Cabbage white caterpillars can be a problem, shredding leaves by their hundreds. You can grow them under a brassica net (see page 187).

Harvesting Eight weeks from sowing. Eat the small leaves, flower buds and flowers. They all have a distinctive peppery, caper-like taste.

US hardiness zone 10 (but grown as an annual).

Primrose

Description A pretty perennial that covers lanes and wood edges in the spring, flowering from March until May (see picture, page 71). They have a mild, slightly sweet, honey-like taste. *Primula vulgaris* does contain primin, however, which some people are allergic to.

Propagation From seed or by division.

Sowing time If plants grown from seed sown in late spring, they won't flower the same year.

Successional sowing No – they are perennials.

Final planting/thinning distance 15cm (6in).

Special growing requirements They thrive in humus-rich soil in sun or partial shade.

Harvesting Early spring.

US hardiness zone 4.

Salad rocket

Description Pretty, cream flowers of the well-known salad plant. As the temperatures begin to rise in late spring, the autumn-sown plants often quickly run to flower. Leave the plants in to harvest the flowers for a while. They have the characteristic rocket flavour.

Propagation From seed.

Sowing time Early autumn and mid-spring, straight into the garden or into guttering (see page 144).

Successional sowing Yes.

Final planting/thinning distance 10cm (4in).

Special growing requirements Runs up to flower almost instantly in the hot and dry, so is better sown to grow at colder times of year. Then you'll get a bit of flower with the leaves, not all flower!

Harvesting You need to keep cutting flowering stems back to within 2.5cm (1in) of the ground in order to prolong rocket leaf production. Rather than compost-ing the flowers, eat those too.

US hardiness zone 7.

Garlic

Viola

Description Small-flowered varieties such as *Viola. odorata* and *V. tricolor* (heartsease) are the best, pretty and delicate to eat (see pictures on pages 66 and 67). I love this native British wild flower, with its cheery yellow and purple flowers. My large-flowered favourite is 'Universal Purple' in a rich, velvety purple.

Propagation From seed.

Sowing time Sow under cover, or direct into the garden any time from mid-spring to late summer. Plant out six weeks later.

Successional sowing Shouldn't be necessary. Once in the garden, the species varieties self-sow.

Final planting/thinning distance 15cm (6in).

Special growing requirements Seed needs to be fresh or it can be very slow and difficult to germinate. Putting the packet of seed in the freezer for a week may help it germinate.

Harvesting Eight to ten weeks from spring sowing.

US hardiness zone 5.

Garlic is indispensable in cooking and is used in almost every cuisine in the world, but it is easy to buy, so why bother to grow it? It's very easy to grow, needing almost no attention, and fresh, green garlic, particularly of the mammoth 'Elephant' kind, is milder and sweeter than any you can buy. It's also a good companion plant, repelling insects like carrot fly. You could plant garlic you have bought for cooking, but you will get a healthier, bigger crop from buying special garlic bred for propagation. This also avoids virus troubles. Garlic bought in a shop is almost always grown in a hot country and therefore the wrong variety for our cooler climate.

Variety description Garlic divides into varieties for planting in the autumn and others that can be planted in the spring.

There are 'short storage', or 'short dormancy' varieties that will be good for only about four months, and 'long storage' or 'long dormancy' varieties, which will store from lifting until the following spring – six or seven months. Most of the autumn-planting varieties are 'short storage', but 'Cristo' is useful because it can be planted in autumn or spring and is long dormancy. It produces large bulbs, with white skins and cloves, weighing in at around 75g (3oz), with eight to ten cloves per bulb. The flavour is excellent, and it stores well.

I also grow 'Elephant' garlic – *Allium ampeloprasum* – which produces huge cloves, with a bulb as big as a man's hand (see picture, page 63). It's much milder than normal garlic, and is excellent roasted with meat or potatoes.

Propagation From garlic cloves planted upright, with the base of the clove downwards.

Planting time 'Cristo' can be planted in the autumn or the spring (see above). Autumn is recommended for 'Elephant' garlic, although you can plant until late winter. If you plant in the spring, there's an increased chance of producing a solid bulb, instead of a bulb with cloves. Push the cloves into the soil deep enough to leave no tip visible. For normal-sized garlic, this means putting the cloves at a depth of about 8cm (3in), for 'Elephant' garlic a bit deeper. Otherwise the birds will pull them up.

Successional sowing No.

Final planting/thinning distance Space them at 15cm (6in) between cloves and 30cm (12in) between rows. For 'Elephant' garlic, space them at 30cm (12in) between cloves and between rows. Garlic will try to flower. If you cut the flower stem down, you will encourage larger bulb formation. You can just nip off the green 'beak' bud and cook it. To make good use of garden space, sow lettuce in between.

Special growing requirements All garlic likes light, free-draining soil in a sunny position.

Harvesting Summer, as soon as the leaves turn yellow. Dry them out of the ground and then store them somewhere dry at a minimum of 5°C (40°F).

US hardiness zone 4.

Opposite **Calendula 'Indian Prince'**.
Above **Garlic 'Cristo'**.
Left **Viola 'Universal Purple'**.

Herbs

You can't have a productive garden without herbs. They are ornamental, easy and make almost any food taste better. These should qualify to fill up lots of your precious space.

Herbs divide into several different plant groups, with annuals – both hardy and half-hardy – forming an important part, as well as herbaceous and woody perennial plants. I choose ones I use at least once a week. There are others, but this is my selection – all easy and rewarding to grow.

Hardy annual herbs, and herbs treated as annuals

Chervil

Description This is a small relative of cow parsley and its leaves and white flowers look similar on a smaller scale (see picture, page 102). Chervil leaves have a fine, tender texture and delicate, aniseedy taste. It's invaluable in the winter, when it will happily grow outside in a protected spot. Scatter a handful of leaves over a mixed leaf salad. When making an omelette, add it right at the end: then the essential oils – and hence the flavour – are not dispersed by cooking.

Propagation From seed.

Sowing time Late summer for winter picking, or early spring for spring and summer. To have it all year, sow two to three times. My first and last sowings are done under cover in Jiffy 7s, or guttering, in early March and early September, but the other sowing is direct into the garden. Chervil is slow to germinate and does not like root disturbance.

Successional sowing Yes, little and often, although you may not need to as it self-sows. You can transplant the seedlings to where you want them.

Final planting/thinning distance 20cm (8in) apart.

Special growing requirements It prefers to grow in moist soil in light, dappled shade and is best grown in the cooler months. In heat, it rapidly runs up to flower and the leaf flavour is decreased.

Harvesting Six to eight weeks from sowing. Leaf production lasts four to five months (longest in the winter). This is the hardiest of these herbs and in a sheltered spot in my garden grows right through the winter, resprouting leaves within a week. I love the taste of chervil, so usually grow it for the spring and summer too, planting it in the shade. In the summer sun it makes a scrawny plant.

US hardiness zone 4 (but grown as an annual).

Coriander

Description Rich-green, lobed leaf with slightly serrated edge. There are two different types of coriander, one for seed (Moroccan) and one for leaf (I grow 'Leisure'). The first forms hardly any basal leaves before it flowers and creates seed. The second forms leafy rosettes, but you need to keep picking them to stop the plants trying to flower. The leaves have a characteristic, unmistakable flavour and a soft texture. Coriander is an essential flavour in oriental cooking, and I love it with ratatouille and with borlotti beans (see page 47). You must be careful not to cook the leaves. The essential oils and flavours are easily destroyed. Add a handful of leaves as you take the dish off the heat.

Propagation From seed.

Sowing time As we now all know, coriander has a fantastic flavour, but it is one of the quickest herbs to bolt. The only way round this is to sow every month to six weeks and keep hacking away at it to stop it running to flower. It does well from an early spring and late summer sowing, lasting longer in the cooler months than when it's hot and dry. Sow into guttering or direct where it is to grow. It does not like root disturbance. Keep it well watered.

Successional sowing To have it all year, sow four or five times. My first and last sowings are done under cover in Jiffy 7s, modular trays or guttering in early March and early September, but the rest are sown direct into the garden. Coriander self-sows with me, germinating in early spring on my south-facing bank.

Final planting/thinning distance 20cm (8in).

Special growing requirements Easy to germinate, hardy and quick to produce, but it also bolts quickly. It prefers very freely drained soil. Add grit to rich, clay soils to increase drainage and decrease fertility. When it does run to seed, I use the seeds green in salads and hot, spicy food.

Harvesting Six to eight weeks from sowing. Leaf production for four to six weeks. You also want to collect and dry the seeds. Pick the seed pods on the stem and hang them upside-down in a cotton bag or pillow case. The seeds will then drop out into the bottom of the bag as they dry.

US hardiness zone 5 (but grown as an annual).

Dill

Description Pretty, feathery leaves in dark green. It has beautiful, acid-green flowers, very fashionable for flower arranging, but you want to delay the formation of these by regular picking every three or four days. The leaves have an invaluable, mild aniseedy, fresh, grassy flavour. I love it raw and use it in marinades. This herb is as ubiquitous in north European cooking as parsley is in British and basil is in Mediterranean, which gives you an idea where it grows best.

Propagation From seed.

Sowing time I sow dill direct into the garden from the mid-spring. It does not like root disturbance and will shoot up to flower quickly. If you want to start it early, use guttering or modules inside.

Successional sowing If you have decent enough drainage for the plants to be happy, they will self-sow and you may not need to sow again. Like coriander, however, dill is quick to run up to flower, and successional sowing is the key to a continuous supply.

Final planting/thinning distance 20cm (8in).

Special growing requirements It likes bright light, but cool temperatures. On my heavy soil, I add grit to the sowing position of dill to encourage good germination.

I have a beautiful self-sown combination of dill with orach (see page 224) in a corner of my garden. I just let them get on with it from one year to the next, thinning seedlings of orach to 45cm (18in) spacings – it's a large plant fully grown – and dill to 20–25cm (8–10in). Many people don't bother to thin seedlings that are self-sown, but this is a mistake. Too closely spaced, the plants will compete with each other for nutrients, water and light, and quickly run up to flower, seed and die.

Opposite, clockwise from top left **Lettuce-leaved basil, dill, sweet marjoram and coriander 'Leisure'.**

Harvesting Six to eight weeks from sowing. Leaf production for two months. Dill doesn't like the damp and dies off in the autumn outside, but I've picked from the same line in the greenhouse right the way through the winter. Dill has very tasty seeds too, which store well.

US hardiness zone 8 (but grown as an annual).

Par-cel

Description Another biennial grown as an annual that tastes like a cross between parsley and celery. It has a strong flavour, invaluable for food where you would use these two flavours together – salads, risottos and stocks. Botanically, it's a curly-leaved celery, not related to parsley at all.

Propagation From seed.

Sowing time Any time from mid-spring to late summer outside. If you want to sow earlier, sow into guttering for transplanting outside when the seedlings reach about 25cm (1in).

Successional sowing A couple of times a year.

Final planting/thinning distance 20cm (8in).

Special growing requirements It has a strong tendency to rust (see page 168). Keep it well watered to avoid this.

Harvesting Eight to ten weeks from sowing. Leaf production for two to three months. You must keep harvesting regularly for the texture to remain soft. Leaves left on the plant for several weeks become tough and leathery, better for cooking than eating raw.

US hardiness zone 6.

Parsley – flat-leaved

Description Parsley is in fact a biennial, naturally flowering in its second year, but as you grow it for its leaves not its flowers, treat it as an annual. The flat-leaved is my favourite form, much more popular on the Continent than the curly-leaved kind. The taste is much the same, but the texture is softer and it has flat, lobed leaves.

Propagation From seed.

Sowing time Mid-spring and late summer straight into the ground, or into guttering under cover almost any time.

Successional sowing Yes, but for year-round picking you won't need to sow more than a couple of times.

Final planting/thinning distance 30cm (12in) plus.

Special growing requirements Of all these herbs, parsley is the slowest to germinate, taking two to three weeks in the colder months. To speed it up, give the seeds a swirl in a cup of warm water to remove the natural germination inhibitor in the seed coat. Parsley likes a rich, moist soil in a slightly shaded position.

Harvesting Ten to twelve weeks from sowing. Leaf production for five to six months. In the south of England you can pick parsley outside all year from two sowings, one in August/early September and one in May. By June the first sowing is determined to flower, however much you cut it back. Get rid of it – the second group can take over. When you pull it up, eat the roots too. You can grate them or slice them finely and they have a delicious, intense parsley flavour. In the north, grow the winter crop under cover.

US hardiness zone 5.

Summer savory

Description The flavour resembles thyme's, but is a little stronger. I sowed this plant first for its famed protective effects against blackfly on broad beans. I then picked it and loved the taste. It has quite insignificant white flowers, but try to prevent these forming. The leaf flavour and texture are better before the plant blooms.

Propagation From seed.

Sowing time Any time from mid-spring to late summer outside. If you want to sow earlier, sow into guttering for transplanting outside when the seedlings reach about 2.5cm (1in).

Successional sowing A couple of times a year.

Final planting/thinning distance 30cm (12in).

Special growing requirements Summer savory grows well on my heavy soil, unlike thyme, although it too likes a sunny spot, in soil that is well drained. On a heavy, wet soil, increase the drainage, adding a spadeful of grit to every square metre (11 sq ft) of soil before you sow.

Harvesting Six to eight weeks from sowing. Leaf production for two to three months. Summer savory dries very well. After it has flowered, cut the whole plant and hang it up to dry.

US hardiness zone 6.

Left **Par-cel.**
Opposite, near right **Sweet basil.**
Opposite, far right **Lemon grass.**

Half-hardy annual herbs

Basil

There are many different basil varieties, most of which are well worth growing. This is a selection of my favourites, which I use almost every day when they're in the garden or the greenhouse during the summer and early autumn (see picture, pages 138–9).

Variety description Sweet basil, *Ocimum basilicum* 'Genovese', has the best flavour and is reliable and easy to grow. It has superb, aromatic leaves to eat raw or lightly cooked. It's perfect raw with tomatoes and is also the main component of pesto. 'Lettuce-leaved' basil (see picture, page 201) is also worth a try. This is a basil with huge leaves, some of which will cover the palm of your hand. It's useful for cooking and salads for large numbers, but the flavour is not quite as good as that of sweet basil.

I sometimes also grow bush or Greek basil, *Ocimum basilicum* var. *minimum*, a small-leaved variety. It produces neat, perfect domes of small basil leaves that look superb in terracotta pots or in a series of painted tin cans that have had a few holes pierced in the bottom. Line them up on a window ledge – they'll look good and you can harvest from them too. The leaves are tasty, but their flavour is less intense than that of sweet basil. Height 20cm (8in).

Purple-leaved basil, *O. basilicum* var. *purpurascens*, is in fact a dark crimson form of the well-known herb, at its best raw in salads. Beautiful, but with a flavour less intense than that of sweet basil and not as good cooked in sauces. In the UK it is also more prone to damping off and fungal problems, even when fully grown.

Of the unusual-flavoured basils, I grow 'Mrs Burns's Lemon' basil, for making delicous herb teas and salad dressings, and Thai basil, *O. basilicum* 'Horapha', a pretty, small basil; the undersides of its stems and leaves are deep purple. It's the crucial ingredient in lots of oriental cooking. It has a very distinctive, strongly aniseedy taste, closer in flavour to dill than to sweet basil.

Propagation From seed.

Sowing time Sow in April/May under cover, or direct into the ground from early June (see page 104).

Successional sowing Yes. Every couple of months to ensure almost year-round production.

Final planting/thinning distance 20cm (8in).

Special growing requirements Thai basil is slower to germinate than other basils and needs more heat: 21°C (70°F). In a grey year, with any of these basils, you may have problems with damping off. This is caused by a mix of soil-borne fungi and wipes out small seedlings. Avoid it by general glasshouse hygiene, including cleaning pots and trays, and by making sure the plants have good ventilation. Pinch out the growing tips, so plants bulk out, and never send them to bed wet. Depending on rainfall, plants outside may not need watering. Inside, water in the morning only. Evening watering encourages botrytis – a potential killer in the cold and wet. Basil in particular likes it hot, but humid and moist, so water liberally if growing inside. Don't plant it outside until cold nights are likely to be over. This is early June in Sussex. Give the plants a sheltered spot in a rich soil, with good drainage. Keep well watered for a couple of weeks, until they are firmly rooted.

Harvesting Six to eight weeks from sowing. Remove individual leaves, or whole stems – don't cut the plant to the ground.

Pinch off flowers as they appear – they coarsen the leaves.

Leaf production continues for two months if you keep basil well watered. It will go black outside in mid-September, so pick the lot to make pesto or basil oil before you lose it.

US hardiness zone 10 (but grown as an annual).

Lemon grass

Description Lemon grass is in fact a tender perennial, which will over-winter in a frost-free environment inside. If not, treat it as an annual, sowing it every year. It forms 60cm (2ft) grassy clumps of grey-green. I cut the leaf bases for oriental curries and soups and use the leaf tips for teas.

Propagation From seed or division in the spring.

Sowing time Early to mid-spring. It is slow to germinate and grow, so an early start is a good idea.

Successional sowing Not necessary. As a perennial, it will keep sprouting new leaves after they have been cut.

Final planting/thinning distance 30cm (12in).

Special growing requirements I have only just started growing this, but it is easy to germinate

from seed and then simple to grow. It does need some spring and autumn protection at night in the UK, so we have it in pots in the greenhouse, harvesting it from there. If kept frost-free in the winter, the plants will survive.

Harvesting From early summer to late autumn, when the leaves lose their green.

US hardiness zone 10.

Sweet marjoram, (or half-hardy oregano)

Description The grey-green leaf (see picture, page 201) has an intense, warm flavour, with three times the taste of the perennial or pot marjoram.

Propagation From seed.

Sowing time Sow under cover in early spring and plant out, or sow directly into the ground in late spring.

Successional sowing Not necessary.

Final planting/thinning distance 20cm (8in).

Special growing requirements This likes very free-draining soil and a sunny, sheltered spot.

Harvesting Give this a regular shear as and when you want it through the summer. Harvest the whole plant before the nights get cold in September and hang it upside-down to dry for use through the winter. Dried, it retains most of its flavour, ideal for zizzing up dishes based on tomato, cheese or fish.

US hardiness zone 7.

Opposite, clockwise from top left **Lovage, green fennel, Moroccan mint and French tarragon.**

Hardy perennial herbs

Fennel – bronze and green

Description The classic, feathery-leaved, aniseed-tasting plant. Many people are confused by its relationship to the bulb Florence fennel – the two plants are cousins. It is one of the easiest and most prolific herbs. I use the flowers and seeds as well as the leaves.

Propagation From seed or division. Lift and divide plants every three or four years.

Sowing time In spring. It germinates in seven to ten days and will freely self-sow. You can then use the plants as seedlings or allow them to reach full – 1.5m (5ft) – size.

Successional sowing No.

Final planting/thinning distance 60cm (2ft).

Special growing requirements A very easy and tolerant plant that prefers full sun and deep, moist soil with good drainage. It benefits from a severe haircut in June. It will leaf up quickly and then go on producing for much longer than if left to flower. Beware of flowers and seeds anyway – it is a prolific self-seeder. I looked out of my bathroom window the other day and couldn't work out what on earth a bronze carpet was doing in the dahlia garden below. When I went down I realized it was a thousand tiny fennel seedlings which had appeared in the warm, wet weather of the previous few days. Bear this in mind when you plant it! Fennel has a noticeable tendency to aphid attack, which will invade the growing tips. The aphids are hard to see, so careful checking or soaking in strongly salted water before you put leaves into a salad is a good idea!

Harvesting Six to eight weeks from seedlings is possible, but it will grow to 1.5m (5ft). Leaf production lasts two to three months, or more if you cut it down before it flowers in June. The great advantage of fennel is that it's very early to emerge in the garden. I start picking it from outside in early March, sometimes even in February, and, by continually hacking away at it, keep it going, sweet and soft in texture, until mid-summer. The seeds are good for baking, pickling and mixing with rice to stuff red peppers and aubergines.

US hardiness zone 5.

Horseradish

Description It's very difficult to find fresh roots of horseradish at the greengrocer's. You might not want much of it, but growing it somewhere in the garden to transform dishes of smoked fish and red meat is an easy thing to do. It's not an elegant plant, and looks like a dock, so don't put in anywhere too prominent.

Propagation From division.

Sowing time Not applicable.

Successional sowing Not applicable.

Final planting/thinning distance 45cm (18in).

Special growing requirements A word of warning about horseradish: it's very invasive, so plant it with care, in a deep pot, or plonk it in a place where it won't matter if it runs riot. Don't grow it if you have a small garden. It's in the cabbage family, so has a tendency to the same pests and other troubles (see page 168).

Harvesting Dig up the roots as and when you want them. You can even harvest roots of this very hardy plant in the winter.

US hardiness zone 3.

Lovage

Description A statuesque 1.8m (6ft) plant, with bold, architectural leaves and a distinctive, strong celery flavour. Use the small, young leaves chopped finely in salad or add it to flavour Hungarian goulash and meaty casseroles and soups. If you get a lettuce glut, it's a fantastic herb to add to lettuce soup. It's also a great-looking plant in a border, and I pick it for foliage in arrangements.

Propagation From seed or division.

Sowing time It can be sown straight in the ground in mid-spring, or under cover in spring or late summer. Germination under cover usually takes just over a week. Outside, expect it to take twice as long. If your clump gets too big, lift and divide in spring.

Successional sowing No.

Final planting/thinning distance For full-sized plants, space at 1m (3ft).

Special growing requirements Benefits from a severe haircut in June. Cut it right back hard, water and wait for it to regrow. You can plant it in sun or partial shade, where it thrives in a deep, rich, moist soil.

Harvesting This is another perennial herb that, like chives, emerges very early in the year. You can pick within six to eight weeks from new seedlings, but it will grow to a plant of about 1.5m (5ft). Don't be tempted by the old leaves. They are unpalatably tough and bitter. Young shoots can be blanched in spring and eaten like celery.

US hardiness zone 4.

Mint

Variety description There are many different mints, but I have three clear favourites. The first is apple (*Mentha suaveolens*), which is very similar to 'Bowles' mint (*M. x villosa* var. *alopecuroides* – see picture, page 102), with soft, velvety leaves that have excellent flavour for cooking and using in drinks. I use spearmint (*M. spicata*) almost daily too, which has a similar flavour, but a smooth, more tender texture raw. I also grow Moroccan mint (*M. spicata* var. *crispa* 'Moroccan'). The flavour of different mints varies in intensity, with Moroccan spearmint being the strongest of all. It is therefore perfect for making strong herbal teas. In Morocco you would sweeten it with lots of sugar, but I prefer it without.

Propagation From division. You need buy only one small plant of each. Mint is rampant and will spread itself quickly. So that mint does not take over when you plant it in the garden, enclose the roots in a large plastic pot sunk in the soil with 5cm (2in) of the rim above the ground so the runners don't creep over the side. We grow ours in an old water trough.

Sowing time Not applicable.

Successional sowing Not applicable.

Final planting/thinning distance 45cm (18in).

Special growing requirements The secret to growing good mint is to realize that it is not one of the typical Mediterranean herbs that like hot, sunny conditions, but a plant that likes moist soil and tolerates some shade. It is also critical to cut plants down before they flower, to keep the leaf flavour and texture good. Just hack it back and it will be ready to pick again within a week. If you have roots enclosed, to keep the flavour strong you must change the soil in the container every two or three years and start off a new plant from healthy runners from the parent plant.

Harvesting Let it settle in for a couple of weeks after planting and then you can pick the leaves to your heart's content. This is a rampant grower and will thrive on being picked.

I pick mint from April to September outside and extend this period through the winter by planting up a large pot for inside. Dig up a pot of mint that has become congested and tip it out. Select some runners and cut them off. Plant them in a pot and cover with 2.5cm (1in) of soil.

US hardiness zone 3–5.

Sorrel – common

Description There are two varieties of sorrel worth growing – *Rumex acetosa*, the common form, closely related to wild sorrel, with long, thin, mini dock-shaped leaves, and *R. scutatus* (buckler-leaved), which is softer, with rounder leaves (see page 222). Sorrel takes its name from the old French word *surelle*, meaning 'sour', and it does have a distinctive, citrus-flavoured leaf, wonderful scattered through salad, or used – just wilted – in sauces and soups.

Propagation Sow under cover any time in spring. You can propagate by division in the autumn or the following spring.

Sowing time Sorrel is a very hardy herbaceous perennial that can cope with shade and most types of soil. It germinates quickly from seed and will appear in five to ten days if sown under cover, or in two to three weeks if sown straight into the ground.

Successional sowing No.

Final planting/thinning distance 15cm (6in).

Special growing requirements A short-lived perennial plant that will produce leaves well for two to three years. Typical of the leafy, luscious, quick-growing herbs, it's best planted in partial shade in a soil rich with organic material. In hot, dry conditions it runs up to flower and the leaves quickly lose their softness and intensity of taste. Keep it well watered, but if it bolts, cut the plants down to within 2.5cm (1in) of the ground.

Be brutal – keep hacking away and you'll get a much longer picking season. Sorrel survives on alkaline soils, but prefers acid, so if it's in a pot, plant it in ericaceous compost. A warning: if you let it flower and run to seed, it freely self-sows, so in a tidy garden, cut it back before the ripe-seed stage. Or, if you have the room, plant it somewhere you're happy for it to run riot.

Harvesting You can pick this from early March until November, with light pickings through a mild winter. When you harvest, shear a plant, picking all the leaves in one go. It will have grown again in about a fortnight. A friend cooked me the Jane Grigson (originally Elizabeth David) recipe for sorrel sauce with some turbot the other day, and it was one of the simplest and most delicious things I've had this year. You strip the green from the stems and wilt the sorrel for a couple of minutes in a knob or tablespoon of butter. Then pour in large amounts of single and double cream – 120ml (4fl oz) of each – lots of freshly ground black pepper and, before you pour it on to the plates, add a slurp of the fish juices into the creamy pan.

US hardiness zone 3.

Chives

Description A lush, grass-like herb with a well-known, characteristic flavour, perfect in potato salad. The flavour resembles that of spring onions, but is a little milder. Chives have a round cross-section and mauve flowers. They are invaluable for being one of the first perennial plants to appear in the spring. In the south, you can start picking them for sauces, dressings and soups from late February onwards.

I also grow garlic chives – with a definite garlicky taste – and they're particularly delicious in cold cucumber soup and tsatsiki. Garlic chives have white flowers and flat leaves. In a mild winter, new plants won't die back at all, so you can harvest right through the leaner season.

Propagation From seed or division.

Division They can be built up more the same year by dividing clumps into smalller clumps 2.5cm (1in) wide, and immediately replanting.

Sowing time From a spring sowing, chives germinate in ten to fifteen days.

Successional sowing A perennial, so this is not necessary.

Final planting/thinning distance 15cm (6in).

Special growing requirements Chives like full sun and an open position, without overcrowding from lots of other plants. Both varieties make excellent edging, but it's important to cut them to within 2.5cm (1in) of the ground in June. The plants will regrow within ten days for picking right the way through the rest of summer. Left to their own devices, they will flower, die back and stop producing good, tasty leaves even as soon as early summer. Ordinary chives in particular have a tendency to rust.

Harvesting Eight to ten weeks from seedlings is possible. From plants already in the garden, I pick chives from early March to September outside and extend this period by six weeks at the end of the season by planting up a pot for inside. I pick the flowers (see page 196) as well as the leaves.

US hardiness zone 3.

Tarragon

Description Tarragon is the herb to cook with chicken, and its soft flavour is excellent with fish. It also makes one of the best-flavoured vinegars for excellent salad dressings and Béarnaise. Grow the French variety of tarragon (*Artemisia dracunculus*), not the Russian. The Russian is easy to grow from seed, but has almost no flavour. Taste a plant before you buy; if there's no tongue tingle, you know it's Russian.

Propagation French tarragon has to be propagated by division or from softwood cuttings, which is harder to do, so it is less available.

Division It takes two or three years to form a sizeable clump, about 60 x 60cm (2 x 2ft). At that

stage you can lift and divide it and replant the separate sections straight away.

Successional sowing Not applicable.

Final planting/thinning distance 45cm (18in).

Special growing requirements French tarragon needs nurturing, a warm, sunny, sheltered spot and good drainage. It is not fully hardy. It usually survives the winter in my garden, mulched in up to 10cm (4in) of mushroom compost. It is also fairly slow-growing, so is easily swamped by more vigorous neighbours in a mixed herb plot. I have a permanent and very successful bed of tarragon in my greenhouse.

Harvesting Leaf production lasts five to six months. I pick tarragon from April to September outside and extend this period by a few weeks by planting up a large pot for inside.

US hardiness zone 5–9.

Marjoram

Description Golden marjoram, *Origanum vulgare* 'Aureum', is one of the best of the hardy herbaceous perennial marjorams. It's lovely and bright and easy to maintain lining a path in a herb garden.

Propagation From division or cuttings (see page 108).

Sowing time Named varieties are not available as seed.

Successional sowing Not applicable.

Final planting/thinning distance 45cm (18in).

Special growing requirements A warm, sunny position and a light, well-drained soil. It thrives on chalky soils and butterflies love it.

Harvesting Almost immediately after planting as this is a quick-growing herb. Leaf production for four months or more if you cut it down before it flowers in June.

US hardiness zone 6.

Lemon balm

Description This is similar in taste to lemon verbena, but the flavour is not quite so intense. It's one of the best herbs to use for making tisanes – hugely prolific and easy to grow. The tea has good effects, too, relieving tiredness and providing an excellent morning pep-me-up.

Propagation From seed, division or cuttings.

Sowing time Sown in mid-spring, direct into the ground, it germinates in seven to ten days. You can sow under cover in early spring for planting out a month later.

Successional sowing Not applicable.

Final planting/thinning distance 45cm (18in).

Special growing requirements A very tolerant plant that thrives in partial shade in my garden and has self-sown into dry cracks on sunny walls. Some would say it self-sows too much.

Opposite **Ordinary chives.**
Left **Golden marjoram.**
Above **Lemon balm.**

Harvesting Six to eight weeks from seedlings is possible, but it will grow into a 1m (3ft) plant. Leaf production for three to four months or more if you cut it down before it flowers in June.

US hardiness zone 5.

Winter savory

Description An invaluable winter perennial herb with a thymey flavour. The winter variety grows strongly through the winter months when my thyme looks tired and ill.

Propagation Propagate it from seed or cuttings.

Sowing time Spring-sown, it germinates in seven to ten days and will freely self-sow.

Successional sowing Not applicable.

Final planting/thinning distance 20cm (8in).

Special growing requirements Easy to grow even on heavy clay soil. Cut back in early spring to prevent it sprawling.

Harvesting Five to six months or more, including the winter.

US hardiness zone 5.

Woody perennials

Lemon verbena

Description Lemon verbena (*Aloysia triphylla*) is a deciduous woody perennial with the most wonderfully scented foliage. Crush it in your hand or hang a bunch under the hot tap for your bath. It also makes fantastic herb teas and sorbets.

Propagation Propagate it from cuttings. The hit rate is small, so I tend to buy my plants.

Sowing time Not applicable.

Successional sowing Not applicable.

Final planting/thinning distance 1m (3ft).

Special growing requirements Grow it under cover in a conservatory or greenhouse, or find it a sheltered, south-facing spot with excellent drainage to survive the winter outside.

Harvesting Only a little in the first year. It's deciduous, and the plant looks dead from October to April, so you'll think the frost has killed it, but then the leaves start to sprout. Once a plant is large and well-established – in two or three years – you can pick handfuls of leaves almost every day from May until September outside. Extend this period by about four weeks at the beginning and end of the season by having a plant in a bed in the polytunnel or greenhouse.

US hardiness zone 9.

Rosemary

Description I prefer the dark blue-flowered *Rosmarinus officinalis* 'Sissinghurst Blue', *R. o.* 'Benenden Blue' and *R. o.* var. *angustissimus* 'Corsican Blue' to the pale, grey-blue-flowered forms. As an evergreen plant, rosemary is invaluable for flavouring food in the winter. Use the leaves with chicken, potatoes and almost any red meat, and use the stems as skewers for kebabs and mini meatballs.

R. 'Miss Jessopp's Upright' is a very upright kind that throws up vertical branches, making it ideal to use as a hedge in a sheltered spot.

R. o. Prostratus Group 29 (see picture, page 109) is a weeping rosemary, which reaches only 15cm (6in) in height. If you have a flower-bed along the top of a low retaining wall, or want to grow rosemary in a window-box, this is the one for you. It looks wonderful tumbling down over brick or stone. But this rosemary is the least hardy, so don't go for it where winter temperatures are severe.

Propagation Propagate it from softwood cuttings or seed. It roots in about four weeks.

Sowing time You can collect seed from the species, but the named hybrids must be propagated from cuttings (see page 109).

Successional sowing Not applicable.

Final planting/thinning distance Final planting distance 1m (3ft). For a hedge, plant at half that distance.

Special growing requirements It thrives in a sunny, well-drained corner and does well in a pot. There has been a problem with a virus infecting these plants in recent years. All you can do to avoid this is improve drainage as far as you can.

Harvesting It's an evergreen, so you can pick it all year.

US hardiness zone 8–9.

Sage

Description There are lots of different types of sage, but the soft, grey-leaved *Salvia officinalis*, rather than the purple or variegated types, has the best flavour. *Salvia* 'Berggarten' is also excellent, with large, rounded leaves, ideal for delicious, crispy tempura.

Propagation Propagate it from seed or softwood cuttings. It will root in about a month.

Sowing time You can grow some forms from seed in spring. It germinates in ten to fourteen days.

Successional sowing Not applicable.

Final planting/thinning distance 45cm (18in).

Special growing requirements Cut back to 15–20cm (6–8in) above ground every year in early spring and again if it flowers in July. This hard pruning prevents plants become leggy. Old plants, even well-pruned, tend to get woody at the base, so it's a good idea to replace your plants every few years with your own home-grown ones (see page 109 for technique). It is said that sage dislikes acid soils, but it survives on mine.

Harvesting Sage is an evergreen, so if you grow enough, you can pick it right through the winter.

US hardiness zone 5–6.

Thyme

Description Common thyme, *Thymus vulgaris*, is the one usually used for cooking. My favourite thyme is the lemon variety, *T. x citriodorus*, which has a citrus scent and taste and is wonderful cooked or very finely chopped and added raw to vegetables or salads.

Propagation You can grow good varieties from seed or cuttings (see page 109 for technique).

Sowing time Spring-sown seed germinates in ten to fourteen days.

Successional sowing Not applicable.

Opposite, clockwise from top left **Rosemary 'Miss Jessop's Upright', grey-leaved sage, lemon thyme and lemon verbena.**

Final planting/thinning distance 20–25cm (8–10in) depending on variety.

Special growing requirements Thyme hates my heavy soil and, even with lots of grit added to improve drainage, often needs replacing. The shrubby varieties like lemon and orange thyme are tougher and better able to resist the British damp than the creeping ones.

Harvesting Should be all year, as it's an evergreen. In Britain it's best to leave it for the winter and start the harvest again in late spring. When I have plenty of thyme in the summer, I make flavoured vinegars for dressings.

US hardiness zone 4–6.

Below **Flowering bay tree.**
Opposite top **Sea kale.**
Opposite bottom **Kohlrabi 'Delikatess Witte'.**

Bay

Description I love confit of duck or chicken, and cloves and bay are the two essential flavours to add to the meat. Rip or crush bay leaves to release their taste.

Propagation From semi-ripe cuttings in late summer or autumn with high humidity.

Sowing time Not applicable.

Successional sowing Not applicable.

Final planting/thinning distance An unpruned tree can be huge, but clipped they rarely exceed 1m (3ft).

Special growing requirements An evergreen that is only moderately hardy. Bay tolerates sun, shade and all soils except very wet ones. It easily gets wind burn at the edge and tips of the leaves in an exposed place with cold winds. In colder areas, it's a good idea to protect the rootball of container-grown trees from freezing. Move the plant under glass or lag the container with hessian or bubble wrap.

Harvesting As and when you want it.

US hardiness zone 6–7.

Kale (or borecole)

I love kale. It's one of my favourite vegetables. I love its robust flavour, incredible productivity and the lack of TLC needed to produce plants that crop for five or six months at a stretch. Not nearly enough of us grow kale.

Variety description 'Red Russian' (see picture, page 116) is my favourite, with its grey-green leaf and purple midrib and veins. We eat this variety raw in winter salads when its leaves are only a few centimetres tall (see page 115), and grow some plants on to maturity to steam chopped into fine ribbons with olive oil and soy sauce. It's also lovely mixed up with anchovies over pasta and, deep-fried, it makes fantastic Chinese 'seaweed' (see page 115).

Cavolo nero – black Tuscan kale – is another good variety, with elegant, upright, dark silver-green leaves with a smooth edge, but deeply indented vein markings.

For autumn, winter and early spring picking every year, I also grow the tall 'Redbor' (see picture, page 162), an F1 hybrid with leaves that look like curly-leaved parsley, but in a rich crimson-black. It's a superb ornamental and edible addition to any productive garden.

Propagation From seed.

Sowing time You can sow kale almost any time and get good germination. For spring and summer picking, sow in March. For autumn and winter, sow in May or June. Brassicas don't like root disturbance, so for the early sowing use modular trays or Jiffy pellets for full-sized plants, or guttering for closely planted cut-and-come-again salad leaves (see page 144). For the later sowing, sow 1cm (½in) deep in seedling rows straight into the garden, 15cm (6in) apart in late spring. Transplant in mid-summer.

Successional sowing Twice a year, as above.

Final planting/thinning distance Plant seedlings for cut-and-come again use in salads at 8–10cm (3–4in). For fully grown plants, space your seedlings more generously, 45–60cm (18–24in) apart. All kales make big plants.

Special growing requirements Plant your kale with plenty of well-rotted manure or mushroom compost in the planting hole. These plants love it rich. Firm soil is also essential to grow good brassicas. They are tall plants with shallow roots, so they need a compact soil to help them stand upright. In the summer most varieties need netting against pigeons and cabbage white butterflies, and the net needs to go right over the plants to protect them against egg laying. 'Redbor' doesn't require protection. The caterpillars don't seem to like its flavour. You may need to protect against flea beetle too, which will pepper the leaves with tiny holes (see page 168).

You want to avoid clubroot disease, which is more likely on acidic soils, so lime the soil before planting and don't plant brassicas in the same ground for three years. Move all kales and cabbages around in a rotation (see page 166).

Harvesting You need only do two sowings a year to get all-year-round picking. Pick the tiny leaves for salads and the larger leaves for greens, and don't forget the flower buds. If you let your winter plants come up to flower in the spring, you can eat the immature flower shoots like purple-sprouting broccoli and the flowers make a delicious and pretty addition to salad. Wash all the summer and autumn leaves carefully. Whitefly is easily hidden in the wrinkles. You can soak

them for half an hour in strongly salted water to make sure you've got rid of any insect pests.

US hardiness zone 6.

Sea kale

Description A cabbage-like perennial, with gorgeous blue-grey leaves and spectacular cream umbels of honey-scented flowers, which looks as good in the ornamental border as it does in the veg garden. You can force this plant for delicous, tender, winter leaves, which are one of my mother's favourite things to eat, with a distinctive, very mild cabbagy flavour, with a hint of bitter overlay.

Propagation From root cuttings or 'thongs'. Sea kale can also be grown from seed, but this is trickier.

Sowing time Early to mid-spring.

Successional sowing No; it's a perennial.

Final planting/thinning distance About 60cm (2ft).

Special growing requirements Patience! Sea kale requires forcing like rhubarb. In the autumn, cut the plant down to a few centimetres and, late in November, cover them. Only plants at least two years old repay forcing, and then they need a year's rest before you can force again, if they recover from the first forcing.

Harvesting In January, cover the crowns with a sea kale forcing pot – or raked leaves or straw about 30cm (12in) deep and a box over the top – and cut the shoots at 15cm (6in).

US hardiness zone 5.

Kohlrabi

This turnip-like root vegetable has a milder flavour than most turnips and is wonderful steamed and then served with meat or fish with dollops of hollandaise.

Variety description Use white varieties like 'Delikatess Witte' for early, and purple 'Delikatess Blauer' for late. The different colours suit different temperatures and do best at these separate times.

Propagation From seed.

Sowing time Sow the white from mid-spring to early summer, and the purple in late summer.

Successional sowing Yes.

Final planting/thinning distance Sow rows 30cm (12in) apart, with seedlings thinned to 15cm (6in).

Special growing requirements They prefer light soil with a high pH. Keep plants well watered in a dry spell to prevent the roots becoming woody and bolting.

Harvesting Roots are best eaten at about the size of a cricket ball. One of the good things about kholrabi is their speed from seed to harvest, which is about ten weeks.

US hardiness zone 4.

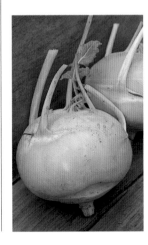

Leeks

Leeks are one of the easiest and hardiest productive plants you can grow. If you select the hardy winter forms, they will be out there for picking right the way through the leanest vegetable months of the year. Leeks are great for soups and make a fantastic winter savoury *tarte tatin*, with rosemary added to the butter and sugar beneath the flaky pastry base. Left to flower – and their seed pods to dry on the stem – they're one of the best ornamental additions to any vegetable patch.

Variety description 'Hannibal' is an excellent autumn/winter type with long, straight, thick, white shafts and dark green leaves. I also always grow 'D'Hiver de Saint-Victor' for the winter garden, an old French variety with a lovely wash of purple over the leaves. It too has long, straight, thick shafts and a good flavour. Interplanting it with kale 'Redbor' makes a wonderful-looking winter vegetable garden combination (see picture, page 162).

Propagation From seed.

Sowing time Early to mid-spring – leek seed germinates at the fairly low temperature of 7°C (44°F). Plant out early to mid-summer to follow early crops such as peas, broad beans or early potatoes. Make seed drills in the garden in spring, 1–2cm (½–¾in) deep and 15cm (6in) apart. Sow fairly thickly, as the thinnings can be used like spring onions for salads. You can also sow inside. I use guttering, sowing seed 2.5cm (1in) apart.

Successional sowing Do a couple of sowings, spaced about one month apart, one for autumn and one to give you a generous winter harvest.

Final planting/thinning distance Thin or transplant seed rows to a plant every 4cm (1½in). When they reach 20cm (8in) high and the thickness of a pencil, dig them up and trim the root to 5cm (2in). Insert each plant into a hole 15cm (6in) deep, made with a dibber, with a plant every 15cm (6in) in rows 30cm (12in) apart for average-sized leeks. The deeper the hole, the longer the blanched stem will be, but ensure some of the leaves are above soil level. Fill the hole with water, not soil.

Special growing requirements For a long white section, draw dry soil around the stems during the summer and autumn, trying not to get the soil in between the leaves. A loo roll tube round the leaves helps to prevent earth getting in. In general, leeks are a trouble-free crop, but they are prone to rust. Plant rotation is important to prevent build-up of the fungus in the soil, but once you have it, there is little you can do. Mildly affected plants are still edible and will stand fine through the winter. Those badly affected must be burnt (not composted). The self-blanching variety 'Titan' is said to have rust resistance.

Harvesting These varieties are for harvesting in autumn, winter and early spring. The flowers and seed pods of leeks look statuesque and impressive in the late spring and summer garden, so leave a few in the ground to flower. The seed is very easy to collect too, although it will not come true if more than one variety flowers nearby at the same time. Pick the browning flowers and hang them upside-down in a cotton bag. All the seed will drop to the bottom.

US hardiness zone 6.

Lettuce
(see Salad leaves, page 221)

Above **Onion 'Sanguigna di Milano'.**
Right **Okra 'Pure Luck'.**
Opposite **Shallot 'Creation'.**

Okra

I like okra, or ladies' fingers, as a vegetable to eat with any hot oriental food in a sort of ratatouille. But it's a tender plant and our climate is not quite hot enough for it. You can grow it in earth beds in a greenhouse or polytunnel, but even with protection it doesn't crop heavily.

Variety description 'Pure Luck', an F1 hybrid, is said to be a vigorous-growing variety of okra, but even this form has not produced much for me.

Propagation From seed.

Sowing time Early spring under cover, maintaining a temperature of 10–15˚C (50–60˚F) during germination and seedling development. I've repeatedly tried to grow okra, but out of ten seedlings germinating, I get left with less than half to plant in the greenhouse, the remainder succumbing to fungal disease.

Successional sowing No.

Final planting/thinning distance Either into 20cm (8in) pots, or 30cm (12in) apart in a greenhouse border.

Special growing requirements Okra grows to 1.2m (4ft) and needs supporting.

Harvesting Pick seed pods when 8cm (3in) long.

US hardiness zone 10 (but grown as an annual).

Onions and shallots

Growing onions and shallots is very easy and they fill the ground over the autumn and winter, when there's less pressure on space. I tend to choose onions with unusual shapes and colours, which are more difficult to buy, and always grow a few shallots. They are oddly expensive to buy, and I like being able to walk outside all through the summer, pulling up a clump that will hang above the cooker and last me for a couple of weeks.

You can grow onions and shallots either from seed or sets (mini onions). Not all varieties are available as sets, so you get a greater choice from seed and, if you're going to grow lots, seed is much cheaper.

Sets are very easy to grow, with a small set turning into a full-sized bulb without any attention from you during the summer. Sets are the immature plants that were raised from seed the previous summer. Because they were sown at very high density, they do not reach sufficient size to bolt. They just carry on growing instead. Sets can be heat-treated by suppliers to kill the flower embryo and so prevent bolting. These tend to

be more expensive, but generally store better.

Variety description One of my favourite onions is 'Rossa Lunga di Firenze', a torpedo-shaped, purple-red bulb with a mild, sweet flavour. These are easy and ideal for scattering, thinly sliced and raw, over a summer tomato salad with lots of parsley or basil, salt and olive oil. I also grow plenty of the sweet Italian variety 'Sanguigna di Milano', which has characteristic flat shoulders at the top of the bulb. It's a huge cropper and slow to bolt, easy to grow, and produces sweet onions. I usually also grow the widely available 'Red Baron' from sets in spring and the yellow 'Radar' for autumn. 'Red Baron' is an excellent red-skinned maincrop variety with high yields and not much of a problem as regards bolting. This stores very well through the winter. I am also very keen on 'Senshyu Yellow', a Japanese variety of early autumn sowing onion, which is easy to grow from seed.

For shallots from sets, I have grown the lovely red 'Delicato', which produced good numbers of sweet bulbs and stored well. From seed, try 'Creation', a high-yielding, yellow-skinned form. There is a move in France to stipulate that shallots grown from seed are a lower form than shallots from dividing bulbs and should be sold under a different name and at a lower price as they are much cheaper to produce. They still taste the same!

Propagation From seed or sets.

Growing from seed You sow most onion and shallot seed in open ground in early spring 1cm (½in) deep in rows 15cm (6in) apart as thinly as possible. I also sow in late winter into guttering using the same spacing. The seed will germinate quickly at 10–15˚C (50–60˚F).

Sow 'Senshyu Yellow' in late summer/early autumn 2.5cm (1in) apart.

Successional sowing No; use alternative, e.g. autumn-sowing types (see above).

Final planting/thinning distance Thin seedlings to 2.5–5cm (1–2in) apart. Onions and shallots are well suited to 'multi-seeding', where you sow six to eight seeds together in an 8cm (3in) pot and do not thin the seedlings. Plant them all out together about 15cm (6in) apart. As the bulbs grow, they push each other apart to make clumps of small, round onions. Final spacing for 'Senshyu Yellow' is 10cm (4in), but wait to thin until the spring.

Growing from sets Plant sets in early to mid-spring, or mid-autumn for an early crop next summer, pushing them gently into the soil so the tips are level with the surface. It's a good idea to cover them with pea sticks or fleece to prevent birds pulling them out. For lots of small bulbs about 5cm (2in) in diameter, plant the sets 2.5cm (1in) apart in rows 15cm (6in) apart. For

larger bulbs 10cm (4in) across, widen the spacing of sets to 10cm (4in).

Special growing requirements The chance of bolting is decreased if you avoid planting in cold, wet soil. They thrive in a sunny, well-drained situation. Both onions and shallots are very susceptible to competition from other plants – usually weeds, so keep your rows weed-free. This is especially important early on. Its also important to move the onion bed around every year to prevent the build-up of diseases like onion white rot (see page 168).

Harvesting 'Senshyu Yellow' is ready in early summer, a full month before other forms. The rest are harvested in mid-summer. The foliage will yellow and fall over naturally. Lift the bulbs with a fork to break the roots and leave them on the soil surface to ripen fully in the sun. In a wet summer, move them to a greenhouse bench to ripen them fully.

US hardiness zone 5.

Ornamental plants for the vegetable garden

There are some non-edible, colourful flowering plants, or ornamental fruiting or podding ones, that are natural partners for vegetables in a productive patch. Like many vegetables, they thrive in an open, sunny position with fertile, free-draining soil. Their presence makes the vegetable garden a lovelier place to be.

Asparagus pea

Description Beautiful, velvety, rich crimson flowers with finger-like vetch leaves. After the flowers come winged pods, which are tasty when eaten small – 3cm (1¼in) long (see picture, page 214).

Propagation From seed.

Sowing time They are half-hardy annuals that do not like root disturbance, so sow them direct into the ground in late spring/early summer.

Final planting/thinning distance 30cm (12in).

Special growing requirements They thrive in full sun in a rich, freely drained soil.

Harvesting Flowers from mid-summer on. You can pick the pods in late summer and autumn.

US hardiness zone 9 (but grown as an annual).

Broad bean – crimson-flowered

Description An old-fashioned, variety with blooms the colour of Rioja. This is the least productive broad bean I've grown, but it looks wonderful.

Propagation From seed.

Sowing time Direct sow in lines, or blocks, straight into the ground from February to May. You can also sow seeds into long, thin pots or root trainers to fill in any gaps in the garden.

Successional sowing Yes. Aim to sow a couple of batches if you want them in the garden for as long as possible.

Final planting/thinning distance Plant seeds 5cm (2in) deep, spaced 20–25cm (8–10in) apart in both directions.

Special growing requirements Easy, hardy plants.

Harvesting Pick these beans young – they become tough with age – from early summer. Dead-heading this ornamental bean just as the pods start to form will prolong its flowering season, but obviously stop any crop.

US hardiness zone 7.

Cup and saucer plant

Description A wonderful tender perennial climber with large, bell-shaped flowers that thrive in similar conditions to veg – a sunny, sheltered spot and a rich, freely drained soil.

Propagation From seed or cuttings from last year's plants.

Sowing time Late winter inside. Sow early so they reach flowering size by mid-summer. If sown late, they may be cut to the ground by frost before they flower.

Successional sowing Not necessary. If you keep picking these, they keep flowering.

Final planting/thinning distance 30cm (12in).

Special growing requirements I have these cladding the walls in the school greenhouse and they look wonderful. They flower solidly from July to November, with a light sprinkling of flowers through winter and into spring. They grow happily outside too, but will be killed by frost.

Harvesting Pick regularly and they will keep flowering.

US hardiness zone 9.

Opposite, top row from left **Asparagus pea, crimson-flowered broad bean and cup and saucer plant.**

Middle row from left **Dahlia 'Happy Romeo', squash 'Turk's Turban' and sweet pea 'Matucana'.**

Bottom row from left **Pumpkin 'Munchkin', pea 'Purple Pod' and zinnia 'Cactus Orange'.**

Dahlia

Description These tender tubers make excellent flowering plants for the vegetable garden. They thrive in similar conditions, loving a sunny, sheltered spot with plenty of manure and water at their roots.

Propagation Seed, division or basal cuttings.

Sowing time Early spring for a few varieties.

Successional sowing No.

Final planting/thinning distance Sizes vary, but many dahlias are large and need to be spaced 1m (3ft) apart.

Special growing requirements Easy, prolific flowering plants. In the north, they will need lifting for the winter and storing cool and dry until the spring. In the south, I mulch mine in 5–10cm (2–4in) of mushroom compost and leave them in the ground.

Harvesting Buckets and buckets of flowers to pick from mid-summer until the first frosts. The petals are actually edible, with some tasting nicer than others.

US hardiness zone 10.

Gourds – ornamental

Description 'Crown of Thorns' is shaped like a medieval goblet in green, cream or yellow. I also grow the fig-leaved gourd purely for ornament. This looks like a water melon and can comfortably reach football size (see picture, page 52). 'Turk's Turban' is another brilliant-coloured variety – good for soup and spectacular growing and arranged in a bowl (see picture, page 151).

Propagation From seed.

Sowing time Sow two seeds to an 8cm (3in) pot, 1cm (½in) deep, placing them vertically in late spring. If you sow these

large seeds flat, they may rot off before they germinate. Once the plants have their first pair of leaves, remove the weakest-looking seedling. They don't like any root disturbance and, sown like this, they won't need pricking out, but potting them on once is a good idea. When the roots have filled their second pot, and they have three pairs of leaves, plant them out, but you'll need to wait until the beginning of June.

Successional sowing No.

Final planting/thinning distance These varieties are tremendous sprawlers and climbers that will grow and cover a 3m (10ft) frame. Space plants 30cm (12in) apart with at least one vertical support per plant.

Special growing requirements Prolonged low temperatures, even without frost, will damage seedlings. Choose your seedlings a sheltered spot. The wind can cause havoc with their huge leaves. Leave the fruit to ripen on the vine as long as you dare in the autumn.

Harvesting Autumn for arranging and storing through autumn and winter. Fig-leaved gourd will store for three to four years without rotting. After harvesting, continue ripening them somewhere bright but cool for a further ten days.

US hardiness zone 10 (but grown as an annual).

Lablab purpureus

Description *Lablab purpureus* (formerly *Dolichos lablab*) has beautiful, large, crimson-purple bean pods that follow purple-coloured, black-stemmed flowers on strongly growing climbers.

Propagation From seed.

Sowing time They are half-hardy annuals, which can be difficult to germinate in our cool climate,

but it is certainly worth a go. Sow them in early spring with some heat. If you get plants going early under cover, you should have them producing plenty of pods from late summer on.

Final planting/thinning distance 15cm (6in).

Special growing requirements They thrive in full sun in a rich, freely drained soil.

Harvesting The pods are highly ornamental and can be picked for bowls inside. Most lablab seed is grown in North Africa, and seeds are being naturally selected for a much warmer climate than ours. Try to collect your own seeds from year to year – you'll be more likely to succeed with germination.

US hardiness zone 10 (but grown as an annual).

Pea – 'Purple Pod'

Description A beautiful, purple-flowered, purple-podded pea that is good when eaten small. But it's really there to make the garden look lovely, rather than to produce a heavy crop. Height 1.8m (6ft). This is in fact what is called a *pois gris* (grey pea), grown to be used dried. The tips are as tasty as those of any pea, but the green shelling peas are sugar-free and rather nasty.

Propagation From seed.

Sowing time Mid-spring to mid-summer. Sow 5cm (2in) deep in 15cm- (6in-) wide zig-zag trenches, seed 8cm (3in) apart.

Successional sowing Yes.

Final planting/thinning distance Grow them on a teepee, or sow them in pots and plant them out with sweet peas.

Special growing requirements Never sow peas in cold, wet conditions. With their large

seeds, they rot easily. Protect against mice at the seed and seedling stages. Peas thrive in fertile soils and will need support.

Harvesting Mid-summer on.

US hardiness zone 7.

Pumpkin 'Munchkin'

Description Similar to 'Jack Be Little', this is a pretty, miniature, orange-skinned pumpkin, only 8cm (3in) across, ideal for adding colour to the late summer and autumn vegetable garden (see picture, page 172). With very sweet flesh, it's good for baking or roasting. Once cooked, its flesh becomes sticky in texture. You can also stuff and then steam or boil it for five minutes. The skin is thin enough to eat the fruit whole.

Propagation From seed.

Sowing time Mid- to late spring inside, or straight into the garden in early summer.

Successional sowing No.

Final planting/thinning distance This is a trailing type, ideal for covering teepees and frames after your sweet peas have gone over. Plant one plant at the base of every other upright.

Special growing requirements These are best grown in a sheltered spot, so the wind doesn't rip the large leaves.

Harvesting Time to maturity: 85 days.

US hardiness zone 10 (but grown as an annual).

Sweet pea

Description These highly scented climbers are another ideal ornamental, non-edible plant for the vegetable garden (see picture, page 156). They thrive in ground with lots of organic material added. The strongest

perfumed varieties are 'Painted Lady' and 'Matucana'.

Propagation From seed.

Sowing time Autumn or early spring.

Successional sowing As above.

Final planting/thinning distance 15cm (6in) apart at the bottom of a frame.

Special growing requirements These vigorous climbers need regular tying in to a frame. Keep picking the flowers so they don't run to seed.

Harvesting Pick their highly scented flowers from late spring until mid-summer.

US hardiness zone 6.

Zinnia

Description Flamboyant, ornamental, non-edible flowers that thrive in similar conditions to veg – a sunny, sheltered spot and a rich, freely drained soil.

Propagation From seed.

Sowing time Mid-spring inside, or outside from late spring on.

Successional sowing Not necessary. If you keep picking these, they keep flowering.

Final planting/thinning distance 30cm (12in).

Special growing requirements They don't like root disturbance, so sow into modules or Jiffy 7s or direct where they are to flower. Don't sow them too early, as they are prone to fungal diseases if sown when light levels are low and nights are cold. Slugs and snails love them!

Harvesting Keep picking these regularly and they will flower for twice as long, from mid-summer until the first frosts.

US hardiness zone 10 (but grown as an annual).

Parsnips

Parsnips are an easy winter crop. You sow them in the spring and simply leave them in the ground until you want to eat some during the winter. They need very little attention, but do take up space for a long period before reaching cropping size. If you have a restriction on space, these may be vegetables to buy.

Variety description Select a modern variety with good resistance to canker such as 'Gladiator', an F1 hybrid and a very vigorous parsnip with good flavour. It grows more quickly than most, with a smooth skin. 'Avonresister' is shorter-rooted and is a good choice for stony, heavy or compacted soil. This is the one I grow on my heavy clay.

Propagation From seed.

Sowing time Sow from early spring inside into guttering, or outside in mid- to late spring. Don't sow if the soil is still cold and wet, as parsnip seed is slow to germinate and will rot before it does if conditions aren't right. Wait until conditions improve. Sow a quick-growing crop like radish in the same drills as a marker. The radishes will be out of the way and eaten before the parsnips need the space.

Successional sowing No.

Final planting/thinning distance Sow three seeds per station, at 15cm (6in) intervals for most, but 20cm (8in) for 'Avonresister', with 30cm (12in) between the rows. Once they've germinated, remove the weaker plants.

Special growing requirements Parsnips do best on deeply dug, fertile soil with a mildly acid pH of about 6.5. Ideally they should follow a previous crop that has been well manured rather than going into soil that has just had manure added. Parsnip seed loses its viability more quickly than other seed, so buy it fresh each year. Parsnips can sometimes be attacked by carrot fly.

Harvesting Autumn and winter, once the tops have died off. They can be left in the ground, where they will stay in good condition until spring, and the flavour is said to improve with frost. In very cold areas, cover the row with straw to stop the ground freezing solid. Parsnip flowers are beautiful, golden-green, dill-like umbellifers that appear in early summer, and the seed pods are loved by goldfinches. I leave some plants unharvested to give colour and height to the late spring and early summer garden.

US hardiness zone 5.

Peas

Home-grown, just-picked peas are one of the most triumphantly delicious vegetables you can produce from your patch. They bear little resemblance to the starchy things, harvested several days or perhaps over a week earlier, that you buy frozen or at the greengrocer's. You really have to make room for at least one or two rows of peas.

Variety description 'Hurst Green Shaft' is my favourite sweet-tasting, wrinkle-seeded variety, with some resistance to powdery and downy mildew (see page 25). It's a heavy-cropping, so-called 'second early', mid-season form that matures over a long period, so is excellent if you want to sow only one lot in the spring. It grows to 1m (3ft). 'Feltham First' is a very hardy pea and one of the tastiest round-seeded forms, with large, well-filled pods. It's the one I use for autumn sowing. Height 45cm (18in). For picking several weeks earlier than any spring-sown.

Getting away from the usual shelling peas, I also love sugarsnap, an edible-podded variety that is very sweet and slow to form strings (see picture, page 64). You can either pick it young and eat the whole thing or allow it to grow on and then shell the peas as normal. This is also an excellent quick-growing form to use for pea tips, the neat, succulent growth tips of an edible pea (see picture, page 65). All peas form them, but the quick-growing, tall and prolific mange-touts and sugarsnap types produce most of all. To get them at their tenderest, pick them before the tendrils start to unfurl. Height 1.8m (6ft).

Propagation From seed.

Sowing time
Peas 'Hurst Green Shaft' and sugarsnaps should be sown in mid-spring on freely drained soil.

'Feltham First' is hardier than most so can be sown in the autumn and early spring. Sow 5cm (2in) deep in 15cm- (6in-) wide zig-zag trenches, with seed 8cm (3in) apart. Peas have large seeds and so are likely to rot if the soil is still cold and wet. On my clay, I therefore sow my early peas into compost in guttering under cover in a double zig-zag line (spaced as above). Once the seedlings reach about 5cm (2in), plant them out (see page 22).

Pea tips Can be sown any time in the year, even in the winter if you have a warm place in bright light. I sow my pea tips in deep trays – wooden or plastic vegetable boxes or polystyrene fish crates work well – with holes made in the bottom for drainage. Fill the trays with at least 25cm (10in) of multi-purpose potting compost and sow the pea seeds closely. Water well and you should have seedlings emerging in one to two weeks. Leave them until they grow to 5cm (2in) tall and start harvesting. For a seamless supply, regular sowing once a month or so is important with these. No thinning is required.

Successional sowing Yes. Taller varieties will crop over a longer period than the shorter forms. It's a good idea to do several sowings of the smaller forms throughout the summer, or make one sowing of an early (e.g. 'Feltham First') and one of a maincrop (e.g. 'Hurst Green Shaft').

Final planting/thinning distance The distance between the rows should be equal to the expected height (see above).

Special growing requirements Peas thrive in fertile soils with plenty of organic material added. On poor soil, it's worth preparing a trench over the winter and filling it with a mixture of soil and well-rotted organic material.

Don't manure immediately before planting, as this will encourage lush leaf growth at the expense of pods.

All tall peas will need support. I use twiggy silver birch or hazel, but you can also get pea netting from garden centres. It looks less nice but does the job, stretched tightly and vertically along the row.

Protect against mice at the seed and seedling stages. Mice love peas! And never sow peas in cold, wet conditions. With their large seeds, they rot easily.

Pea and bean weevils may nibble semicircular notches out of young leaves in spring. They rarely cause a problem, whereas pea moth and its grub can be a pain. They burrow through the pod into the peas. The simplest way to avoid this pest is to concentrate on sowing early and late. The moth lays its eggs on pea flowers during June and July. Early spring crops will flower in May and early June, and lates will flower after July, so both will escape!

Harvesting
Fully grown peas Late spring onwards for 'Feltham First' sown the previous autumn, and throughout the summer for 'Hurst Green Shaft'. You can harvest sugarsnaps from mid-summer on for pods and then shelling peas.

Leaving pods on the plants for too long will shorten the cropping season.

Pea tips By picking pea tips heavily, you will decrease the harvest of mature peas you've sown in the garden, so either pick lightly at their early and most active stage of growth, or do several special sowings of peas to crop for their tips (see above). For picking pea tips, harvest at about 5cm (2in) tall, within three to four weeks of sowing. Slice the tips off about 2.5cm (1in) above the soil. You'll get three or four cuts from one batch in a box.

When any pea crop is finished, cut the tops off the plants at ground level. Leave the roots with their nodules to fertilize the next crop.

US hardiness zone 7.

Opposite **Parsnip 'Gladiator'.**
Above **Mangetout peas.**
Right **Chilli 'Hungarian Yellow Wax Hot'.**

Peppers

Peppers come in hot (chilli) and sweet forms. It was surprising to me that sweet peppers, like peas, taste three times better and are many times sweeter when they're home-grown. They are also very ornamental in the greenhouse or against a sunny wall, and are worth growing for their brilliant-coloured fruits alone.

With the hot varieties, I use them fresh and to make chilli oil for pepping up food in the winter.

Variety description

Hot 'Hungarian Yellow Wax Hot' (aka 'Hot Banana' – see picture, page 60) is an incredibly versatile pepper that can be eaten young and very mild, or left to mature and develop heat. It is hugely prolific. 'Filius Blue' is a very beautiful chilli with almost black leaves and purple, exceptionally hot fruit, ripening to orange with milder heat (see picture, page 61).

Sweet My favourite of all sweet peppers is 'Marconi Rosso'. It's two or three times more prolific than other quite large-fruited varieties I've tried. Its fruits are long and thin – the shape of a horn – and it has a lovely, crunchy texture and a sweet taste. F1 hybrid 'Jingle Bells' or 'Mini Bell' is another very

Potatoes

worthwhile form. It's a very prolific miniature bell variety in yellow-orange, in a perfect eat-in-one-bite size. This is ideal for eating whole in a late summer garden mixed tempura.

Propagation From seed.

Sowing time Late winter, with temperatures of 15–21˚C (60–70˚F). I sow two seeds into a Jiffy 7 pellet or small pot. If both germinate, remove one.

Successional sowing No.

Final planting/thinning distance 23cm (9in), in 2-litre pots in mid-spring and on into 5-litre pots by early summer.

Special growing requirements Most grow best indoors with high levels of humidity and good ventilation. When the plants reach 20cm (8in) high, pinch out the tips to encourage more side shoots and hence more peppers. Also remove the first fruit that forms, to encourage more. Feed regularly with high-potash tomato feed once the fruits start to form. Sweet peppers have heavier fruit and may need some support. Hot peppers should be fine without.

Harvesting From late summer almost until Christmas. You can dry chillies and freeze them. For drying, choose the long, slim types, drying them overnight in your oven on its lowest possible setting. It's the chemical capsaicin concentrated in the seeds and flesh around them that is responsible for the heat. If you remove these before using the chillies, you have a much milder fruit. Milk or yoghurt, not water, are the best antidotes to the heat.

US hardiness zone 10 (but grown as an annual).

Earlies All early potatoes are best home-grown. They taste much better eaten straight from the garden, as their flavour disappears fast once they've been dug up.

The first early group is the first to plant and crop. These varieties are hardier than most and tend to produce potatoes that won't store well, dehydrating (wrinkling) and turning green quickly however you store them. Second earlies share many of the characteristics of the first earlies, but they are slightly later to crop.

Maincrops are later to plant and produce their crop. They tend to be good storers, happily sitting in the cool and dark for several months before deteriorating.

You also distinguish potato types according to their texture. Waxy-fleshed potatoes are best boiled and used in salad. Floury types are good for mashing, baking and chips.

First earlies

Variety description 'International Kidney' is my favourite first early, with excellent flavour, waxy texture and good productivity. This is the variety better known as 'Jersey Royal'. 'Winston' is another very early, high-yielding form, with delicious waxy flesh. This has the RHS Award of Garden Merit and is a very useful form. You can eat it young and small, or leave it in the ground to grow – it develops into a large potato and is then perfect for baking. It also has good disease resistance and medium productivity.

'BF15' is another first early variety with a lovely yellow skin and light, waxy flesh (see picture, page 34). This is a very popular choice with foodies – I first came

across it in Raymond Blanc's hotel kitchen garden.

'Dunluce' (see picture, page 33) and 'Swift' are the final first earlies that I grow. 'Dunluce' is a heavy cropper with an excellent flavour and 'Swift' is a round, white potato with fine skin, good disease resistance and medium productivity, but the outstanding thing about this one is that it matures in about 70 days and is a very compact plant, ideal for growing in pots, under polythene or in cold frames. We grow lots of these for early forcing, so we have potatoes to eat from the middle of May, about a month before the others in the open garden are ready.

Second earlies

Variety description 'Charlotte' is a French second early variety. It forms one of the biggest salad potatoes, with excellent flavour. It has been awarded the RHS Award of Garden Merit but has lower yield than the others mentioned.

Propagation From tender tubers.

Planting time
Summer potatoes Plant these in mid-spring after chitting in late winter. Chitting (see picture, page 33) encourages the tubers to sprout and gains a few precious weeks while the soil is too cold for them to grow outside. To do this stand them in trays, 'rose' end up – the end with the greatest concentration

of eyes – in a cool, dry place with good light, but not direct sunlight. Rub off all but four of the strongest sprouts at the rose end before planting. If you leave them on, you will grow lots and lots of very small potatoes. To plant, take out a trench about 25cm (10in) deep and 30cm (12in) wide. Dig in manure to the bottom, forking it over well, and plant the tubers about 40cm (15in) apart. Refill the trench so that the tubers are about 15cm (6in) deep, leaving any surplus soil for earthing up later.

Spring potatoes Use a quick-growing early form like 'Swift' or 'International Kidney' and plant one tuber in compost bags or at least 10-litre pots in early spring. (If using bags, empty them first and turn inside out – with black plastic now on the outside – to conserve the heat.) Three-quarters fill the containers with compost (molehills are another good addition if you have any) and plant one sprouted tuber in each, so that it's covered with compost. Put them somewhere light and cool. Bottom heat will force them into growth sooner. As the plants grow, keep adding more compost so as just to cover the growing tips, adding compost until it almost reaches the rim. Keep the containers moist but not too wet and leave the plants to grow more and flower. The flowers are the sign that tubers are starting to form. At the beginning of the season try to rummage around gently at the edges to harvest what you need, leaving the plants to grow on and produce more. When the tops begin to die down, tip out the containers and collect the tubers.

Autumn potatoes When you plant your earlies in spring, hold some back. Store these somewhere cool and dry, but with good light. They will start to sprout. In early June, plant each tuber individually

in a 15cm (6in) pot and keep it well watered outside. The tubers, though shrivelled, will burst into life. From late June onwards, when you have space in the garden, plant the contents of the pots, burying the base of the shoots as well as the roots. Cover them with straw in November and December and harvest straight from the garden.

Sweet potatoes such as 'Beauregard' can be grown like potatoes, but they're more tender and will crop well only with the protection of a polytunnel. I've grown them outside in the garden and the crop has been very small. Our frosts cut them down too early for the tubers to swell to a decent size.

Successional sowing
Plant earlies and maincrops in succession.

Final planting/thinning distance
Earlies make smaller plants than maincrops, so space them 40cm (15in) apart with 45cm (18in) between the rows.

Special growing requirements
When the first shoots appear, start to draw the earth from between the rows up over the centre to cover them. Earthing encourages underground shoots and hence more tubers. It also prevents tubers pushing above the surface and turning green and protects plants from frost

and blight. In dry weather, water earlies thoroughly once a week.

Harvesting You harvest earlies when they finish flowering, before the haulms have died back. For 'International Kidney', 'Swift' and 'Winston' this is in June/July. For the others it's July or August.

Maincrops

Variety description My favourite maincrop is 'Pink Fir Apple', which has fantastic flavour and texture, and is good eaten in salads, just straight boiled or sautéd in a slurp of olive oil. This is an old English, pink-skinned late potato with a very irregular shape. Because it's late to harvest it's prone to blight, which can be a major problem with the later cropping forms.

'La Ratte' and the similar 'Belle de Fontenay' (see picture, page 30) are old French early maincrops with a nutty flavour. They are a salad potato and not quite as tasty as 'Pink Fir Apple', but easier to grow because they mature before the worst of the blight. They're also good for boiling, making dauphinoise and any dish that requires a potato that won't disintegrate. Flavour improves with storage, so they are useful through the winter.

'Santé' is a very good potato for organic growers, as it has

excellent resistance to slugs and eelworm, and it's not susceptible to blight. It's a good boiler and roaster with mild, creamy flesh.

'Highland Burgundy Red' and 'Salad Blue' are both unusual-coloured late maincrops (see picture, page 31). Use them to make multi-coloured chips (see picture, page 10).

Propagation From tender tubers.

Planting time Mid- to late April.

Successional sowing
Plant earlies and maincrops in succession.

Final planting/thinning distance
Space the tubers 45cm (18in) apart with 60cm (2ft) between the rows.

Special growing requirements
Water maincrops when they flower, not before or they'll form lots of leaf at the expense of root.

Harvesting August for immediate use, but potatoes for storage should be harvested in September or early October when the plants have died down completely. 'Pink Fir Apple' matures late and so can be badly affected by blight. 'La Ratte' and 'Belle de Fontenay' mature before the worst of blight in the autumn.

US hardiness zone 10.

Pumpkins and squash

There are bush and trailing varieties. Go for bush types if you're short of space. In our cooler climate, it is also advisable to select varieties that fruit early. The fruit needs time to enlarge and ripen before frosts are forecast and you have to bring them inside. In the sun, the skin ripens and hardens. With this leathery exterior, they'll store for months without rot setting in.

Variety description My favourite pumpkin is 'Uchiki Kuri' (also called 'Red Kuri' and onion squash – see picture, page 162), for its delicious, waxy, nutty-tasting, deep orange flesh and high production of fruits perfectly sized for eating in one meal.

I also love butternut squash, with its dense, waxy texture and sweet flesh, but many varieties of butternut need a longer growing season than we can give them in the UK. I have had success with 'Early Butternut', which is quick to mature in about 85 days. It's a typical bell-shaped squash with beige skin and a tight, flavoursome, slightly nutty flavour, but it's not prolific in its production of fruit. It is, however, an excellent storer.

'Blue Ballet', a so-called Hubbard squash, is a small and more usable version of the famous 'Blue Hubbard', widely held to be the most delicious squash you can grow. 'Blue Ballet' produces 1.75kg (4lb), blue-grey fruits, with fibre-less, orange flesh and is very popular in America. It's also a first-class storer.

'Buttercup' is another excellent one, which is very fast-growing with firm, dense flesh and a sweet flavour – golden, fluffy and delicious. It has dark green skin, with lighter stripes, and deep orange, fibreless flesh with an oily texture. This is superb baked, roasted, mashed, deep-fried for squash chips, or used in a risotto. 'Buttercup' is quicker than most, with time to maturity of about 90 days and the average fruit weighing 1–2kg (2¼–4½lb). It keeps well.

'Atlantic Giant' (see pictures, pages 54 and 57) is a vast pumpkin – the variety you want to choose for the giant pumpkin competition. Each plant may produce only three or four fruits, but they're worth it. I was recently sent a photograph of a monster specimen of this variety hollowed out and used with a paddle in a children's boat race.

At the other end of the size scale is gem squash, which is prolific and produces baskets and baskets of small, round, dark green fruit a little bigger than a cricket ball. I first ate these in southern Africa, where they are on every market stall. I brought home some seed and they've grown here brilliantly every year since. The good thing about this variety is that they taste delicious, and have an ideal size for one fruit per meal per person. Bake or boil them whole and scrape out the flesh, or eat it straight from the skin.

The final one worth mentioning is 'Jack o'Lantern', the traditional Halloween pumpkin, with orange skin and flesh. It will grow to 4.5–6.75kg (10–15lb), so it's not a mammoth. This is ideal for lanterns and soup served in the shell, but there are better-textured and -flavoured varieties. If you make a lantern, remember to line the hollowed flesh with tin foil, so it doesn't cook in the heat of the candle flame. If you then keep the carved fruit cool, storing them outside at night, they'll last over a week before rot sets in. Their time to maturity is about 100 days and they are not great storers.

Propagation From seed.

Sowing time Sow two seeds to an 8cm (3in) pot, 1cm (½in) deep,

placing them vertically in late spring. If you sow these large seeds flat, they may rot off before germinating. Once the plants have their first pair of leaves, remove the weakest-looking seedling. They don't like any root disturbance, and sown like this they won't need pricking out, but potting them on once is a good idea.

When the roots have filled their second pot, and they have three pairs of leaves, plant them out, but you'll need to wait until the beginning of June.

If you garden in the south, you can sow squash direct into the ground outside. The key thing with direct sowing is warm soil. These plants will not germinate if the soil is below 13°C (55°F) and they prefer it warmer than this. If you're sowing straight into the garden, wait until early June. Sowing this late outside, it's only in the south with its longer growing season that you'll get any chance of fruit at the end of the season.

Dig out a hole at least 30–45cm (12–18in) square, fill with well-rotted manure and cloche the soil for a week before you sow. This will warm the soil up more quickly. Make a mound above

the manure and sow two seeds 2.5cm (1in) deep in the centre of the mound. Cover again with a cloche or horticultural fleece. Wait for the seedlings to appear and remove the weaker-looking plant. After a couple of weeks, remove the cover.

Successional sowing No.

Final planting/thinning distance Many pumpkins and squash are tremendous sprawlers – they will spread a metre or so in each direction. Space them 1.2m (4ft) apart with 1.8m (6ft) between rows.

Special growing requirements Prolonged low temperatures will damage seedlings, even without frost, and the longer the period of cold, the worse the harm. Choose your seedlings a sheltered spot. The wind can also cause havoc with their huge leaves.

Harvesting You harvest pumpkins and squash in the autumn. Leave the fruit to ripen on the vine as long as you dare in the autumn, laying the fruit on a tile to protect it from rot on damp soil. After harvesting, ripen them somewhere bright but cool for a further ten days.

US hardiness zone 10 (but grown as an annual).

Radish

Radish are generous, quick and easy plants to grow. You can sow them straight into the ground or into guttering inside and be eating the swollen roots in three to four weeks' time. The best way to eat them is from a big bowl in the middle of the table with a pot of Maldon salt and some good, sweet butter by your side – treat each radish to a smear of butter and a sprinkle of salt.

There are some amazing-looking long-taproot radish – which can be grown as a winter crop – and I have grown rat's-tail radish, where you eat the strong-tasting pods rather than the roots, but the usual mini roots remain my favourites.

Variety description The three radishes I grow are 'French Breakfast', with long, pink-red roots with white tips, 'Cherry Belle', which forms perfect, red-pink globes (both are quick-growing and remain crisp and dense over a long time), and 'Sparkler' (see picture, page 175), which stays crunchy to a big size.

Propagation From seed.

Sowing time Sow straight into the ground from early spring until mid-summer. Sow thinly, 2.5cm (1in) apart in rows spaced at 15cm (6in).

Successional sowing Yes, every couple of weeks to guarantee a regular supply.

Final planting/thinning distance No need to thin.

Special growing requirements Flea beetle can be a pain (see page 168). If it's a problem, grow them under horticultural fleece.

Harvesting Within three to four weeks of sowing – the quickest veg from seed to harvest that you can grow. When you pull them up, don't forget that the leaves make a delicious salad too.

US hardiness zone 6.

Salad leaves and lettuce

Continental loose-leaf lettuce and salad leaves are the most-picked plants in my garden. There is hardly a day in the year when I don't pick at least a bowlful to eat. They're easy, hugely prolific, tasty and beautiful. You can want no more of a productive plant!

The important thing with cut-and-come-again salad leaves, is that you grow the right plant for the right season. There are some that like it cold and dark, and others that need bright sunshine. If you go for a plant in the wrong season, it won't perform.

When you're choosing what to sow, select a variety of flavours, textures and colours, so you're able to make a beautiful, tasty salad any week of the year.

All-year salad leaf crop

The tolerant group of plants that grow well outside from spring to autumn, as well as growing slowly in the garden, or better still under cover, all winter. Direct sow them in lines, or blocks, straight into the ground from April to early September. You can sow them under cover, cloches or mini-polytunnels a month to six weeks before or after these dates, depending upon where you are in the country and how mild the weather is. In those periods I sow them into guttering (see page 98).

These are the mainstay for autumn, winter and early spring salad, but they're excellent at any time of year. For winter picking, one sowing in August/September will see you through. In the spring and summer – as with all these plants – serial sowing is the key (see pictures, pages 26–7).

Opposite '**Early Butternut**' **squash.** Right **Mibuna.** Above right **Mizuna.**

Chard – multi-coloured

Description Cut-and-come-again leaves of deep green, with stems bright red, tangerine, yellow and cream. The varieties 'Rainbow' and 'Bright Lights' are amazing sights in the garden and brilliant-coloured additions to a salad bowl. The young leaves are good eaten raw. Larger leaves should be cooked like spinach, or finely sliced or shredded and added to a colourful winter risotto. Leaf height reaches 15–20cm (6–8in) but, for eating raw in salad, try to pick them at half this size. Flavour – mild and earthy. Texture – robust.

Propagation From seed.

Sowing time Slower to germinate and grow than other salad leaves, so don't leave sowing too late in autumn or you won't get a crop that year. It's easy to give up on trays or lines of this newly sown in the garden. Other things are up and away and there's still no sign. Hang in there – germination can take three times as long as rocket.

Successional sowing Two or three times a year.

Final planting/thinning distance 10–15cm (4–6in) if growing as cut-and-come-again leaf; 30cm (12in) if you want the whole plant for spinach-like leaves.

Special growing requirements Very easy to grow – hardy and slow to bolt. Chard thrives in soil following a crop like potatoes that has had manure added.

Harvesting Ten to twelve weeks from sowing, i.e. slower than most. Leaf production for four to six months – one of the longest-producing salad leaves you can grow.

US hardiness zone 5.

Mibuna

Description Hardy annual. Oriental salad and stir-fry type of cut-and-come-again leaf, very like the more famous mizuna. It has a similar mild but very characteristic flavour, a cross between peppery rocket and cabbage, but has smooth-edged leaves about 15cm (6in) long,

Propagation From seed.

Sowing time March until September.

Successional sowing Yes – every couple of months during this time.

Final planting/thinning distance 10cm (4in) if growing as cut-and-come-again leaf; 23cm (9in) if you want whole plants for stir-fries.

Special growing requirements Very easy – it's very hardy, quick to produce and slow to bolt. It will need protecting against flea beetle in the spring and maybe in the summer too (see page 168).

Harvesting Six weeks from sowing, depending on the time of year. Leaf production for two to three months – less in the heat of summer, when it will bolt if not kept well picked.

US hardiness zone 7.

Mizuna

Description Hardy annual. Oriental salad and stir-fry type of cut-and-come-again leaf. A very productive salad plant with jagged, deep green leaves. The great thing about this plant is that it doesn't become too hot and strong, like rocket, even when mature. Leaf height 15–20cm (6–8in), but try to pick them at half this size. It has a mild but very characteristic flavour, a cross between peppery rocket and cabbage.

Propagation As for mibuna (see left).

Sowing time As for mibuna (see left).

Successional sowing As for mibuna (see left).

Final planting/thinning distance As for mibuna (see left).

Special growing requirements As for mibuna (see left).

Harvesting As for mibuna (see left).

US hardiness zone 7.

Opposite, top row from left **Pak choi, 'Red Russian' kale and buckler-leaved sorrel.**

Middle row, from left **'Red Giant' mustard, red orach and 'Bull's Blood' beetroot.**

Bottom row, from left *Chenopodium giganteum*, **edible chrysanthemum and summer purslane.**

Pak choi

Description Hardy annual (it will tolerate light frost). Oriental salad and stir-fry, cut-and-come-again leaf which is delcious raw or cooked. It has smooth-edged, rounded leaves about 8cm (3in) long, with prominent, white stems and a mild cabbagy flavour. Tat soi is a similar-looking and tasting leaf that is slightly hardier for winter outside growing.

Propagation From seed.

Sowing time March until September.

Successional sowing Yes – every couple of months during this time.

Final planting/thinning distance 10cm (4in) if growing as cut-and-come-again leaf; 23cm (9in) if you want whole plants for stir-fries.

Special growing requirements Very easy – hardy, quick to produce and slow to bolt. It will need protecting against flea beetle in the spring and maybe in the summer too (see page 168), and will need to be grown with a little protection in the coldest winter spells. A mini-polytunnel is ideal.

Harvesting Six weeks from sowing, depending on the time of year. Leaf production two to three months – less in the heat of the summer, when it will bolt if not kept well picked.

US hardiness zone 9.

'Red Giant' mustard

Description Hardy annual. Another oriental salad and stir-fry type of cut-and-come-again leaf. It has a pretty, red-veined, crimson leaf, and is a productive, fast-growing salad plant. In cool weather the red colouring is at its deepest. Leaf height 15–20cm (6–8in), but try to pick them at half, or better still one-third, of this size. Otherwise the leaves can take your head off like very strong mustard, and the texture is better when they're small – the size of a plum is ideal. With its hot, mustard flavour and soft texture, this is one of the strongest, punchiest plants, excellent when added to any salad – and superb if a few leaves are added to a roast beef sandwich!

New to me this year is another type of mustard – 'Komatsuna' or spinach brassica (see page 95). Its taste is milder than 'Red Giant' but still mustardy, and it has a crunchier, more lettuce-like, water-filled texture. It's as hardy a leaf as any I've tried.

Propagation From seed.

Sowing time March until September.

Successional sowing Yes – every couple of months during this time.

Final planting/thinning distance 10cm (4in) if growing as cut-and-come-again leaf; 30cm (12in) if you want whole plants for stir-fries.

Special growing requirements Very easy to grow – hardy, quick to produce and moderately slow to bolt. It will need protecting against flea beetle in the spring and summer (see page 168).

Harvesting Six to eight weeks from sowing. Leaf production for three months. Best as a baby leaf – a bit coarse later on. When leaves are large, it's best used in a stir-fry or is delicious in soups. Just whizz it up with a tin of coconut milk.

US hardiness zone 7.

'Red Russian' kale

Description Hardy annual. This is a beautiful plant with silver-green leaves and red-purple stems and veins that is also good to eat. Leaf height 15–20cm (6–8in), but try to pick them at one-third to half of this size. It has a mild, cabbagy flavour and robust texture. The leaves become tougher as they increase in size, and although still very tasty, will need cooking.

Propagation From seed.

Sowing time March until September.

Successional sowing Yes – every couple of months during this time.

Final planting/thinning distance 10cm (4in) if growing as cut-and-come-again leaf; 45cm (18in) if you want whole plants for stir-fries or as all-year greens.

Special growing requirements Very easy – hardy, quick to produce and one of the slowest to bolt. It needs protecting against cabbage white butterflies and flea beetle in the summer (see page 168).

Harvesting Six weeks from sowing. Leaf production for six months plus – the longest I know. You can use larger leaves whole, steamed as a vegetable, or chopped finely in a stir-fry. They have a strong, delicious kale flavour, perfect with soy sauce.

Sorrel – buckler-leaved

Description Hardy perennial. Delicious, sharp little shield-shaped leaves. I prefer *Rumex scutatus*, buckler-leaved sorrel, to the ordinary sorrel *R. acetosa* (see page 207). The latter can become fibrous in texture to eat except when young, but is more prolific. If you love sorrel, grow both. It's the most lemony-tasting leaf you'll find and, with *R. scutatus*, the texture is soft and not stringy. It has a strong flavour, so don't pick too many for a salad, but they make an excellent sharp addition to a mix of leaves.

Propagation From seed or division.

Sowing time Sow under cover any time in spring, and then plant out in sun or light shade. You can propagate by division in the autumn or the following spring.

Successional sowing A couple of times a year between April and September outside, or a month before or after into guttering.

Final planting/thinning distance 15cm (6in).

Special growing requirements Very easy. In fact a short-lived perennial plant, but this form of sorrel is best treated as an annual. Plants will try to flower. Keep picking and cut back flowering stems as soon as they form.

Harvesting Six to eight weeks from sowing. Leaf production for three months.

US hardiness zone 3.

Rocket – wild

Description Short-lived perennial. A slower-growing, more prostrate plant, with leaves more finely cut and a stronger flavour than conventional salad rocket (see page 226). It's also slower to bolt in heat, so more suitable for summer growth. As a perennial, it keeps producing some leaves all winter if in a sheltered spot or grown under cover. Height 10cm (4in).

Propagation From seed.

Sowing time March until September.

Spring-sowing salad
leaves for late spring
summer picking

As well as trying some of the plants on pages 221–2 that can be sown all year, sow a few from this section in mid-spring. All these plants thrive in warm conditions, with good light levels. They are hardy, but will not continue to grow in the winter months. Each one can be direct sown from April to July, in lines or blocks, straight into the ground, or sow them a month to six weeks earlier under cover for an early harvest. I recommend at least two, possibly three sowings to provide salad from May until September.

Beetroot leaves

The beetroot varieties 'Globe 2' and 'Bull's Blood' have delicious leaves (and roots) when eaten very small. Harvest the leaves regularly as a cut-and-come-again crop for salad, and then thin and leave some to grow on for roots.

Propagation From seed.

Sowing time This shouldn't be sown until the second half of May or it may bolt.

Successional sowing Yes, particularly if you like adding beetroot-flavoured leaves to your salads.

Final planting/thinning distance Because beetroot are cluster-seeded – several seeds together in a lump – you need to sow them widely spaced, at 10cm (4in) intervals in 2.5cm (1in) drills. Space lines 30cm (12in) apart.

Special growing requirements Soak the beetroot seed in warm water for half an hour. Some beetroot contain a natural germination inhibitor that slows or prevents germination. You need to wash this off before you sow. Beetroot do well on most soils, but do best in well-manured ground in full sun.

Harvesting For leaf crop, harvest within six weeks. The roots won't have filled out properly for another six.

US hardiness zone 5.

Garland chrysanthemum (or chop suey greens or shungiku)

Description Garland chrysanthemum (*Glebionis coronaria*) has dark green leaves, cut around the edges. If allowed to flower, it has pretty, single blooms, yellow, usually tipped white, the petals of which (not the middles) are edible too. Plants can reach 1m (3ft). Young leaves can be eaten raw and larger leaves cooked like spinach, with a soft texture and fragrant, chrysanthemum flower taste.

Propagation From seed.

Sowing time Mid-spring to late summer straight into the garden or into guttering inside.

Successional sowing Do two or three sowings in the year.

Final planting/thinning distance 10cm (4in).

Special growing requirements Very easy.

Harvesting Six to eight weeks from sowing. Leaf production for three months – a good long producer. This summer salad crop will withstand a few light frosts, so can start earlier and continue to produce longer than the other summer salad leaves.

US hardiness zone 9.

Red orach

Description A hardy annual, edible and ornamental plant. Pick the youngest leaf shoots of this handsome crimson-foliage plant (*Atriplex hortensis* var. *rubra*) to mix in salad. It's one of the darkest colours in my bowl, good in contrast to bright green, bronze and pink, and the backs of the leaves have an amazing sparkle when they catch the light. Small leaves and side buds can be eaten raw, larger leaves steamed and eaten like spinach. Height when full grown 1.5m (5ft), but it's best to pick it at the seedling stage. The flavour is mild and earthy, rather like spinach, and the texture is soft. This is not the tastiest leaf, but is here for its coloured leaves.

Propagation From seed.

Sowing time This is one of those odd plants where germination initially can be a problem – particularly without very fresh seed – but once you have one plant flowering in the garden, it will be there for ever because it prolifically self-sows. Just dig up the self-sown seedlings and put them in a row. If you don't want it to run riot, pull out the plants when the seeds begin to turn from crimson to brown.

Successional sowing To keep the plant small and tender, do two or three sowings in the year, but you should find that it self-sows enough, and you don't need to.

Final planting/thinning distance 20–25cm (8–10in) if for using as a salad leaf; 45cm (18in) if for full-scale plant with larger leaves.

Special growing requirements Easy, particularly on a rich, moisture-retentive soil.

Harvesting Six to eight weeks from sowing. Take the tips out and pick leaves off the central stem. Leaf production three to four months. Keep cutting it back hard if you're growing it for eating rather than ornament.

US hardiness zone 6.

Successional sowing Yes – every three months during this time.

Final planting/thinning distance 15cm (6in).

Special growing requirements Will grow in part shade. It's important to water regularly to prevent it becoming too hot and sour. You need to protect against flea beetle for a pristine crop (see page 168).

Harvesting Eight to ten weeks from sowing – considerably slower to germinate than most. As a perennial, it will keep going for many months, particularly if you nourish it with a balanced feed.

US hardiness zone 7.

Above **Wild rocket.**
Opposite **Corn salad.**

Summer purslane

Description Round, fleshy stalks that bear a rosette of succulent, tasty leaves at the top. I grow two varieties of summer purslane: the ordinary species, with mid-green leaves, and the golden variety, where the whole plant is a bright acid-green. Height 30cm (12in). Mild flavour and invaluable succulent texture that reminds me of mangetouts and pea tips.

Propagation From seed.

Sowing time It needs a sunny, open spot with well-drained soil.

Successional sowing A couple of times during late spring and summer.

Final planting/thinning distance 20–25cm (8–10in).

Special growing requirements An easy tender annual, very tolerant of heat. This will survive a baking summer in Greece, and purslane is widely used there for summer salads.

Harvesting Eight to ten weeks from sowing. Take the tips out and pick leaves off the central stem. Leaf production for three to four months. For the longest salad season, keep picking regularly and don't let plants flower and run to seed.

US hardiness zone 10 (but grown as an annual).

Tree spinach (or magenta spreen or lamb's quarters)

Description A hardy annual, edible and ornamental plant with young foliage in the brightest fuchsia pink. It's an essential part of a bold bowl of salad with green, pink and crimson leaves (see picture, page 93), and orange nasturtium flowers scattered over the top. The older leaves are a dull grey-green, but their undersides are brushed with the same intense pink. Pinch out the central stem to promote the formation of side leaf buds and so get the punchy colour. This leaf has not yet been discovered by the supermarket salad-bag brigade, so you won't see it on sale. Height in flower 1.5m (5ft). The young leaves have a gentle spinachy flavour and soft texture. Not the tastiest, but an incredible colour.

Propagation From seed.

Sowing time Freely self-sows. Once you've introduced it into the garden, you won't need to sow again. Transplant volunteer plants to where you want them.

Successional sowing To keep the plant small and tender, do two or three sowings in the year, but you may find that it self-sows enough and you don't need to.

Final planting/thinning distance 20–25cm (8–10in) if for use as a salad leaf.

Special growing requirements Easy, although germination can be erratic. Best sown direct into the garden.

Harvesting For salad, six to eight weeks from sowing. Take the tips out and pick leaves off the central stem. Leaf production for three to four months.

Late summer/autumn sowing salad leaves for autumn/spring picking

These are the salad leaves sown in late summer/autumn for autumn and winter, with a second sowing in late winter to pick in the spring. These bolt and their flavour changes quickly in summer when they are exposed to drought and sun. A spring sowing of these plants may give one or two cuts, whereas August and early September sowings remain productive over many months, especially where grown under cover. They won't grow quickly in very cold weather, but will start into growth again as soon as temperatures rise.

Sow them in lines, or blocks, straight into the ground in early spring and late summer/autumn, or into guttering inside. Sown in autumn, under cover or cloches, they will provide valuable winter salad.

Corn salad (or mâche or lamb's lettuce)

Description Delicious, mild flavour that reminds me of fresh hazelnuts. In Swiss German it's called *nüssli salat* – nutty salad. The leaves have a soft, slightly succulent texture. 'Verte de Cambrai' has the best flavour and is the hardiest of the lot, superb eaten on its own with grilled meat or fish, or used in a mixed-leaf salad. I love it in a quick, easy first course with roughly chopped, roasted hazelnuts and a rich salad dressing with hard-boiled egg yolks added to the oil and vinegar mix. Rosettes of oval, deep-green leaves. Height 8cm (3in).

Propagation From seed.

Sowing time Sow from August to October for winter picking and again in February for early spring. Soak the seed overnight to soften the hard coat and speed up germination.

Successional sowing Yes, a couple of times from late summer until mid-autumn. These should keep producing until mid-spring.

Final planting/thinning distance 15cm (6in).

Special growing requirements Easy, although can suffer from mildew and rot off in damp, very cold winters. It self-sows in my polytunnel and a little in the garden.

Harvesting This is slower growing than other leaves, taking eight to ten weeks from sowing. 'Verte de Cambrai' has a small leaf, so pick the whole rosette, once it has six to eight leaves. The spring crop will probably start to flower if you don't keep picking it regularly. Leaf production for three to four months.

US hardiness zone 5.

Cress

Description There are several varieties of this fast-growing cut-and-come-again salad plant. My favourite is 'Cressida' (see picture, page 226), and I also like curly-leaved 'Wrinkled Crinkled' and Greek cress. I'm not so keen on American land cress as a salad plant. It quickly gets very hot and strong and is then good for soup, but not eaten raw. They all have that characteristic zippy, cress-like flavour.

Propagation From seed.

Sowing time To have enough to pick, sow in a wide band or block. Its leaves are small, but very strong in taste, so you won't need much to flavour a salad. Cresses are always the first to bolt and run to flower in my garden, so regular serial sowing, once a month, is the only way to ensure a steady crop. 'Wrinkled Crinkled' cress is the slowest to bolt and can be sown from April to August for the summer months too.

Below left **Cress 'Cressida'.**
Below right **Lettuce 'Black-seeded Simpson'.**

Opposite, clockwise from top left **Lettuce 'Merveille des Quatre Saisons', Cos 'Little Gem', Cos 'Freckles' and Cos 'Lobjoit's Green Cos'.**

Lettuce

Successional sowing Yes, crucial.

Final planting/thinning distance 8–10cm (3–4in)

Special growing requirements Easy. Will grow in part-shade or sun. Water regularly to prevent it becoming either too hot or quickly bolting.

Harvesting Four to six weeks from sowing. Leaf production for one to two months.

US hardiness zone 7.

Rocket – salad

Description A very productive, fast-growing cut-and-come-again salad plant, which is good raw, or wilted over pasta or pizza. Leaf height 15–20cm (6–8in), but try to pick them at half this size. Flavour strong and peppery.

Propagation From seed.

Sowing time From late summer until mid-spring.

Successional sowing Yes, crucial. I sow it every six weeks or so to ensure a regular crop.

Final planting/thinning distance 8–10cm (3–4in).

Special growing requirements Easy. Will grow in part-shade. Water regularly to prevent it

becoming too hot and sour. It is hopeless to grow it in the summer – it will immediately run up to flower. You need to protect against flea beetle (see page 168) for a pristine crop .

Harvesting Six to eight weeks from sowing. Leaf production for two to three months. The flowers are edible and tasty too.

US hardiness zone 7.

Winter purslane (or miner's lettuce)

Description Shield-shaped leaves at the top of succulent stems in neat rosettes of bright green leaves. It produces edible white flowers in the spring. Eat it raw or cooked like spinach. Leaf height 15cm (6in). Delicious, mild cut-and-come-again salad leaf with succulent texture.

Propagation From seed.

Sowing time It will germinate only in the cold, so sow in the autumn or winter.

Successional sowing Not necessary. It crops well over a long season and will self-sow, germinating often in the depths of winter.

Final planting/thinning distance 8–10cm (3–4in).

Special growing requirements Easy. Very hardy.

Harvesting Six to eight weeks from sowing. It has small leaves, so you need to pick a lot to fill a bowl. Cut the whole plant in one go. Leaf production for three to four months – and pick the lovely, honey-scented flowers when they appear.

US hardiness zone 5.

I love cut-and-come-again salad leaves and I love lettuce. You need to grow both, so you can mix one with the other. The lettuce is there for the bulk and noisy crunch, the leaves for the main taste. Deprived of salad or wilted greens dressed in olive oil and lemon juice – warm salad – life feels bad.

I also love the look of lettuce in the garden, the lines of different shapes and colours to edge paths or provide the undulating under-storey to taller-growing peas and beans (see picture, page 41). Lettuce are also ideal for making effective use of space. Use the early sowings for inter-cropping between slow-developing plants like onions and shallots (see picture, page 170). The late sowings go in between lines of parsnips, kale or purple-sprouting broccoli. You will have harvested all the lettuce by the time the others are ready to be picked and, decently spaced, the one will not crowd or overshadow the other.

Lettuce divide into soft-textured Butterheads, upright and crunchy Cos, Iceberg-like Crispheads and cut-and-come-again, loose-leaf Continental varieties. Most of them are really a mid-spring-sowing, summer- and early autumn-harvesting crop, but you can grow the loose-leaf varieties for eight months of the year. They'll grow fast enough to make it worth it from early spring to mid-autumn; but, even under cover, most grow

too slowly in the depths of winter to earn their space. Lettuce that have been grown slowly can be very bitter, so the hardy salad leaves are a more reliable and productive crop at the colder times of year.

US hardiness zone 6.

'Black-seeded Simpson'

Description A very handsome, tall Crisphead lettuce with large, crunchy, upright leaves, rather like a giant, more crinkly Cos. With every vein, there is an indent on the leaf. It has a superb taste and firm texture.

Propagation From seed direct into the garden, or under cover into guttering or Jiffy 7s.

Sowing time This is excellent for sowing in late winter under cover. February sowing will give valuable, hardy early lettuce, but it can be sown February to September. Plant out in March, or continue growing under cover to give you your first spring lettuce in May with a brilliantly crunchy texture.

Successional sowing Yes, three or four times from late winter to mid-autumn, starting under cover and then moving outside to sow direct (see page 140).

Final planting/thinning distance 40cm (15in). It's a huge lettuce.

Special growing requirements Easy. Slower to bolt than most, but you'll need to keep them well watered if you hit a dry spell in May.

Harvesting Ten weeks from sowing for full-sized, hearted lettuce. Harvest the whole plant at once, or treat it as a cut-and-come-again. Leaf production for two to three months.

Cos – 'Little Gem'

Description The famous, short Cos type which you can often buy at the greengrocer's, two lettuces in a bag. It's quick-maturing and is almost all crunchy heart. One of the best and sweetest Cos lettuces there are.

Propagation From seed direct into the garden, or under cover into guttering or Jiffy 7s.

Sowing time You can sow under cover in early spring – late February/early March for a May and June crop. I do one more sowing inside about a month later. A month after that, you can sow straight into the ground outside and keep sowing a short line at a time regularly until mid-August.

Successional sowing As above.

Final planting/thinning distance 20cm (8in).

Special growing requirements None.

Harvesting Quick to mature at only eight weeks from sowing. Harvest the whole plant at once. The root won't resprout. This is a mainstay for summer, autumn and early winter picking – I usually pick my last plants just before Christmas. I then pick the first spring one in May. I don't recommend storing, as it's always better for flavour and texture to pick your lettuce fresh, but this one lasts longer in the fridge than any other lettuce I grow. It's still fine after a week in a bag. Leaf production for two to three months.

Cos – 'Lobjoit's Green Cos'

Description A Cos lettuce with that fantastic Cos crunch. This is my main summer lettuce – I grow lots of it. It's the key ingredient of a Caesar salad – large, crunchy and brilliant green. Can be grown as a hearting lettuce or as a cut-and-come-again. Firm enough texture for the leaf to be used as a scoop for houmous and guacamole, and the heart is brilliant green with a bright-white stem. Picked as soon as the heart bulks out, this has one of the sweetest flavours you'll get in a lettuce.

Propagation From seed direct into the garden, or under cover into guttering or Jiffy 7s.

Sowing time Ideal for spring or summer sowing. I start sowing these under cover in March, for planting out six weeks later. From mid-April to August, I sow a short line at least once a month, straight into the ground. This variety can also be grown as a cut-and-come-again seedling leaf and is often a feature of supermarket Continental mixed salad bags.

Successional sowing Yes, several times.

Final planting/thinning distance 40cm (15in) for hearting lettuce, 10–15cm (4–6in) as cut-and-come-again.

Special growing requirements Easy. Look out for slugs when you're washing it. They seem to love this one and are able to hide easily between the outer leaves and the heart. I look on both sides of every one of these middle-section leaves before I put them in a bowl!

Harvesting Eight to ten weeks from sowing.

Cos 'Freckles' (or 'Forellenschluss')

Description This beautiful, crimson-splotched, bright-green leaf is surprisingly hardy with me. It has good taste and crunchy texture, but it's really for its looks that you're growing it.

Propagation From seed direct into the garden, or under cover into guttering or Jiffy 7s.

Sowing time March and September under cover. April to July outside.

Successional sowing Yes, three or four times through the growing season.

Final planting/thinning distance 20cm (8in).

Special growing requirements Easy and slower to bolt than most, but keep them well watered if you hit a dry spell.

Harvesting Eight weeks from sowing. Leave the root in the ground when you harvest: it will resprout. Leaf production for two to three months.

'Merveille des Quatre Saisons'

Description Butterhead type. It looks great in the garden, with its big, generous balloons of green leaves, heavily tinged with bronze crimson. You can treat it as a cut-and-come-again plant or leave it to grow on to form a heart, or semi-heart – it doesn't make a dense, true heart. Added to a green salad, it's a perfect match to bronze fennel and is one of the essential colours for the best-looking bowl. Excellent flavour, soft texture, with a waxy sheen to the leaves.

Propagation From seed direct into the garden, or under cover into guttering or Jiffy 7s.

Sowing time Can be sown from late winter onwards under cover and mid-spring to late summer outside.

Successional sowing Yes, every couple of months.

Final planting/thinning distance 35cm (14in) if you want the whole plant. Also good as a cut-and-come-again crop, for which space them much closer, at 10–15cm (4–6in).

Special growing requirements Easy.

Harvesting Eight to ten weeks from sowing for full-sized plant; six weeks for seedling leaves. When you're picking, slice the lettuce off an inch above the ground. Don't pull the roots up – they will sprout leaves again. Leaf production for two to three months.

Oak Leaf (or 'A Foglia di Quercia')

Description Hardy annual. This is a Continental, non-hearting type of lettuce. You can pick as many leaves as you want at a time, or treat it as a cut-and-come-again crop, slicing the whole plant 2.5cm (1in) above the ground. It is a wonderful lettuce, bright green, with a pretty, undulating edge. The green form has a better taste than the 'Red Oak Leaf' variety, which has a crimson colouring to the leaves. There are two very similar lettuces, 'Green Salad Bowl' and 'Red Salad Bowl', which also have a good, sweet flavour and a soft texture. I like the similar 'Bronze Arrow' with more upright growth (see picture, page 41).

Propagation From seed direct into the garden or under cover into guttering or Jiffy 7s.

Sowing time March until September.

Successional sowing Yes – every couple of months.

Final planting/thinning distance 25cm (10in) if you want the whole plant. Space them much closer at 10–15cm (4–6in) if you want to pick them at the seedling stage.

Below left **Lettuce 'Reine des Glaces'.** Below centre **Lettuce 'Triumph'.** Below right **Spinach 'Dominant'.**

Special growing requirements Very easy – hardy, quick to produce and the slowest lettuce to bolt that I know.

Harvesting Eight weeks from sowing for full-sized plant; four to six for seedling leaves. Start cutting when the leaves are about 5–10cm (2–4in) high. At the seedling stage, these plants are naturally so vigorous they will resprout, each plant producing endless new leaves within a week or so. It's important to keep picking them regularly. The leaves become slightly bitter as they age. Leaf production for three to four months.

'Reine des Glaces'

Description An old French Crisphead type with large, jagged-edged leaves with very crunchy texture and good taste. Chefs love this one as it is as good cooked as raw, the stems having an excellent, mildly bitter taste.

Propagation From seed direct into the garden, or under cover into guttering or Jiffy 7s.

Sowing time I sow this direct into the garden from late April to late July. It's one of the best for a summer crop.

Successional sowing Yes, several times, at intervals of about one month.

Final planting/thinning distance 30cm (12in).

Special growing requirements Very hardy.

Harvesting Eight to ten weeks from spring sowing. Harvest the whole plant at once. The root won't resprout. It lasts well into maturity and is more resistant to bolting than other types.

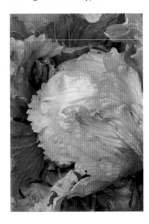

'Triumph'

Description A new and excellent Crisphead type producing large hearts of curled and crisp leaves.

Propagation From seed direct into the garden, or under cover into guttering or Jiffy 7s.

Sowing time I sow this direct into the garden from late April to late July. It's one of the best for a summer crop.

Successional sowing Yes, several times, at intervals of about a month.

Final planting/thinning distance 40cm (5in).

Special growing requirements Very hardy.

Harvesting Eight to ten weeks from spring sowing. Harvest the whole plant at once. The root won't resprout. It lasts well into maturity and is more resistant to bolting than other types.

Salsify

Salsify looks like a thin, straight parsnip and is very popular with foodies. It has an almost oyster-like taste, hence its common name – 'vegetable oyster'.

Variety description I grow a variety called 'Giant', but apparently there is little to choose between the different cultivars.

Propagation From seed.

Sowing time Sow in mid-spring, placing three seeds per station 15cm (6in) apart in 30cm (12in) spaced rows. Remove the weaker seedling as soon as possible.

Successional sowing No.

Final planting/thinning distance As above.

Special growing requirements Salsify needs deep, stone-free soil. Do not put it in newly manured ground, or it will fork.

Harvesting Autumn. You can leave the roots in the ground until you want to eat them. Then dig them up carefully, as they are very brittle and go very deep.

US hardiness zone 5.

Spinach

The well-known leafy green that also makes a superb cut-and-come-again salad leaf. I love this as the main leaf in a salad with blue cheese, bacon and walnuts.

Variety description I use 'Winterreuzen' (or Giant of Winter) for autumn sowing and late autumn and winter picking, 'Trinidad' for spring sowing and summer eating, but 'Dominant' – my favourite – I sow and grow almost all year. It is the slowest to bolt of all the varieties I've tried. It has good disease resistance and a characteristic earthy flavour and lovely soft texture, particularly at the small-leaf stage.

Propagation From seed.

Sowing time Sow every three to four weeks from early to late spring for a summer harvest. Sow in late summer for picking in winter right through to early summer.

Sow *In situ* thinly 2.5cm (1in) apart and 1–2cm (½–¾in) deep in rows 30cm (12in) apart, or into guttering at the same spacings. Cover with soil. Germination usually takes less than a week.

Successional sowing For a bumper crop, sow in long rows and, between spring and summer, sow three or four times. Remember that a few spinach leaves don't go very far once cooked.

Final planting/thinning distance 20cm (8in).

Special growing requirements Easy. It tends to bolt quickly in the hot and dry, so water summer lines. Choose a position in light shade with moist ground. It needs a rich, fertile, moisture-retentive soil. Dig in well-rotted organic matter before planting. A leaky-pipe irrigation system will prolong the summer-picking season of spinach.

Harvesting Six to eight weeks from sowing. Leaf production for two to three months. Pick continually so that fresh growth is encouraged.

US hardiness zone 5.

Spring or salad onions

Spring onions are wonderful finely chopped for dressing, and I love them griddled to eat with dry-cured ham and salami. They are also an invaluable companion plant that helps protect carrots against carrot fly (see page 38). Mix the two packets up in your hand and sow them together in lines (see picture, page 171).

Variety description My favourite spring onion is a deep red variety, North Holland Blood Red (or 'Noordhollandse Bloedrode'). It can be eaten small and young, or you can let it grow into an excellent, full-sized onion.

Propagation From seed direct into the garden, or under cover into guttering or Jiffy 7s.

Sowing time Can be sown from late winter under cover, and from mid-spring to late summer outside.

Successional sowing Yes, every couple of months.

Final planting/thinning distance 2.5cm (1in), in rows 10cm (4in) apart.

Special growing requirements Easy.

Harvesting Six weeks for spring onions, ten weeks for full-sized bulbs.

US hardiness zone 5.

Swede

The orange-fleshed root vegetable known colloquially as 'neeps' in Scotland is superb mashed and served with haggis. I love it like this, or roasted with other mixed roots, but I have to confess that I tend to buy swedes rather than grow them. They fill the ground for a very long time before reaching harvestable size, and I don't eat them often enough for them to make it worthwhile. I have, however, recently discovered a great recipe. Peel them and cut them into segments, like a chocolate orange, then steam them gently for fifteen minutes. Remove them from the pan and then wrap each chunk in a slice of dry-cured ham or pancetta. Roast them in the oven for another fifteen minutes until the ham is cooked and brown. You can also use this recipe for celeriac, and both are delicious.

Variety description 'Ruby' has excellent flavour and deep orange flesh.

Propagation From seed.

Sowing time Sow from late spring to early summer very thinly with 45cm (18in) between the rows.

Successional sowing No.

Final planting/thinning distance 15–20cm (6–8in) apart.

Special growing requirements It suffers from the same pests and diseases as other brassicas: cabbage white butterflies, flea beetle and clubroot (see page 168).

Harvesting Four to five months from seed to harvest, so it's not a good plant to grow when space is short.

US hardiness zone 7.

Right **Spring onion North Holland Blood Red.**
Opposite top **Tomato 'Brandywine'.**
Opposite bottom **Sweetcorn 'Sweet Nugget'.**

Sweetcorn

Sweetcorn is another of the veg-garden musts, a different-tasting thing eaten straight out of the garden from the shop-bought kind. It looks good too, with tall, luscious, grass-like leaves. Sweetcorn has deep roots, so won't suffer from inter-planting with climbing nasturtiums or small, trailing squash. Try growing it with pumpkins 'Munchkin' and 'Red Kuri'.

Variety description I grow 'Sweet Nugget', a tried-and-tested, mid-season, supersweet variety with a good yield of long, uniform cobs (see picture, page 29). I also grow an F1 hybrid called 'Red Strawberry' for my daughters, who love popcorn. This is an amazing variety – round, red and covered in shiny kernels – and ideal for popcorn. I also grow the ornamental 'Inca Rainbow' (see picture, page 12).

Propagation From seed.

Sowing time Sow under cover in mid- to late spring straight into 8cm (3in) pots, at a temperature of 13˚C (55˚F). The large seeds are ideal for this. The plants resent root disturbance so I use biodegradable coir pots that can be planted straight into the ground. Alternatively sow *in situ*

in early summer. The supersweet varieties need warm conditions to do well.

Successional sowing Yes, two or three times, about one month apart.

Final planting/thinning distance Space them at 40cm (15in) intervals each way.

Special growing requirements Because of cross-pollination, supersweet varieties should not be grown near other forms. Plant in blocks, not lines. Sweetcorn is wind-pollinated, and neat rows make pollination less likely. Blocks allow pollination whichever way the wind is blowing. Water well at all times, especially during dry weather. Earth up stems in summer for better root anchorage.

Harvesting Pick them as the tassels on the cobs start to shrivel. To check they're ready, peel back the husk and press one cob with your thumbnail. If it's ready, a creamy liquid will squirt out. If it's still watery, leave the cobs another few days. 'Red Strawberry' needs to be dried well to make good popping corn.

US hardiness zone 10 (but grown as an annual).

Tomatoes

Tomatoes are an absolute must-have home-grown vegetable. Greenhouse, no greenhouse, you've got to give them a go. Just bear in mind that, outside, they are more prone to blight (see page 16).

.

Which to grow

There is a huge range of different tomatoes which it is exciting to get to know. They divide into three groups:

Bush (or determinate) varieties will grow to a predetermined height and then stop, so don't need pruning or pinching out. They tend to produce most of their fruit over a period of about four weeks, and so are popular commercially as they can be machine-harvested. They need less support than cordons, but a mesh cage to keep the fruit off the ground is a good idea.

Cordons (or indeterminate varieties) will grow as tall as you wish. They'll keep going until you stop them. They flower in succession and will keep fruiting over a long period. They will need support.

Tumbler types are for growing in pots and tend to crop for a season mid-way between the two above in length.

Size This also varies hugely, from large beefsteaks to small cherries, with plenty of sizes in between. As a rule, large-fruited varieties ripen best in a cold greenhouse. The fruit is too big to ripen properly outside.

US hardiness zone 10 (but grown as an annual).

'Brandywine'

Description Traditional Amish, pink cordon type famous for its huge fruits and superb flavour. We always grow this one. It comes in various different

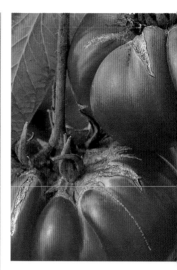

colours – yellow and crimson, which are also superb. An excellent salad tomato.

Propagation From seed.

Sowing time Late winter until mid-spring.

Successional sowing No (see 'Gardener's Delight' on page 232).

Final planting/thinning distance 45cm (18in).

Special growing requirements With 'Brandywine' productivity is low, but much improved by watering from above, so the pollen from the higher flowers fertilizes those on the lower trusses, causing fruit to form.

Harvesting This is a very large-fruited variety that will be ready to harvest only from late summer on. In a cold, grey year, this form does not do well, with some of the fruit rotting before they ripen.

'Costoluto Fiorentino'

Description This is my favourite variety of cordon tomato, with the best flavour and firm, juicy texture for eating raw. Its fruits are middle-to-large-sized, but

Opposite **Turnip 'Blanc De Croissy'.**

Turnips

not too large to be difficult to ripen in our grey climate (see picture, page 16).

Propagation From seed.

Sowing time Late winter until mid-spring.

Successional sowing No (see 'Gardener's Delight' below).

Final planting/thinning distance 45cm (18in).

Special growing requirements A reliable and easy form to grow.

Harvesting Ready to harvest from mid-summer on.

'Gardener's Delight'

Description 'Gardener's Delight' (see picture, page 19) is the well-known red cherry variety, superb for all-round use, with good flavour, perfect eaten raw, whole or sliced. On the down side, it has a tendency to greenback (that disc of hard, green flesh around the stem) and splitting. It has a long season and is very productive of large cherry tomatoes. A cordon type that grows to about 1.5m (5ft) tall.

Propagation From seed.

Sowing time Late winter until mid-spring.

Successional sowing It's only worth doing two sowings of the small cherry varieties, which will continue to ripen late into the autumn. I sow one lot of 'Sungold' and 'Gardener's Delight' in late winter and another in late spring and then can pick tomatoes from mid-summer to early winter.

Final planting/thinning distance 45cm (18in.)

Special growing requirements A reliable and easy form to grow inside and out.

Harvesting This is a large cherry-sized variety that will be ready to harvest from mid-summer on.

'Principe Borghese'

Description A very recognizable, small plum tomato with a characteristic nipple at the tip of the fruit. This is a hugely prolific form, with good flavour, particularly when cooked. It's the one I sow for tomato sauce and soup.

Propagation From seed.

Sowing time Late winter until mid-spring.

Successional sowing If you like making lots of tomato sauce, try sowing this variety a second time too. It will crop and ripen well under cover until early winter.

Final planting/thinning distance 45cm (18in).

Special growing requirements A reliable and easy form to grow.

Harvesting A cherry-sized variety that will be ready to harvest from mid-summer on.

'Sungold'

Description Bright orange-yellow cordon, producing small tomatoes with superb flavour. Some find the fruit too sweet to eat all the time. Another good all-rounder, excellent both raw and cooked. A cordon type 1.2m (4ft) tall.

Propagation From seed.

Sowing time Late winter until mid-spring.

Successional sowing It's only worth doing two sowings of the small cherry varieties, which will continue to ripen late into the autumn. I sow one lot of 'Sungold' and 'Gardener's Delight' in late winter and another in late spring, and then I can pick tomatoes from mid-summer to early winter.

Final planting/thinning distance 45cm (18in).

Special growing requirements A reliable and easy form to grow.

Harvesting They are heavy-cropping and have a very long season. They have a tendency to split as soon as they're ripe, so pick as regularly as you can.

'Tumbling Tom Red'

Description This is the only non-cordon variety of tomato I grow. I plant three to a window-box or pot and leave it to trail down the side. With no training, these plants will produce bowls and bowls of sweet, tasty, small tomatoes. Its an ideal variety for children, and Rosie, my elder daughter, grows this in her patch.

Propagation From seed.

Sowing time Late winter until mid-spring.

Successional sowing If you have limited space, it's worth doing two sowings of this variety, one in late winter and one in late spring for cropping through most of the summer and autumn.

Final planting/thinning distance 30cm (12in).

Special growing requirements A reliable and easy form to grow. If you're growing it in pots, remember to water and feed.

Harvesting It is heavy-cropping and has a very long season.

Turnips

There are some very tasty, nutty-flavoured turnips, and some bitter ones that I don't like, but whichever you choose, eat them young and small to enjoy them at their best. The good thing about small turnips is that they take only eight weeks from sowing to eating, so they make the perfect catch crop when you have a slot that you don't know how to fill.

Variety description I've recently started growing 'Blanc De Croissy', an old French variety of turnip that looks like a large, white radish. It's delicious raw, sliced into salad, or cooked, steamed whole or slow-roasted with other roots, and it has a distinctive, nutty taste.

Propagation From seed.

Sowing time Sow maincrop turnips like this one from mid-spring to mid-summer outside. You can also start them off earlier by sowing into guttering.

Successional sowing Yes.

Final planting/thinning distance 10cm (4in).

Special growing requirements They thrive in a moist, fertile soil and are happy in a little shade in the summer.

Harvesting Summer and autumn.

US hardiness zone 7.

Calendar of jobs to do

Note to gardeners The dates on this calendar are based on my own experience in south-east England. As all gardeners know, conditions vary enormously with location. If you are an experienced vegetable grower you will know how to adapt these dates to suit where you live. If in doubt, ask your friends, neighbours or local garden centre for advice.

January
Gardening

Have a rest or do hard landscaping and ground preparation

Buy your seed potatoes as early in the year as possible so you get a good selection, and start chitting earlies

Harvesting

Salad leaves – there are many hardy types: rocket, mizuna, mibuna, 'Red Giant' mustard, winter purslane, corn salad – and chard. Both may need a cloche or polytunnel

Parsnips

Leeks

Kale

Red and green cabbage and Brussels sprouts

Hardy annual herbs – parsley and chervil

Evergreen herbs – rosemary, sage, bay and winter savory

February
Gardening

Dig and prepare soil on light ground when there's a dry day

Plant salad leaves and annual herbs into Jiffy 7s or guttering

Start sowing half-hardy annuals – those slow to develop like cucumbers, tomatoes, chillies and aubergines – under cover

Start sowing plug-grown hardy annuals – chard, spinach and broad beans – under cover

Put a few potatoes in big pots (5 litres) or in beds in the polytunnel or greenhouse

Harvesting

Salad leaves

Chard – this may need a cloche

Parsnips

Leeks

Kale

Cauliflower

Red and green cabbage and Brussels sprouts

Hardy annual herbs – parsley and chervil

Evergreen herbs – rosemary, sage, bay and winter savory

March
Gardening

Dig and prepare soil on light ground when there's a dry day

Continue sowing half-hardy annuals – like cucumbers and courgettes – under cover

Continue sowing plug-grown hardy annuals – leeks, coriander, dill and beetroot – under cover

Sow globe artichokes

Sow peas under cover into guttering

Aim to plant your first early potatoes at the beginning of the month, followed by a second batch at the end of the month

Chit maincrop potatoes

Plant asparagus crowns

Plant perennial herbs – tarragon, mint, rosemary and lovage

Harvesting

Salad leaves and pea tips

Spinach

Chard – this may need a cloche

Leeks

Kale

Cauliflower

Purple-sprouting broccoli

Red and green cabbage and Brussels sprouts

Hardy annual herbs – parsley and chervil

Perennial herbs poking up now – sorrel, lovage, chives and fennel

Evergreen herbs – rosemary, sage, bay and winter savory

April
Gardening

Continue to sow half-hardy annuals, the quick-growing ones like butternut squash, sweetcorn, pumpkins, basil, French beans and runner beans, and Florence fennel

Direct sow hardy annuals – salad leaves, lettuce, carrots, beetroot, chard and spinach

Plant second early potatoes at the beginning of the month, followed by the maincrops at the end of the month

Plant tomatoes and cucumbers into their beds under cover at the end of the month

Harvesting

Salad leaves and pea tips

Spinach

Chard

Kale

Cauliflower

Purple-sprouting broccoli

Hardy annual herbs – parsley, chervil and now coriander

Mint now joins other perennial herbs

Evergreen herbs – rosemary, sage, bay and winter savory

May
Gardening

Plant out half-hardy annuals

You can now direct sow half-hardy annuals – French beans, squashes and pumpkins

Start lifting your early potatoes if they begin to flower

Ridge (or earth up) second early and maincrop potatoes

Harvesting

Salad leaves and the first Cos lettuce

Spinach

The first broad beans

The first peas – at the end of the month

Hardy annual herbs – parsley, chervil, coriander and now dill

Mint and other perennial herbs

Evergreen herbs – rosemary, sage, bay and thyme

New potatoes raised inside

June
Gardening

Direct sow hardy annuals.

Make second sowing of courgettes and tomatoes to continue cropping late in the year

Give your herbs a shear. Cut them right back to within a few centimetres of the ground

Lift your early potatoes when they begin to flower

Harvesting

Salad leaves and lettuce

Lots of broad beans

Lots of peas

The first new potatoes from the garden

The first carrots

Baby beetroot

The first outdoor courgettes

Hardy annual herbs – parsley, chervil, coriander and dill

Tender herbs – basil

Mint and other perennial herbs

Evergreen herbs – rosemary, sage, bay and thyme

July
Gardening

At the end of the month make your last sowing of any hardy or half-hardy annuals, e.g. French beans that you want to eat in the autumn

Plant your potatoes for Christmas

Make successional sowing of salad leaves and roots

Harvesting

Salad leaves

Early potatoes

Carrots

Peas and broad beans

Hardy annual herbs – parsley, chervil, coriander and dill

Tender herbs – basil and oregano

Mint and other perennial herbs

Evergreen herbs – rosemary, sage, bay and thyme

The first tomatoes and cucumbers

Courgettes

August
Gardening

Towards the end of the month, start your autumn sowing of salads and herbs for autumn and winter picking

Harvesting

Salad leaves

Second early potatoes

Carrots

Calabrese

French and runner beans

Sweetcorn

Hardy annual herbs – parsley, chervil, coriander and dill

Tender herbs – basil and oregano

Mint and other perennial herbs

Evergreen herbs – rosemary, sage, bay and thyme

All half-hardies – tomatoes, cucumbers, aubergines, chillies, sweetcorn and courgettes

September
Gardening

Sow salad leaves under cover

Make last sowing of spinach and chard by the middle of the month

Sow broad beans direct into the soil

Sow peas in guttering for planting out

Harvest seed, e.g. beans and tomatoes

Harvesting

Salad leaves

French and runner beans

Maincrop potatoes

Carrots and beetroot

Tomatoes

Sweetcorn

Squash

Cucumbers – these will be coming to an end

Courgettes from the second sowing

Hardy annual herbs – parsley, chervil, coriander and dill

Tender herbs – basil and oregano

Mint and other perennial herbs

Evergreen herbs – rosemary, sage, bay and thyme

October
Gardening

Sow broad beans into root trainers for putting out by the end of the month

Plant out guttering of peas

Make last sowing of salad leaves

Plant cauliflowers

Clear the garden

Harvest seed

Dig in lots of well-rotted farmyard manure in the patch allocated for potatoes next year

Harvesting

Salad leaves

Tomatoes – these will be coming to an end

Maincrop potatoes

Carrots

Butternut squash and pumpkins

Hardy annual herbs – parsley, chervil, coriander and dill

Evergreen herbs – rosemary, sage, bay and thyme

November
Gardening

Clear the garden

Dig and prepare soil on heavy ground when it's a dry day

Plant shallots and garlic

Harvesting

Salad leaves

Chard – this may need a cloche

Parsnips

Leeks

Kale

Red and green cabbage and Brussels sprouts

Hardy annual herbs – parsley and chervil

Evergreen herbs – rosemary, sage, bay and winter savory

December
Gardening

Plant shallots and garlic if you haven't done so already

Take a break

Harvesting

Salad leaves and chard – both may need a cloche

Parsnips

Leeks

Kale

Red and green cabbage and Brussels sprouts

Hardy annual herbs – parsley and chervil

Evergreen herbs – rosemary, sage, bay and winter savory

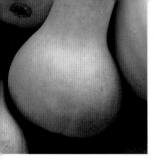

There are many people I would like to thank for their help over the long evolution of this book. My vegetable gardening friend Matthew Rice has been a constant source of inspiration, as has Jane Dunn and her garden at Stone House. Several friends have helped me by reading and advising me at the research and proof stages – Clare Smith, Tam Lawson and Lou Farman, with Derek Bice and Frances Smith being the final, sage-like pairs of eyes.

Warm thanks also to Viv Bowler for following through with the idea over several years, Andrew Barron for taking so much trouble to get the book looking just as I wanted, and Sarah Reece for her detailed editing.

Most of all I want to thank Jonathan Buckley and Adam, Rosie and Molly Nicolson. Jonathan and I have been thinking about this book now for five years, chipping away together at the huge number of pictures that we wanted to take. We've learned a lot and become great friends.

Adam, my husband – not a born veg or salad enthusiast – is still prepared to read every word I write. And thank you to my two lovely girls, Rosie and Molly, for putting up with my vegetable passion.

Sarah Raven's Cutting Garden

Seeds, baskets and other gardening products.

Mail order

Raven Direct
6 Castleham Road
St Leonards-on-Sea
East Sussex TN38 9NR
Telephone 0845 0504848

Garden and cookery school

Perch Hill Farm
Brightling
Robertsbridge
East Sussex TN32 5HP
Telephone 0845 0504849

For more information about courses, events, and shop and garden opening times at Perch Hill, or to order a catalogue, visit www.thecuttinggarden.com or telephone 0845 0504849.

Acknowledgements

Opposite **The shepherd's hut displays some of the items to be found in the shop at Perch Hill.**

Index

This book is published to
accompany the television series,
Gardeners' World, produced for
BBC2 by BBC Birmingham.

Series producer:
Sarah Moors

Published by BBC Books,
BBC Worldwide Limited,
Woodlands, 80 Wood Lane,
London W12 0TT

First published 2005
Reprinted 2005 (three times), 2006 (twice)
Text copyright © Sarah Raven 2005
The moral right of the author
has been asserted.

Photographs copyright
© Jonathan Buckley 2005

ISBN-10: 0 563 48817 4
ISBN-13: 978 0 563 48817 0

Commissioning editor:
Vivien Bowler
Project editor:
Sarah Reece
Designer:
Andrew Barron
@ Thextension
Copy editor:
Steve Dobell
Illustrator:
Cedric Knight
Horticultural consultant:
Tony Lord
Production controller:
Kenneth McKay

Set in Modern 216 & Swiss 721
Colour origination and printing
in Great Britain by
Butler & Tanner Ltd

For more information about
this and other BBC books,
please visit our website at
www.bbcshop.com
or telephone 08700 777 001.